Public Education for Children with Brain Dysfunction

SHELDON R. RAPPAPORT

Foreword by
WILLIAM M. CRUICKSHANK

SYRACUSE   UNIVERSITY   PRESS

Public Education for
Children with
Brain Dysfunction

This book is dedicated in loving salute to Bruce Abrams, a brilliant youngster who helped me realize what it is like to live with brain dysfunction and seizures — the ultimate cause of his death. Its writing is an effort to keep faith with him and with God: ". . . I will show thee my faith by my works." — James 2:18.

Sheldon R. Rappaport has had many years of experience in developing methods and materials for teaching children with brain dysfunction. After spending thirteen years in private practice, he is now president and founder of The Pathway School, Norristown, Pennsylvania, a unique institution dedicated exclusively to children who have learning and behavioral difficulties. The object of Pathway is to provide them the opportunity to overcome their handicaps and thereby become self-respecting, contributing members of society.

Dr. Rappaport is a member of the Pennsylvania State Teacher Education Advisory Committee and the Editorial Advisory Board, *Journal of Learning Disabilities*, and is consultant to various state and local educational organizations. He is also a diplomate of the American Board of Examiners in Professional Psychology and a member of the American Academy of Psychotherapists, the New York Academy of Sciences, and the American Association for Children's Residential Centers.

Dr. Rappaport is widely known as a lecturer and author of books and articles on the problems of teaching children with learning and behavioral disorders. He received both his A. B. and A. M. degrees from Temple University and was awarded his Ph. D. by Washington University, St. Louis.

Foreword

Brain dysfunction in children, as an aspect of the broad area of mental retardation and mental disease, constitutes one of the chief educational, social, medical, and economic problems of our time. The significance of this problem area is to be observed in the dramatic action that has taken place at both the federal and state levels of government since 1955 and in the unique position that it is accorded in all phases of government. Both professional and lay people were galvanized into action by the leadership of the late President John F. Kennedy, who in October of 1961 convened the President's Panel on Mental Retardation. He served as a catalytic agent for the diverse groups that for a decade previously had been exerting pressures, oftentimes without too much direction or vision, and that were calling for the solution of at least the most immediate problems, if indeed not the long-term national issue of retardation.

The President's Panel on Mental Retardation and its subsequent report (*Report to the President: A Proposed Program for National Action to Combat Mental Retardation, 1962*) calling for national action culminated in the first presidential message to Congress in the history of the United States on such matters as mental retardation, mental illness, and related problems. While not specific to the child who has brain dysfunction, this document is historically significant and is closely related to that problem. Congress simultaneously had been making its own investigations, and it was furthermore not lacking in socially-minded leadership. The President's message was warmly received. It was blended with the findings of congressional studies and thought and, with the precedent of earlier legislation behind it, Congress ultimately presented to the nation Public Law 88-164, an amendment of Public Law 85-926. In this legislation is the germ that will provide the force for breakthrough in the area of mental retardation and brain dysfunction. In this legislation is the stimulus for basic and applied research, the nature of which ultimately will change understandings of the problem of mental deficiency. In this legislation is the format for remodeling the total educational and social direction of programs for all aspects of mental deficiency in children and for the preparation of a modern core of professional personnel to replace the inbreeding of past generations. The nation has provided the professions with opportunities for the key to doors that when properly opened, will result in new vistas and new horizons of experience and understanding of those who have brain dysfunction and the mentally retarded. The professions now are faced with a challenge that they have been begging for, for many years. The professions must now confront this issue with the same energy as they have exerted toward such problems as civil rights, immunization, atomic research, cultural deprivation and housing, retrolentil fibroplasia,* and other human problems, large and small. They must bring solutions to the complex issues of brain dysfunction, the results of which will make human life better here and abroad.

Although mental retardation is one of the oldest recognized social problems in our country, it is always a source of interest to me that we are still faced with some of the same unsolved issues as were apparent more than 100 years ago when Horace Mann, Samuel Gridley Howe, Dorothea Dix, and others began demanding solutions to what they then saw only as a social problem. (I speak here of mental retardation because in its broadest sense brain dysfunction is an aspect of the retardation of mental ability. I am not thinking solely of the traditional concept of retardation and intelligence quotient.) Mental retardation later was seen solely as a custodial and medical problem. It was looked upon as an ill that society would have to accept, since no treatment could be envisioned. Still later, although

*Opaque tissue behind the lens of the eye, leading to retinal detachment and arrested eye growth, traced to the use of highly concentrated oxygen for premature infants.

accepted also as an educational problem and one requiring training, mental retardation has for a hundred years reflected little change in methods of teaching, in teacher preparation, or in the goals of special education.

Teacher education has been characterized by little creativity, by failure to utilize all the resources at hand, and by a tendency to become parochial and isolated. While, of course, there are exceptions to what I say, this phase of special education has not always attracted the best of the teaching profession either in colleges and universities or at the service level in public school systems. Parochial school systems have largely ignored this problem completely until the past few years, when a few individual schools have attempted what for the most part are ineffective programs.

Certainly this issue has not attracted the best of the profession within institutional settings. Inbreeding has been rampant; creativity, at an absolute minimum. Even in very recent years the records show that dynamic systems of education for the mentally handicapped and those with brain dysfunction have been aggressively rejected by those who found the status quo more comfortable. Individuals of foresight and understanding who have advocated change toward greater reality of programming for the retarded have been attacked, have been replaced, and have been removed from their positions of leadership by people of little professional stature and of limited educational vision. As concepts of brain dysfunction, perceptual disturbance, and visuomotor problems are added to the concept of mental retardation, changes in these attitudes are mandated.

Medical research in mental retardation and brain dysfunction, until very recently, has been limited to institutional settings that have lacked both the adequate laboratories and competent personnel sophisticated in modern technique needed to attack the complex problems. Institutional personnel, with few exceptions, have been insular in their point of view. Most of that research that has taken place has been internally directed for institutional convenience rather than externally directed for universal application. Our best professional minds have not always occupied positions in institutional settings. These centers have been egocentric and have rigidly contained both the retarded and ideas about them rather than being allocentric agencies challenging stereotypes and suggesting remedies.

Recent decisions of the Congress and the President—to say nothing of the decisions of foresighted legislators, governors, and citizens at the state level—belie the historical past. They give new direction, not to education alone, not to medicine as a single profession, not to public health or nursing or social work or law in isolation, but to all professions as equals among equals and in concert, challenging them to an interdisciplinary attack on the many tentacles of this complex and sometimes staggering problem.

The problem of brain dysfunction is at least twofold. First, intelligent opportunism requires that there must be servicing of the present generation of these children and their families. Secondly, there is the problem of the solution of neurological disability itself for the alleviation of future generations. Let us examine the latter first.

The goal of all professions working with any facet of the disability is that of professional self-extinction. We have seen this goal modestly achieved in some areas of physical handicap. Retrolentil fibroplasia, to which reference was made earlier, is a case in point. Osteomyelitis (infantile paralysis), so common a crippling condition a few years ago, is now seldom seen in classes for crippled children. The Salk and Sabin vaccines have markedly changed the complexion of educational programs for crippled children. The development of ophthalmological and optometric techniques, the refinement of lenses, and the creation of specialized teaching techniques have reduced by more than a thousand classes the number of educational programs specifically devised for the partially sighted in the United States in the past twenty years. Equivalent gains have not been experienced in the area of mental retardation.

We are reminded of the fact that routine measures, when universally applied, could effectively control the clinical problem of phenylpyruvic oligophrenia. Understanding the role of kernicterus in mental retardation has also made a significant stride ahead. Furthermore, very recently developed vaccines may make the issue of rubella and the resulting mental retardation, brain dysfunction, cerebral palsy, deafness, cardiac disorders, and a myriad of other disabling conditions, singly or in combination, inconsequential. Although important, percentage-wise these are but small inroads on the major problems of mental deficit.

The great problems of genetics in relation to the endogenous mentally retarded have yet to be mastered and to be understood to a point where acceptable preventative measures can be initiated. Such problems account for much more than half of the total area of retardation. The significant problems of the exogenous mentally retarded children, who in this country had their stimulus originally from researchers at the Wayne County Training School, have yet to be definitively explored. Prevention and remediation and habilitation are not yet fully understood. The social and educational problems of this group of mentally retarded children have been lost to view in the greater interest that the professions have given to the child with brain dysfunction of normal intelligence. As a matter of fact, it is more common than not that mentally retarded children with brain dysfunction are actually legally excluded from educational programs for children with brain dysfunction. This is true in spite of the fact that much of what is known about the education of intellectually normal children with brain dysfunction came from the initial studies of exogenous mentally handicapped children. This issue must be opened up and these children must be given their rightful opportunity for educational and medical programs conceived to meet their special and unique pathology and need.

One reason why only such modest steps forward have been made in resolving the problems of children with brain dysfunction and retardation is the fact that professions most often have engaged in separatism and have operated in a parallel fashion rather than in a unitary fashion. This is not to be construed to mean that there is no research except interdisciplinary research. Every profession has obligations to solve the problems that are particularly related to it. The broad complex of medically oriented professions must not only initiate studies but continue to pursue those studies that have already been initiated to refine their own diagnostic techniques, treatment approaches, operative interventions, and habilitative procedures.

Pathology and *histology* must continue their separate investigations of cellular and tissue abnormalities, and out of these studies shed new light on the normalcy of living matter. *Embryology* must continue its basic studies of life before birth. *Neurology*, in the most exact definition of that term, must continue to study the function of the cell in a neurological setting, and it must determine the interrelationships that exist between cells and systems of cells in the dynamic action of the organism. *Psychology* must study what goes on at the synapse and shed light on this action in terms of learning and adjustment. *Genetics*, in an ever wider and deeper penetration into chromosomal studies, must seek ways of controlling mutations and of avoiding the union of hereditary systems from which retardation in any form can be predicted. *Law*, in keeping with democratic traditions and respect for human rights, must seek ways and implementations to permit the basis of sound sex education in the schools; to establish birth control programs where needed as a method for protecting the society of which the individual is a vital but still a single element; to permit under careful controls, to be established by the profession and the courts, the legalization of abortion when it is indicated to be in the interest of society; to develop legal concepts that will be accepted as universal truisms to permit all men—regardless of their intellectual status, as well as their race, religion, or creed—to ask for and receive all benefits of society that are within their ability to use appropriately. *Social work* must study the impact of disability on the family constellation and seek ways of more surely maintaining family integrity in the face of the demoralizing effect of disability—particularly long-term disability as is the case in mental deficit. *Education*, not to be ignored in this spirit, has its responsibilities too.

Briefly stated, then, there are for each profession areas that rightfully need its single research thrust. There are problems for which the men of a single profession alone have the training and the techniques at hand for logical attack and solution.

In this vast effort of parallel research activities no one profession can be considered to be the more important. It is truly a matter of equals among equals, for the efforts of all in concert are needed to understand and ultimately to minimize the problem whose solution is sought. One of the very healthy signs of professional maturity that one sees in the United States today, if indeed not in many countries, is the feeling of interprofessional respect that is developing. Gone, except in the minds of a dwindling minority, is the feeling that one profession, medicine, is the capstone of all professional insight and knowledge. In its place is the recognition by the great medical minds of this generation that medicine alone cannot solve all the problems of mankind, but that it too is dependent on the support and understanding and learning from the galaxy of professions that are concerned with human development. Gone in the minds of all those save the most immature is the attitude that medical personnel represent outworn models that must be attacked. In the place of this unfortunate attitude is the reality of the pediatrician or psychiatrist and the pediatric clinical psychologist joining forces as professional partners in a common practice. Thoughtful physicians recognize the skills of the well-prepared psychologist. Certainly if negative attitudes still exist, they cannot be tolerated any longer. As competency appears in the special education classroom, medical practitioners and psychologists are the first to recognize it and cooperate with it.

What we are seeking in these statements is an ecumenical movement among professions. I am not approaching the matter from an emotional orientation whatsoever. I am approaching the issue from the realistic point of view that science today is too complicated to be the province of a single profession. The human organism is not owned by a single point of view. To understand it is the obligation of many professions and many points of view. Each profession can accomplish much alone, but it can accomplish much more for the society that supports it if it harmonizes and amalgamates its interests with its sister professions to the end that a joint attack can be exerted.

Interdisciplinary research, over and above that of the specialized research of a single discipline, is also needed. Here the imagination of men must be given full vent. The limits of interdisciplinary action have not even been initially dented. The long-term interuniversity, interdisciplinary Perinatal Research Project, now in its eighth year, after four years of planning, already is becoming recognized as perhaps the most exciting and most significant action of recent professional history. Fifteen medical centers in the United States have joined with the National Institute of Neurological Diseases and Blindness (NINDB) with all their interdisciplinary ancillary personnel, to study 50,000 mothers from the approximate point of conception, through labor and thereafter, until their offspring complete the first year of school. Geneticists, sociologists, obstetricians, pediatricians, pathologists, psychologists, psychiatrists, speech pathologists, educators, and others in interdisciplinary teams in each of the fifteen locations are simultaneously functioning as a national interdisciplinary research unit to understand, among many other things, the effect of neurological insult on the mother and on the developing human organism. This, in relation to the Perinatal Laboratory for Infrahuman Organisms at Puerto Rico, should provide, among other things, a significant breakthrough in understanding the exogenous mentally retarded and the intellectually normal child with brain dysfunction.

The brain studies, begun originally by the National Society for Crippled Children and Adults under the leadership of Meyer Perlstein and more recently assumed by the NINDB to try to ascertain common pathology in the brains of individuals who had the diagnosis of cerebral palsy, is another example of interdisciplinary research and action that functions at the cutting edge of knowledge. Obviously, in this type of research there is no place for the educator; for in this interdisciplinary action, the educator plays no part in the team. This is not to indicate that the educator is less skilled than those members who are on the team. It is merely to recognize that sometimes teams do not need representatives from every field and that no one profession can serve all fields equally. If the educator is not included in this team action, he must not give way to immaturity that results in failure to cooperate with his professional colleagues on other problems where he does have competency.

Interdisciplinary action can be observed in still another area that at first glance might appear to be outside the professions of medicine and psychology; namely, a study of the competencies needed by teachers of children who have brain dysfunction. Such a study, now concluded (Cruickshank, 1966), was the basis of one of the most satisfying interdisciplinary activities I have ever had. Eighteen persons consisting of general educators, clinical psychologists, a psychiatrist, neurologist, optometrist, educational psychologist, special educators, psychopharmacologist, pediatrician, neuropsychologist, individuals concerned with cognitive structure, speech pathology, and those with other professional concerns worked for some six months to develop a model of the bases of competency of teachers. In a prolonged seminar attended by all of these persons, neurology sought to understand education's point of view, and vice versa, in the development of common operational models; psychopharmacology sought to integrate its knowledge with speech pathology, and both with special education; proponents of cognition and perception assisted in elaborating educational methodology to the end that stronger concepts were possible. It was a demonstration of the best minds of the nation, irrespective of their professional preparation, attacking a problem that affected all of them and seeking a solution that would benefit each ultimately.

So, too, in the area of brain dysfunction, interdisciplinary research must tackle significant problems, solutions to which are still to be sought. This can be done only in those major university complexes wherein are represented all the disciplines needed and where these, in turn, are represented by men of quality who have at their fingertips the scientific armamentarium for modern research: laboratories, statistical services, computers, and systems for information retrieval that support the complete epigenesis of an idea. Some of the elements that I shall mention are, of course, presently under study and have been for many years.

Pediatricians, psychologists, ophthalmologists, optometrists, and educators in union must become concerned with the enigmas of the blind or partially sighted brain-injured child. Neurologists as well as educators, psychologists, and pediatricians must make significant thrusts in better understanding the perceptually disturbed cerebral palsied child. Jointly medical personnel, psychologists, nurses, social workers, and educators must clearly define and study the family adjustment problems that surround the presence of a child with brain dysfunction in the home constellation. Sociologists, psychiatrists, psychologists, and educators must combine their efforts to solve the problems of community acceptance of the mentally retarded worker and to harmonize the conflicts that now exist between the developing self-concept in the retardate and the community's self-concept, middle-class respectability, and guilt.

Genetic psychology, genetics, embryology, and neurology must, as separate disciplines, join together to the single goal of ascertaining the problem of fetal growth in relation to spontaneous developmental arrest and the sequelae to this phenomenon insofar as brain dysfunction is concerned.

Neurology and experimental psychology must join to ascertain what exactly happens at the synapse during conditioning and what is the effect of genetic deprivation on the synapse.

Education, labor economists, and business-administration leaders must study the issue of automation as it relates to brain dysfunction. Is automation in fact a source of economic disruption for the disabled, or may it indeed make it possible for the disabled to compete with individuals of intellectual superiority more equitably? The concept of interdisciplinary effort must expand.

Educators, labor-union representatives, and business management must study and devise ways of serving youth who have brain dysfunction to the end that the transition from the shelter of the school into the competition of the labor market is achieved with the emotional adjustment and community adjustment of the individual intact. Business management, employers, and labor leaders must join with educators in determining what is the most significant curricular program that can be devised to bring those with brain dysfunction to the maximum of their potential with the least trauma to them. to their families, and to the community in the process thereof.

There is indeed a role for theology and ethics to play in an interdisciplinary concept as many theoretical models are suggested for the control of mental retardation and brain dysfunction. There is little need for greater elaboration of what is probably already commonplace—or should be. The point I make is that we need interdisciplinary research that is limited only by the imagination of the individuals involved.

Intradisciplinary research also is needed to drive deep thrusts along parallel lines of scientific investigation. With a well-executed program of both types of activity, there is little question but that solutions will be achieved in a reasonable time and, in terms of the history of this culture, at a reasonable cost. Thus the solution of the broad issue of retardation and mental deficit itself is needed for the protection of future generations of our society, the second of the two aspects of this great problem that was earlier mentioned.

The other aspect mentioned is the realistic fact that the present generation of children who have brain dysfunction and their families must be served. This issue, equally important, can be discussed with greater dispatch, for it is closer to us and is the one we see more frequently.

It is impossible for us to close our eyes ostrich-like and to deny the existence of a great population of children, youth, and adults in our society who have brain dysfunction. They are with us. They defy the ignoring attitude of society. They cannot be written off as can be an international debt, or by agreement be erased. They are indeed in many instances a significant part of our economic structure, and they may make significant contributions to our national economy. The present generation is no longer a problem of genetics, nor indeed is it a problem of medicine, except as medicine may be interested in the long-term chronic aspects of deviation. This is not now a matter of eugenics or prevention. This is a reality. These people exist. They must be served. They must be housed. They must be educated or trained. Their parents must be strengthened and supported. They must be prepared for whatever employment is appropriate to their potential. Thus, vast service programs must be envisioned throughout the country. But, for too long a period, these service programs have been left to chance, to misguided if well-intentioned leadership, or to programming based on fallacious premises. If these are to be minimized and in their stead be achieved the substitution of quality programming based on research and appropriate conceptual model, then demonstrations of broad interdisciplinary dimension must be created that can serve a leadership function. What exactly is meant?

First, for example, in a related field, studies of Kirk (1958, 1962) have indicated the value of preschool programs for the mentally handicapped child. With these, the growth of the child is likely to reach its maximum with less intervening plateaus, with a more intact ego, and thus with a better overall adjustment than would be attained by one who has not experienced this training. Kirk had certain basic notions of what this program should entail, including such things as visual-motor training, eye-hand coordination skills, self-help skills, and socialization activities of a broad nature. In like manner, demonstrations of high quality nursery school programs for children with brain dysfunction are needed as substitutes for the stagnant programs of baby-sitting that are all too often observed.

Secondly, it is my considered opinion that the great majority of educational programs that do exist for children with brain dysfunction, are inappropriate for those they serve. More than a great majority of educational programs are watered-down college preparatory programs or purely remedial involving little or no modification of time in which the content is presented and supposedly integrated by the child. In 1968 teachers are being prepared to teach these children from a point of view that regards brain dysfunction as synonymous to endogenous retardation and from a remedial education point of view when there is nothing to remedy. Somewhere, somehow, a demonstration of what good teaching is for children with brain dysfunction, of how sound curricular concepts are achieved, and of how they are implemented must be established for others to see, to understand, and to use as a model. Pathway School is in large measure serving such a function and is to be commended in this sense.

Teacher-education programs and educational research centers can be conceptualized along with these demonstrations, from which educators, well based in solid educational concepts, will be sent to take their places as community leaders and to serve children and parents. These educational and prevocational demonstrations will also serve as places where young pediatricians, neurologists, psychiatrists, and psychologists will see what comprises a good educational program for those having brain dysfunction. They will see what entails reasonable expectancies for these children. They will see what growth and achievement rates realistically should be for such children. They will be better prepared to serve their patients and clients when, as independent professional workers, they receive them in their private practices and are required to counsel their families.

How many community mental health centers have failed when faced with clients who have brain dysfunction because no one on their interdisciplinary service team knew how to deal with brain dysfunction as an entity; educators in terms of realistic education, psychologists in terms of realistic child-development concepts, social workers in terms of realistic impact of the deviation on family structure, pediatricians in terms of realistic counseling of the parents? A demonstration involving a dynamic child-guidance program for children with brain dysfunction would not only provide direct service, but would again provide a conceptual model for other communities. More important, it would provide a training center in which young people as a normal part of their professional preparation for the above-mentioned disciplines would experience and witness realistic planning.

There *is* something different about brain dysfunction in comparison with normal child growth and development. Psychologists need to understand brain dysfunction per se, not just from the textbooks. Practical experiences must be provided for every school psychologist and clinical psychologist to meet this problem head on, first hand, in terms of psychodiagnosis, psychotherapy, parent advisement, and prevocational guidance. Social workers, public health nurses, and indeed hospital nurses in bedside contact with children need to understand the learning problems and adjustment problems of children with brain dysfunction, for each member of each profession mentioned will have to do teaching of some sort in planning with and for these individuals. This must come through direct contact with an interdisciplinary center. Young medical and dental students, in order to meet the total demands of their profession, must know and understand brain dysfunction also. The dental specialist who has never worked with children who have brain dysfunction is often faced with a new and very perplexing experience when he first receives such a child into his office and into his dental chair. Theological students can receive rich practical experiences that will make them better able to serve the needs of their future parishes if during their preparation they have had experience, under supervision, with disability and its impact on family life and living. The demonstration center is an absolute in considering the responsibility of the professions in meeting society's demands.

The relationship of the demonstration center's activities to the interdisciplinary research mentioned earlier is probably obvious, but this should not be overlooked. One will support the other to a certain extent, although the interdisciplinary and disciplinary research will probably make greater use of the demonstration center than the other way around. Together, the two thrusts will be the ingredients of a nearly perfect program.

There remains still another significant matter to discuss. This is the matter of the interdisciplinary-team concept itself. I have spoken at some length of interdisciplinary research. I have urged interdisciplinary experiences for young people in demonstration centers. I might well have also spoken at length of interdisciplinary teaching, which is both possible and necessary as we envision professional preparation in all professions in this complex field.

We hear on all sides discussions about the interdisciplinary team, an interdisciplinary entente, which is to accomplish all the things I have been suggesting. The implication is that if an interdisciplinary consortium is organized, ends will immediately be accomplished and all goals achieved. The "team" has become a magic word in the professions. As the young person speaks glowingly of "team action," so the more mature person often speaks of the "so-called team," using this term with a bit of wistfulness and with the hope that he will shortly find what he seeks. Still more maturity often brings discouragement on the part of professional people in the knowledge that they have really never seen a team that works effectively and realistically on an interdisciplinary level. That this is indeed a fact is all too true. The team concept has been administratively short-changed and too often fails to meet the expectancies for it. The lay public becomes confused, for all too often again it has been assured that the only way to effect a community program is via the team approach. When the team approach doesn't work, consternation and aggression often result. No one is the winner.

This is true, I believe, because of a misconception of what professional people are and what they need or do not need in order to function adequately on a team. It is too often assumed that because a professional person *is* a professional person he can automatically and spontaneously become a team member who works in harmony with other professional people. It is assumed that this is a part of his preparation, if not indeed innate in professionalism. It is furthermore assumed that all persons have equal ability in getting along with one another and that team members are endowed by the very nature of the team concept with a capacity for intrateam cooperation. Nothing could be further from the truth.

In the first place, it cannot be assumed that every professional person is equally able to participate as a team member. The concept of individual differences is well recognized with respect to children. It is not so well recognized in considering adults. It is essential that we do recognize it in adults, however. Serious problems will be avoided if it is remembered that certain individuals are better soloists than they are members of a quartet or chamber ensemble. For team action, individuals must be selected who are able to participate without threat in the group process.

What is to happen when an individual whose skills are needed is not one who can tolerate a team approach or when the team cannot tolerate the individual? It is quite possible to function well in these situations, not by including the irritating maverick personality on the team but by making that individual a satellite to the team and providing for him a bridge with the team through one member who is able to develop mutual respect between himself and the individual of concern. Remarkable team action has often been observed with an interdisciplinary hard core operating sometimes with as many as three or four satellite members. To accomplish this is the function of administration.

In this respect it is necessary that young people, as a normal part of their professional preparation, not only see teams in action, but actively serve on several to become skilled in the matters of interpersonal relationships. What football coach in his right mind would take a person from the stands and put him on the field without practice in team function? But in the professions we do this every graduation day. Upon graduating young people from colleges and universities, we send them into schools with the dictum, "Function as a team member," whereas most of them have never seen a team. I do not mean to imply that all persons must have the skills for interpersonal contacts, but if these are as important as we are led to believe, then those persons must be selected who have these skills as a part of their dossier of personality characteristics.

Secondly, it is important to conceptualize the team in terms of the minimal number of members needed, not the maximum that might be nice to have. It is not necessary to have a representative of every department in a hospital or school on the team simply to be able to say it is interdisciplinary. In tennis a team is two people. In football it is eleven. In other activities the number is determined by what is necessary—and no extras are allowed! What is the size of an interdisciplinary team in the area of brain dysfunction? It should be only that number minimally required to do an optimal job, and it need not always be the same size for every facet of the work. The teacher, the psychologist, and the pediatrician may be the team insofar as school adjustment is concerned, with the school social worker a member if possible. The teacher, the rehabilitation representative, the school-work coordinator, and the social worker may be the team insofar as the adjustment of the adolescent with brain dysfunction into the community is concerned. The neurologist and the psychologist alone may be the team in a short- or long-term neuropsychological study.

Thirdly, every team will require a captain, or if such structure is too limiting, then certainly a coordinator. It is absurd to think that everyone can participate on an equal footing or with an equal amount of self-developed leadership and motivation. Team function is not merely an exercise in professionalism. Its aim is to accomplish something vital for the child and his family or to participate in ongoing research that must be kept stimulated. Social psychologists could do well to make some very careful studies of the role of the leader in an interdisciplinary situation. The leader must be tolerant. He must respect others. He must have the ability to help individuals face failure or misjudgment. He must be able to synthesize ideas. He must be able to insure the status of each and every member of the team. Finally, he must be able to make decisions and to point up steps next to be taken.

Who is the leader? The leader of the team in most instances should be the person representing the profession that will have final responsibility in that instance. Hence, in a hospital-treatment situation, the team leader should come from medicine or hospital administration. All other team members are ancillary. In a school situation, the team leader is the educator in spite of the fact that school health or physical disability may be the topic for discussion. Legal responsibility is invested by the state in the educator, and in this situation the medical personnel are ancillary—important, but ancillary to the main function of the school. Teams break down in public school systems because historical precedent alone is used to dictate leadership roles. Historical precedent must give way to legal responsibility in service areas, or to professional goals when research is involved.

Finally, in this recital, I would point out that teams of an interdisciplinary nature often fail to function because the element of *time* has not been adequately considered in projecting group action. Professional persons who have been concerned with their own and their profession's problems for a number of years cannot be expected to shift gears at a moment's notice and begin to think in a completely different frame of reference. Teams can be effective constructs only when ample time to practice is available. Medical, educational, and psychological representatives, as well as other professional representatives, need just as much if not more time to become effective members of a team as do baseball, football, or basketball athletes. They perhaps need more time, for their orientation—at least to date—has been directed toward individual participation, not toward responsibility in concert with others. Time is interpreted not to mean a single meeting of the team or a period of one week. In some instances time is interpreted to mean many months. It is an interesting psychological and indeed sociological observation that effective team function requires (a) time for people to appraise themselves in relation to their professional peers, (b) time for individuals to establish their status in the group, (c) time for individuals to inform their associates in one way or another of their competencies, (d) time for leadership to exert its influence and to be tested by team members, and (e) time to group and regroup insofar as intrateam dynamics are concerned. Some individuals, in spite of the fact that they may be leaders in their profession, may not ever have functioned on a team. Such individuals often become exceedingly disturbed in the initial activities of team participation, because decisions are not easily reached or are not reached at all. Neither the degrees following one's name, nor years of experience in professional activities, nor even a long life and staff seniority insure effective team function. Time must be built in administratively for any interdisciplinary venture, or it is likely to be minimally effective, if not completely ineffective.

Interdisciplinary research to provide a frontal attack on the long-term problems inherent in brain dysfunction, demonstration programs to provide leadership in the solution of current problems of service and a basis for short-term research, and a thoughtful appraisal of the dynamics of team function as well as the ingredients of good team operation—these together are the major elements that must be secured in order to attack effectively the problems of disability in the broadest sense and of brain dysfunction in particular.

William M. Cruickshank

Director, Institute for the
Study of Mental Retardation

Ann Arbor, Michigan
Fall, 1968

REFERENCES

Cruickshank, W. M. (ed.). *The Teacher of Brain-Injured Children.* Syracuse: Syracuse University Press, 1966.

Kirk, S. A. *Early Education of the Mentally Retarded—An Experimental Study.* Chicago: University of Illinois Press, 1958.

————. "Effects of Educational Treatment," *Mental Retardation*, eds. R. L. Masland, R. E. Cook, L. C. Kolb, Research Publications of the Association for Research in Nervous and Mental Diseases, XXXIX (Baltimore: Williams and Wilkines, 1962), 289-94.

The President's Panel on Mental Retardation. *Report to the President: A Proposed Program for National Action to Combat Mental Retardation.* Washington, D. C.: U. S. Government Printing Office, 1962.

Preface

This book is a product of twenty years of query, toil, and much help from a myriad of persons. Adult patients in mental hospitals were the first to teach me that it was possible to alter the way a person functioned, even though he had been diagnosed as having a hopeless ailment of the brain. In spite of their own accurately diagnosed chronic brain ailments, many demonstrated that they were affected by the environment, that they could learn a variety of skills, that they could retain and apply what they had learned. They showed me that their outlook on life and their relationships with others improved as they felt pride in their accomplishments. All indicated to me that the way they functioned must be correlated with more than the pathology inherent in certain tissues of their brains.

Children with learning and behavioral disorders due to brain dysfunction have been my main and most admired teachers, however. These youngsters have been cited by me in previous books and in the present one. Although their names are fictitious, their problems have been very real. Sharing those problems with the children and their families and attempting to help find the solutions to them have charted for me the requirements of an effective habilitative program.

During the past seven years, The Pathway School, in Norristown, Pennsylvania, has worked to implement those requirements by building a habilitative program that would enable youngsters with brain dysfunction to graduate into the stream of regular education, where they then could succeed. In keeping with its founding goal of being a demonstration, training, and research organization, Pathway has shared whatever it has learned with various public school agencies. Translating its interdisciplinary program, which employs a full-time habilitative staff larger in number than the student population it serves, into what is needed but feasible for public schools has been a valuable education.

To share with public education in general its current knowledge of concepts and techniques for establishing programs for these children in public schools, Pathway sponsored an institute, "Concepts and Techniques for the Establishment of Programs for Brain-Injured Children in Public Education," held May 5 and 6, 1967, in Washington, D. C. It was attended by representatives of agencies in 26 states and the District of Columbia. Because of his notable leadership in helping public schools to establish programs for these children, Dr. William M. Cruickshank, Director of the Institute for the Study of Mental Retardation at the University of Michigan, was asked to present the keynote address. In his speech he emphasized the inter-disciplinary nature of the service, research, and training necessary today in the broad field of mental retardation and in the field of brain dysfunction. That speech serves as the Foreword to this book. The presentations of the other panelists who participated in the Institute prompted a number of ideas also found in this book.

The participants in the institute were:

William C. Adamson, M. D., Director of Clinical Services at Pathway;

John J. Bassler, M. Ed., English-Reading Supervisor, Office of Public Instruction, Springfield, Illinois;

Marcia Berlin Wicks, M. Ed., classroom instructor at Pathway;

William P. Camp, M. D., Director of Clinical Services at Pathway (he is now Superintendent of Friends Hospital of Philadelphia);

Benjamin W. Champion, M. Ed., Educational Coordinator at Pathway;

Lois Cindrich, B. S., classroom instructor at Pathway;

Bryant J. Cratty, Ed. D., Associate Professor, Department of Physical Education, and Director of the Perceptual-Motor Learning Laboratory, University of California;

Gerald N. Getman, O. D., D. O. S., Director of Child Development at Pathway;

Gertrude Justison, Ed. D., Associate Professor of Education, Graduate School, Howard University;

Leslie W. Kindred, Ph. D., Professor of Educational Administration, College of Education, Temple University;

Rosemaur Leonardo, M. A., classroom instructor at Pathway;

Shirley R. McNary, M. A., Educational Supervisor at Pathway;

Erma C. Metz, M. S. S., A. C. S. W., Chief of Parent Counseling Service at Pathway;

Sylvia O. Richardson, M. D., Assistant Clinical Professor of Pediatrics, College of Medicine, University of Cincinnati, and Editor of Children's House Magazine;

Thomas J. Scharf, M. S., C. A. S., Resource Center Supervisor at Pathway (he is now Supervisor of Special Education of the Department of Public Instruction, Bureau for Handicapped Children, Wisconsin).

Since that Institute, many aspects of Pathway's habilitative program and its underlying concepts have been further refined and elaborated, and they have had additional trial in the field, at public schools. Those which have proven most useful to public education form the essence of this book.

It is not the purpose of this book to provide a recipe for duplicating Pathway's program for children with brain dysfunction. Its intent is to acquaint the entire community and all within, who can offer direct service to this child, with the enormity of his problem and to furnish them with guidelines for his habilitation. Within this framework, the solutions to the child's specific problems in his home community are left to the creativity and sensitivity of the reader. In this way the solutions will be prescriptive to the child's individual needs. Although the guidelines presented in this book have proven helpful and thus far look promising as a route to the habilitation of this child, they are not offered as a panacea. They are not set forth to be automatically and uncritically ingested. To the contrary, these guidelines are offered in the hope of assisting all who are of service to this child and his family to assess more critically the effectiveness of what they do and why they do it. Moreover, it is hoped that these guidelines will be discriminatively evaluated and, as a result, replaced by more effective ones.

Never in the history of education has there been such an opportunity to provide true habilitation for the child with brain dysfunction and for those with other exceptionalities. Today's unprecedented knowledge and technology are the forerunners of every child's being able to develop optimally as a holistically functioning organism. I have no illusion that to achieve this realistically and to instrument it economically will be easy. But we must do it. It is our responsibility to ourselves and to this generation and future generations of children. It is our obligation to utilize all the richness of our present knowledge and technology to provide children with a heritage of freedom for optimal development rather than to allow them to inherit the wind of educational obsolescence.

Sheldon R. Rappaport
President

The Pathway School
September, 1968

Acknowledgments

As implied in the Preface, this book could never have been written without the tutelage of hundreds of children with brain dysfunction and their families. The contribution of the entire staff of The Pathway School, who have worked arduously to examine and refine habilitative concepts and techniques, is also acknowledged with pleasure and gratitude.

To Dr. William M. Cruickshank goes special thanks, not only for his cogent thoughts expressed in the Foreword of this book, but also for the inspiration and help he has provided for many years and continues to provide.

The able panelists who participated in Pathway's 1967 Institute are gratefully recognized for their presentations from which a number of this book's concepts emerged. Special credit goes to Dr. Leslie W. Kindred for ideas that were adapted for use in Chapter II, to Dr. Bryant J. Cratty for ideas that appear in Chapter VII, to Miss Rosemaur Leonardo for the case study in Chapter VII, and to Dr. William P. Camp and especially to Dr. William C. Adamson for their contributions that helped in the development of Chapter IX.

Particular appreciation goes to Dr. Darell Boyd Harmon, Consultant and Non-Resident Research Professor of the Environmental Design Center at the University of Wisconsin and also Executive Director of the Texas Interprofessional Commission on Child Development, for his contributions both to this book and to the development of Pathway's program.

Signal gratitude goes to Dr. Gerald N. Getman. Many of the concepts that appear throughout this book were either contributed or clarified by him, as a result of many pleasant and stimulating hours of discussion and as a result of his vast knowledge of child development that has greatly enhanced Pathway's total program.

Abiding appreciation also goes to Mrs. Shirley R. McNary; without her help, this book would not have reached completion. Despite her already hectic schedule, she gave generously of her time and experience to discuss the contents of this book from the vantage point of the needs of the classroom teacher.

Many thanks go to my charming and most capable secretary, Mrs. Joyce McSurdy, who graciously and efficiently added to her already full complement of responsibilities that of preparing the manuscript for this book.

Finally, for preparing the figures that appear in this book, many thanks go to Joseph R. Tremul, Pathway's Coordinator of Educational Technology, and to Charles Moore, Graphic Technician, of Pathway's Resource Center.

S. R. R.

Contents

Figures

I. Our Current Status

Man did not invent the atom. It always existed. Man merely belatedly discovered its existence. Similarly, the child who has learning and behavioral disorders due to brain dysfunction also always existed. He has but recently been discovered. Although there is no statistical validation of that statement, it is unlikely that in past generations there were fewer biochemical, traumatic, and other organic causes of brain dysfunction than there are currently. Furthermore, since today's children are expected to absorb greater quantities of information and to comprehend more abstract concepts earlier and quicker than ever before, it is likely that these current cultural factors cause learning disabilities due to brain dysfunction to be manifested, whereas the lesser cultural demands of the past did not.

For the sake of accurate communication, the child with whom this book is concerned should be identified. This child has been described as brain-injured and by at least thirty-five additional terms. Terminology will not be discussed here, because it already has been adequately treated by Cruickshank (1966, Chapter I; 1967, Chapter I), and Clements (1966), to name but two. Although it is the child who is important, not the label attached to him, for the purpose of the topics to be discussed in this book, the problems of the child under consideration can best be described as learning and behavioral disorders due to brain dysfunction. The word *disorder* was selected because it is defined as a condition marked by a lack of order, system, regularity, predictability, or dependability. Furthermore, it connotes an undoing of proper order or sequence, which can be returned to an ordered state. The word *brain* was selected to indicate the importance of the central nervous system in its relationship to the functions of learning and

1

behavior. The word *dysfunction* was chosen to suggest that in all cases, regardless of etiology, there is some insufficiency or alteration of function. Moreover, in many instances an actual injury to the central nervous system cannot be specifically demonstrated. At the same time, there is increasing evidence that disorders within the organism's biochemical (including genetic coding), electrochemical, and molecular chemical systems interfere with the functions of the central nervous system. Another decade or more may be required before the relationship between disorder in those systems and the functions of learning and behavior can be specifically demonstrated and the disorder alleviated on a biochemical or related basis. Meanwhile, the main thrust toward habilitation for these children continues to be working with how they function; and this work is accomplished primarily through education.

Specifically, the children referred to in this book have near-average to superior intellectual potential, which is not fully utilized because of learning and behavioral disorders, which range from mild to severe and which are associated with dysfunction of the central nervous system. These disorders do not result primarily from handicaps of sight, hearing, cerebral palsy, mental retardation, emotional disturbance, or cultural deprivation. However, they may be found in tandem with any of these. Most of the children are boys, the ratio of boys to girls being estimated to range from seven to one to twenty-five to one. Although the majority of the children for whom help has been sought come from middle- to upper-income families, that is probably a correlate to being well-informed and to having the finances necessary to seek professional help. It is not necessarily indicative of a lower incidence of brain dysfunction among low-income families. On the contrary, because of inadequate nutrition and other aspects of prenatal care, as well as a host of other factors, low-income families may prove to have a higher incidence of brain dysfunction. Hopefully this question and others will be answered when the Collaborative Perinatal Research Project is completed.

2

The reader who is interested in exploring the syndrome of problems presented by these children and in learning more about their diagnosis may begin with Cruickshank (1966 and 1967), Cruickshank and Johnson (1967, Chapter VI), and Rappaport (1964 and 1965).

Thoughtful estimates indicate that within the United States there is a frightfully large number of children who have learning and behavioral disorders due to brain dysfunction. At the 1967 International Convocation on Children and Young Adults with Learning Disabilities, Harold Howe, U. S. Commissioner of Education, cited 7 per cent of this country's school children as unable to succeed in regular classes because of this handicap. Through his work in the Johns Hopkins Collaborative Perinatal Study, Dr. William G. Hardy reported that in a population in excess of 1,300 children, 10.0 per cent showed abnormal responses to the infant screening tests (for more information about those screening tests see Hardy *et al.*, 1962). Psychological and neurological examinations confirmed the lack of organismic integrity of those children. These examinations also identified children who had passed the infant screening tests, but who showed behavioral and neurological problems, thereby bringing the total number of children thus identified to 18.4 per cent. Hardy predicts that most of these children will show learning disorders due to brain dysfunction. In all likelihood this disorder disrupts the lives of at least 3,000,000, but more likely close to 8,000,000, of our nation's children and their families. Because our public schools have not as yet established preschool programs that could prevent the main symptoms of brain dysfunction from occurring, and because research has not as yet indicated how to prevent this handicap completely, our burgeoning population can only result in an even greater number of children being thus affected.

In an attempt to care for the needs of these children, seven state legislatures have enacted special legislation to establish the necessary educational programs (*Special Education for Handicapped Children*, 1968, p. 32). In a recently completed survey

3

of the education statutes of our fifty states, entitled "Study of State Legislation" and funded by the U. S. Office of Education, the Council for Exceptional Children (CEC) found twelve states to have within their educational code mention of "children with learning disabilities," or comparable terms. Other states operate programs for such children under the legal definition of physically handicapped, socially and emotionally maladjusted, et cetera. CEC cautions, however, that the existence of a law does not imply the existence of a program. Moreover, an enabling law in no way guarantees the adequacy of existing programs. Enabling legislation must be regarded only as a first preliminary step to adequate educational programs for these children in public schools.

In large measure, the impetus behind the legislation already accomplished in some states and in the process of being accomplished in many other states is a growing popular awareness of these children. This has formalized itself into the parent-professional Association for Children with Learning Disabilities, a national organization with over 200 local and state groups that currently represent more than 6,000 families.

To those who have worked with children who have brain dysfunction, it is entirely understandable that the parents of these children should seek prompt action. Because of their plight, it is only just that today the needs of these parents are no longer being stifled in the throat of quiet desperation, but are being voiced and increasingly listened to. Nevertheless, neither these parents, nor their communities, nor their public schools are certain how to establish appropriate habilitative programs for children who have brain dysfunction.

Part of the confusion lies in the fact that this is an age of change, as much for the field of education as for the rest of the world. No longer is the educator permitted to be content because he is upholding tradition by teaching others in the same way he and his forefathers were taught. Today the younger generation is expected to be knowledgeable about much that their parents will never be expected to understand. Today the parent is expected to encourage the child not to be content with

4

the parent's lot, but to exceed the parents in knowledge, in skill, in education, and in social and economic achievements. Today's teacher is charged with the responsibility of providing this generation with the opportunity to learn what it is expected to know. Such a degree of change in role and in goal demanded of the child, the parent, and the teacher is disquieting to each. None are certain of either the role or goal expected of them, and none know exactly how to go about fulfilling them.

Similarly, the public school is no longer the province of the well child; and the parent is no longer expected to keep the exceptional child hidden so that he does not offend the sensibilities of society. Instead, legislative mandate requires the initiation of appropriate educational programs for all exceptionalities. Unfortunately, change in educational ideology, curriculum, teacher training, and administrative policy cannot occur as rapidly as can the mandate for the change.

The educational changes required for the establishment of high-quality, *appropriate* habilitative programs for exceptional children, and for children with brain dysfunction in particular, are still to be accomplished in most states—even in those states whose legislature has mandated the initiation of such programs. Too often special classes are still based on conceptions of normal children founded on nineteenth-century thinking. When dealing with children who have brain dysfunction, which is perhaps the most complex of all exceptionalities, education cannot be encumbered by obsolete concepts. Nor can education be encumbered by interpreting the parental pressure for action as the command, "Don't think, do!" Action *is* needed, but it must be action that is carefully planned and thoughtfully executed. If properly channeled, the pressure for action can be a carrier wave that will sweep away obsolete concepts and replace them with a greater understanding of the phenomenon of learning than ever before known. Whether history records this as education's best of times or worst of times will be determined by how education uses its present opportunities.

To utilize these opportunities successfully, the first goal of education should be, in cooperation with the community and its professional persons, to intelligently direct the popular surge of interest in children with brain dysfunction, before it becomes a headlong plunge into wasted lives, lost opportunity, and misspent funds. Because the dimensions of public education have been stretched to include all exceptionalities, education has the obligation to help the community become aware that special education is not the Garden of Eden; that unless much effort and thought and planning go into its cultivation, its most abundant crop will be weeds.

It is also the obligation of education to enlighten the community to the fact that even when there is an organic basis to the learning and behavioral disorders of children who have brain dysfunction, education is the primary tool of habilitation for these children. This remains true even though in some cases such children require anticonvulsant or other medications, or even neurosurgery. It remains true even though most children who have brain dysfunction also require and are helped by psychotherapy and parent counseling. It remains true even though more is known today about the biochemical, electrochemical, and molecular chemical aspects of brain function than ever before. Certainly there will come a time when the educator will receive direct help with children who have brain dysfunction from his colleagues in biochemistry and related disciplines. However, that time has not yet come. The important and exciting work currently being done in protein metabolism of the brain and in nerve conduction, for example, is still at the frontier in the laboratory. As yet such work cannot be translated directly into help for children with brain dysfunction.

A habilitative program for children who have brain dysfunction should be established in a community only if the first goal is to return these children to regular classes where they can succeed and grow into self-respecting as well as respectable members of society. Babysitting service is too costly, both in terms of dollars and heartbreak. The community's second goal should be for this program to be available to all children. This can be achieved primarily through public, not private, schools. The number of children who need such a program is so large that private schools cannot be expected to provide the service to all. Moreover, the cost of private schools alone would exclude many.

Concerning costs, the community must also recognize that the national average cost per pupil in regular classes in 1966 was approximately $705 per year. The national average cost per pupil in special education has been estimated to be an additional $217.50 per year.* In contrast to that average of $922.50 spent per year on a child in special education, the national average cost per patient in mental hospitals is $2,544.05 per year. When it is recognized that many children who have brain dysfunction and do not receive appropriate help eventually become patients in mental hospitals or similar institutions, it becomes obvious that the funds expended for special education are both disproportionately small and pitifully inadequate for the needs of millions of American children and their families. Moreover, the community must be made aware of the fact that children who have brain dysfunction comprise by far the largest group who receive service under the aegis of special education.

The taxpayer must be helped to see that to deprive the millions of these children of an appropriate habilitative program would add immensely to the economic burden of society. When deprived of the benefit of such a program, these children cannot earn the income needed to contribute to society, which in most cases they would earn otherwise. Instead of contributing to the upkeep of society, they receive welfare subsidy from it. Moreover, without this program, these children often are unwittingly and inappropriately consigned to the ranks of the mentally subnormal or the mentally ill, who require lifelong maintenance in institutions. Even more unfortunate and costly, both in terms of dollars and pain to the families, is that these children often vent their frustrations and hurt pride in antisocial acts. Thus, if not given proper help, by adolescence they frequently become wards of the court.

*Taken from *Education in the Seventies, Report of Program Planning and Evaluation* (U. S. Office of Education No. FS5.210:151 [Washington: U. S. Government Printing Office, 1968]).

7

Today, an astounding 35.9 per cent of those arrested in our country are referred to juvenile court. Five per cent of those incarcerated in correctional and training institutions are under fifteen years of age, and 22 per cent are under twenty years of age. Although there are no statistics on how many of those children got there via the route of brain dysfunction, one may assume that there are many. Thus, added to welfare subsidy and institutionalization costs for those children with brain dysfunction who are not habilitated is some portion of the $1,303,000,000 spent annually (as of 1965) on penal institutions.

The tax payer can see that it is undoubtedly less expensive to provide appropriate habilitation for these children than to offer no special service whatever or classes that only prepare them for being lifelong expenses to society. Then the community must decide whether the comparative pittance spent for these children, thereby dooming them to lifelong ineptitude, will be tolerated. The community must decide if it will allow this nation's greatest resource, its mentality, to be wasted. For this to be a community's decision would surely be a great American tragedy.

As part of community education, the taxpayer should be acquainted with the fact that appropriate habilitative programs *are* emerging today. For example, the one in Bucks County, Pennsylvania, has an annual cost per pupil of $2,800. This is not appreciably more than is currently being spent on patients in mental hospitals. It is financially sound to invest $2,800 per year for two to four years on a child who ultimately can become a self-supporting, tax-paying citizen, than not to make the investment and thereby be forced into spending upward of $2,500 annually for a decade or for a child's lifetime. Thus, appropriate habilitative programs could save society, over a child's lifetime, tens of thousands of dollars for millions of children. In turn, the billions of dollars thus saved would be relatively inconsequential compared to the blessing of well-being afforded to the children's families in communities throughout our nation.

8

Although the past several years have seen state departments of education and school boards increasingly eager to initiate programs for children who have brain dysfunction, their enthusiasm alone cannot produce effective habilitation. Effectiveness requires a conceptual framework that not only permits the inception of such programs, but from the outset insists on their quality. This conceptual framework provides both the administrator and the teacher with an understanding of what needs to be done and why it needs to be done. It provides for the utilization of all relevant knowledge available, and it makes provision for future knowledge to be attained and applied. Without that, there is little hope of refining or determining the true value of what is being done educationally. This does not imply that every program should have the same conceptual model, only that each should not operate without one.

Today, as in the past, not all educators believe a conceptual model to be necessary. There are some who still advocate that all children who have problems need only to be placed in a special-education class—whatever that is—and in some instances it has been the apotheosis of diverse sins. To put children who have divergent needs together in one classroom, under the instruction of a teacher who has but one, inflexible, and often untrained approach to all the children, cannot prove gratifying or successful for anyone, including the teacher. Although it is not important for the teacher to attach a label to children, it is important to identify their individual needs, so that a program can be designed to meet those needs.

As the understanding of why children have certain symptoms is advanced, and as operational conceptual models are refined, the classification of children will undoubtedly change. Classifications will probably become the natural outgrowth and reflection of the child's functional needs that are to be answered by given programs of habilitation. Until that time, the present classification for children who have brain dysfunction, as well as for children who have other exceptionalities, is sufficient to enable the abolishment of the era of the special class.

9

Today, as in the past, some school administrators still advocate that all children, both with and without problems, need only artful teachers who are devoted to them. In the opinion of such administrators, those teachers require no conceptual model or specified approach simply because they are *artful* and *devoted*. To be *only* artful seems much like flying by the seat of one's pants, which is not known to be the most intellectual portion of the anatomy. Although devotion *is* an essential characteristic of a good teacher, no matter how well-meaning its application, alone, devotion is not capable of habilitating. Neither artfulness nor devotion is a substitute for the skillful handling of a child's problems that are well understood. And the skillful handling and understanding are not inborn characteristics; they come only from proper training and experience.

During the recent years in which classes for children with brain dysfunction have arisen in public schools, it has become increasingly apparent that the well-trained and experienced teacher alone cannot habilitate these children, whose needs are both complex and variegated. Nevertheless, throughout our nation, even in its largest and wealthiest cities, school districts continue to have isolated classes for these children sprinkled among their elementary schools. The teacher of such a class, containing eight or more children, is expected to be autonomous and to answer all needs of the class. Without the benefit of preadmission evaluations to provide even some notion of where to begin, without a teacher's aide, without administrative support, without conferences in which to discuss the needs and performances of the children, without another teacher to stimulate ideas, without counsel from a psychiatrist or a psychologist to help with the behavioral disturbances, and without a social worker to aid with the problems of the harassed parents, the teacher is expected to make classroom materials, order supplies, plan daily lesson routines for each pupil, teach the class, cope with behavioral disturbances, advise troubled parents, attend to all paper work, *and* maintain his or her own psychic equilibrium. What chance of success can such a class have? How many such teachers can be expected to survive, and for how long? What percentage of the children in such a class could be predicted to make sufficient gains to be able to handle normal classroom and family situations successfully? One needs neither a Ph.D. in research methodology, nor a crystal ball, to predict the effectiveness of such a program. What, then, is the rationalization for such classes? It is the school district's response to the popular demand for *action*. It is the soporific that such classes are better than none. It is the self-righteous ruse, "*We* have a program for those kids." Obviously, it behooves both the public school and the community to curb the stampede into action, and to proceed instead as speedily as possible to invest their talents, energies, and funds in building quality programs.

Some school districts have accepted the responsibility for providing a well-trained teacher and a classroom aide, but they continue to regard all conjunctive personnel as unessential luxuries. Only rarely have unaided teachers been able to cope with the feelings and responses evoked from these children. Certainly those rare teachers are not among the recent graduates or the unseasoned. When there is an acknowledged scarcity of all teachers, it is apparent that veteran teachers for children who have brain dysfunction will be scarce indeed. Therefore, supportive help from the psychiatrist or psychologist is not a luxury, but a necessity.

In spite of the fact that some school districts do employ social workers, many school systems still regard their obligation to the child as being confined to his hours in class. Thus, they do not deem parent counseling to be their responsibility. Such a viewpoint ignores the fact that the child spends more time at home than at school. It also ignores the fact that what the child experiences at home can very much influence how effectively he can use what is offered to him at school. Finally, it ignores the fact that regardless of the quality of the classroom program, a child who has brain dysfunction requires the opportunity for home-school consistency if any of the gains he makes are to become an integrated part of himself. From the parents' standpoint, there is nothing more degrading and frustrating than

11

to be helpless with one's own child whose need for help is great. Parents require help both in how they can aid their child's progress and in how they can cope with the customary feelings and response patterns within themselves and the child alike. They can, of course, get help privately or in a community mental-health clinic, but much is lost in the fragmentation that results when separate agencies, whose staffs rarely communicate, work with a given family. So much more can be accomplished when one social worker who knows the child both in the school and in the home counsels the parents.

In school districts where the need for supportive help has been disallowed, as classes have failed or as teachers have had nervous breakdowns, the old-guard educators who have damned psychiatrists and other clinicians now find themselves to be cohorts of the damned. As part of the job, a well-trained teacher who works assiduously at habilitation applies knowledge obtained from other disciplines. That teacher does indeed, for example, effect psychotherapeutic good. However, the teacher achieved such skill not by working in a vacuum, but by working with a team and learning from it.

To be optimally effective the teacher must work in tandem with the team. The teacher needs the team's support, the conviction that there is a common shouldering of responsibility for the child's progress, rather than the expectation that he be all things to both the child and his family. The teacher needs specialists to help with stubborn problems, whether they are faulty number concepts or faulty self-concepts. The teacher needs assistance with the management of the inner feelings and the overt responses aroused by those children. It should not be a luxury to feel assured and at ease while teaching, for these feelings serve to insure the success of the program.

If the wave of popular interest in the child with brain dysfunction is to carry education forward to new heights rather than to scuttle it, public schools must formulate programs that: (1) view this child as a total, integrated organism that needs a total, integrated program in order to have the most effective opportunity for learning; (2) insure the consideration of all aspects of his developmental growth and performance within his educational program; (3) acknowledge learning opportunities to be present both before and after school hours, so that more than classroom conditions are considered, and so that the teacher is not charged with the sole responsibility for the child's habilitation; (4) see this child not only as a pupil, but also as a member of a family and of society, with the result that the home and the community assume their responsibilities in providing adequate and appropriate learning environments. The complexity of the problems posed by the child with brain dysfunction dictates such a comprehensive program. Furthermore, when this child is not habilitated so that he can become a self-supporting, taxpaying citizen, the cost to society also dictates that it is more economical to have such a comprehensive program than to waste mentality in institutions. Because this program is comprehensive and requires interdisciplinary teamwork, neither the parents nor the public schools alone can accomplish it. The required habilitative program can be initiated most readily and effectively through the joint efforts of the school district and the community.

REFERENCES

Clements, Sam D. *Minimal Brain Dysfunction in Children.* Public Health Service Publication Number 1415. Washington, D. C.: U. S. Government Printing Office, 1966.

Cruickshank, W. M. (ed.). *The Teacher of Brain-Injured Children.* Syracuse: Syracuse University Press, 1966.

_____. *The Brain-Injured Child in Home, School, and Community.* Syracuse: Syracuse University Press, 1967.

Cruickshank, W. M., and Johnson, G. O. (eds.). *Education of Exceptional Children and Youth.* Englewood Cliffs: Prentice-Hall, 1967.

Hardy, W. G. *et al.* "Auditory Screening of Infants," *Annals of Otology, Rhinology and Laryngology,* LXXI (1962), 759-67.

Rappaport, S. R. (ed.) *Childhood Aphasia and Brain Damage: Volume II, Differential Diagnosis*. Norristown: The Pathway School, 1965.

Special Education for Handicapped Children. U. S. Department of Health, Education, and Welfare, Office of Education, 1968.

II. Preparing the Community

Before a school district embarks on a habilitative program for children who have learning and behavioral disorders due to brain dysfunction, it must be willing to evaluate candidly a number of factors both within its own organization and within its community. These factors will be discussed briefly in this chapter. Because most are the essence of any successful school program, the reader is encouraged to seek a more detailed understanding of them in such works as Dapper (1964), Johnson and Kartman (1964), Kindred (1957 and 1960), and Sumption and Engstrom (1966).

The school district can readily convince itself that historically the community's lack of knowledge or lack of fiscal support concerning exceptional children is in itself justification for not launching a program for children who have brain dysfunction. The school district could also convince itself on those grounds that it is *forced* to initiate a program, necessarily poor to mediocre in quality, for these children. When examined more closely, such a conviction at times serves the public school's purpose of self-deception, of hiding from its own awareness that which needs to be changed or strengthened within its own philosophy and organization. For this reason, before launching a habilitative program, it is safest to begin by evaluating the factors within the school system itself. Another reason for doing so is because ultimately the authority and responsibility for such a program emanate from the school district. Although total community support is needed for the program to be successful, if the school district itself is not geared for it, the program is doomed to failure before its inception.

What motivates a school system to start classes for children with brain dysfunction? Ideally the answer to that question

15

should be that the school board, the school's administrators and faculty, and the community all were so aware of the need for such classes and so convinced of their necessity that together they worked out the policy and program that would, to the best of their knowledge and talent, insure the habilitation of these children. Unfortunately, the ideal is not yet reality. Many times a school district begins such classes because the superintendent of schools or the supervisor of special education has found that thousands of federal dollars can be injected into the school system's budget under the guise of planning such a program and that thousands more can be received for its initiation. Such grants can be impressive on the school administrator's record and pleasing to the fiscally-oriented school board. In such instances, the prime basis for launching these classes is not the hope of habilitating children, but the hope of furthering the administrator's career or of permitting the school board to avoid requesting an increase in taxes. Both the administrators who harbor these hopes and the school boards that put those hopes into action must look this federal gift horse in the mouth. They must do so to insure their future success and status, if for no other reason—and public schools should abound in other reasons. They must realize that to be responsible for initiating a program that fails for lack of proper planning and instrumentation ultimately dooms them to both public and professional disfavor. They must recognize that to believe otherwise is to foster self-duplicity.

In terms of public and professional recognition and self-fulfillment, it is to the administrator's advantage to originate programs that will be successful for the *children*. In this respect, public schools can profit from what the business world has had to learn for its own survival in a competitive market: success is based upon the ability to provide what the consumer needs.

In an era characterized by change, the business world has been forced into constant assessment of its product, the demand for its product, and the efficiency and economy with which its product is manufactured. Whereas businesses have been forced to do this for their own survival, public schools have not been

16

forced into that role of continuous self-assessment because they are tax-supported institutions. Frequently their fiscal basis and organization are dictated by laws that have not been examined for fifty or more years. For those who seek it, this can provide a convenient rationalization for complacency and declension. On the other hand, there are some school boards that are being prodded into self-evaluation by the very nature of our era of change. Their evaluations are accurate, and the resulting recommended changes are aimed at an improved organization and an enhanced quality of service. When necessary, these school boards are also instrumental in changing the obsolete governing laws that have hampered their progress.

To be effective, a school district's self-assessment must clearly define its purpose, its responsibility, its authority, and the fiscal and personnel allocations by which it is to accomplish its goals. Then these factors must be further evaluated in terms of how well they meet the needs of the community as it currently exists and as it will exist in the near future. Perhaps foresight is not listed as an essential duty in the job description of members of the school board, but it is more economical to ascertain the direction of the community's growth and its future needs than to wage a continuous war with obsolescence.

After the initial evaluation is completed, policies need to be erected. Too often policies are confused with rules or regulations. A policy is a generalized statement of goals and the means for their accomplishment. Policy should guide decision-making and action, whereas rules or regulations should implement policy. If policies do not exist, there is no guarantee that decisions will be made within the framework of consistency. Without a policy, there is no baseline for translating ideas or goals into the specifics of a program. To build a program without first establishing a policy has all the dangers inherent in building a car without a steering wheel: one can never be certain of its direction or into which obstacle it will crash.

Usually, the board of education is charged with the responsibility for developing policies, and the school system's administrators are responsible for implementing policy. Nevertheless,

17

school boards typically have neither the technical competence nor the time required to draft policies. Consequently, they delegate this responsibility to the superintendent of schools, reserving the right to approve or disapprove the drafted policy. Under these circumstances, it is not unusual for the superintendent to draft a policy only to have it rejected by the board of education because the latter did not have the technical competence with which to evaluate it. Such a frustrating and unnecessary stalemate can be avoided if the board of education instructs the superintendent to formulate a given policy, in this case concerning children who have brain dysfunction, with the help of experts who are knowledgeable about the subject and with the help of those persons within the school system who will be affected by the policy when it is put into operation. Herein lies a unique opportunity to involve knowledgeable persons within the community and within the school system in a program from its very inception. Once the policy is developed, both it and the reasons for it can be presented to the school board by the experts as well as by the superintendent who helped to formulate it. This course helps to insure the school board's being informed about, and therefore in support of, a policy with which the school system and the community will have to live for a long time.

Once a school board is convinced of the desirability of a policy, the next step is to convince the community. Progress in public education cannot be made without public consent. Public consent cannot be achieved without planning a system of communication with the men and women who staff the schools, with those whose children attend the schools, and with those who pay the school's bills via their taxes. Then, if local or state laws must be changed, either to permit or to instrument the policy, legal changes can be brought about by popular demand. No politician can oppose public demand for very long. Conversely, no politician can venture on an untried path without a sense of popular support. Lack of public support is an epidemic that undoubtedly has buried a vast number of meritorious ideas of the school districts across our nation. It is high time that

18

public education innoculated itself with the vaccine that can prevent this epidemic—the vaccine of community education and positive public relations in equal parts.

Regardless of the excellence of a policy, and regardless of the excellence of the program that is to be an outgrowth of it, the policy or the program cannot be translated into effective practice unless the public understands, believes in, and endorses both the policy and the program. Moreover, a community cannot be expected to pay for a particular program until it is convinced that its children will derive such benefit from it that it must be purchased for them. Without such an attitude, the typical resistance to educational costs will prevail: the community will want to pay the least amount of money possible for public education.

For practical purposes, this means that when a school board wants to initiate a new program for children who have brain dysfunction, it requires the prior policy that these schools belong to the public and that the public is therefore entitled to be well-informed about the school's needs and operations. Part of that prior policy is the further position that the school operates most successfully with community support, which is dependent upon the maintenance of positive public opinion. Recognizing that opinions are formed on the basis of available information, or the lack of it, the school board, as part of its policy, should consider it important that school activities, methods, and objectives be conveyed to the public, to whom the school board is responsible. Such a policy provides the philosophical base on which the superintendent and others in school administration can build. This philosophical base will prove more helpful and gratifying to the school administrators than will the acquisition of federal funds that were obtained simply because they were available. Serious problems require solutions born of excellence, not expedience.

This base can be built upon, first, through the interpersonal contacts between the school and the parents via telephone, correspondence, and visits to the school, especially those involving the parents of children in the new program. A second means to

19

good public relations is the fostering of constructive interest on the part of community organizations. A third deals with utilizing the mass media such as newspaper stories and television programs. By these means the type of adult education that serves to insure the support of the school's new program can be implemented. However, if community support is to be maintained, such communication and adult education cannot stop when the new program begins. Continuous communication concerning the program's operation, effectiveness, results, unforeseen problems, and ramifications for education in general is also required.

How a program is implemented will depend on the needs of a given community. A metropolitan area has needs obviously different from those of a rural area. In a large, urban community it might be best to have two or three such classes within each school. In a smaller community, a cluster of such classes within a single school might be most feasible. In a sparsely populated rural area, a residential center may be required, with children coming by bus for the five weekdays and returning home on weekends. Similarly, whether a school system initiates mobile diagnostic units, a regional diagnostic center, or a central diagnostic center with satellites spread throughout the area must be determined by the needs of the given community and its professional resources.

During the planning stage, a decision must be made to determine which services will be implemented in the program. To be a genuine reflection of the community's needs and professional resources that decision can best be made through a professional advisory or liaison committee. Hopefully, such a committee will already have been in existence as a result of the school board's instruction to the superintendent of schools to utilize such a committee for the formulation of policy. Because ultimate responsibility for the program is vested in the school, the committee should be headed by the person within the school district responsible for the everyday implementation of the program. Usually, that person is the supervisor of special education. The committee should represent those agencies

20

and/or professional persons in private practice whose services are a necessary conjunction to the educational aspect of the habilitative program for children with brain dysfunction. Not every agency or discipline or professional person within the community needs representation on the committee. In fact, the chairman of the committee should diligently try to limit recruitment to those who can supply direct, relevant, supportive service to the educational program, and within that perimeter, only to those who are the most talented, forward thinking, and open-minded. Even then, ample time must be provided to allow these persons an opportunity to get to know and respect each other as individuals and then to learn how to share ideas from the vantage point of different disciplinary backgrounds in constructive and effective communication that focuses on the child's problem that needs solving.

In general, the areas of service required in conjunction with the educational program are: diagnosis or identification, parent counseling, support for the teacher in terms of determining the adequacy of the organs underlying each of the child's information modes and performance systems, support for the teacher in terms of behavioral management of the child (including psychotherapy), and, in some instances, support for the teacher in terms of medication for the child. Additional supportive services for the teacher, such as in reading, arithmetic, speech and language development, and adaptive physical education, are also required if these are not already available within the school system itself. In regard to supportive services, an important function of the committee is to help establish and maintain open channels for referral and continuous communication between the school and the specialists to whom the children are referred. Perhaps the single factor most vital to successful communication is the committee's realization that knowledge is the province of no one profession. When dealing with problems as complex as those of the child who has brain dysfunction, his habilitation requires that all information about him be shared. In some communities, this realization has enabled such arch enemies as an optometrist and ophthalmologist to relegate their

21

rivalry to the past and to focus their specialized talents in a joint effort to find a solution to the child's problem.

An equally important function of the committee is to help the teacher learn to make those observations for which teaching presents a unique opportunity. It is also vitally important to communicate these observations to the other professional persons working with the child. The teacher can learn to make such observations without interpolating them with value judgments or professional jargon aimed at self-esteem in the eyes of the specialists with whom the information is shared. The teacher who can make accurate observations of a child and effectively communicate these to persons in other professions will make a unique contribution not only diagnostically, but also in terms of the continuous assessment and refinement of the child's total habilitative program.

Once a professional liaison committee learns to function smoothly, it can be called upon to focus expeditiously and effectively on the problems confronting a given teacher or a particular school within a school district. In this way, economically, a school district can have the services of an effective interdisciplinary team in all its schools to support the program for children with brain dysfunction.

Whenever possible, it is advisable to have a dentist and an orthodontist on the committee. When a child who has brain dysfunction enters the office of a dentist who is unfamiliar with the nature of this child's problems, the experience can be traumatic both to the child and to the dentist. Moreover, malocclusions and other orthodontic problems often are interrelated with speech difficulties, head tilts, postural warps, and other problems that add to the child's inadequate performance and interfere with his progress.

Often it is helpful to have the local public health agency represented on the committee. Usually this agency offers maternity and infant care and other health services for those who cannot afford to be followed by private physicians. Such cumulative information on a child obviously is important to the school. Another value some communities have found in the public health agency is that their social workers and nurses have been trained to go into the homes to provide counseling to parents about dressing, eating, and other problems presented by the child in daily living.

In addition to learning what professional resources are available in the community, the administrators in the public school district must also carefully assess how they are deploying the talents of those within their own staff. For example, it is not unusual for the superintendent of schools to claim an inability to pay for the services of a psychiatrist or psychologist to help with the behavioral management of a class when within that school district psychologists are being used solely to grind out tests that have no value to the child's habilitative program. Such tests are not translated into indications for the child's educational program, but instead are filed and looked at twice a year only by a clerk in the principal's office when she sends the test results to the state department of education in order to get fiscal reimbursement for the school district. Such rote and unproductive use of professional talent is always uneconomical and undesirable. When working with children who have brain dysfunction, misspent professional talent becomes even more critical because it can undermine the success of the program.

Most schools do have psychologists, guidance counselors, and nurses. If the administration carefully evaluates the roles of these professional persons and effectively redeploys their talents to provide supportive service to the habilitative program, these required services usually can be achieved without enlarging the fiscal base of operation. By investing relatively small sums for training, the school psychologist, for example, can work with the teacher on a system of testing that is meaningful and easily translated into an appropriate educational program for the child. Also, the school psychologist can learn how to provide the required supportive help to the teacher concerning behavioral management. The school nurse can become acquainted with this child's information systems and their accompanying sensory organs, so that her evaluations of the children become meaningful and essential portions of the program instead of just more

23

data to be filed in the child's folder and to serve no purpose other than satisfying the state law. The guidance counselor also can be of greater value to the habilitative program by being shown how to help parents resolve the problems presented by this child in everyday living.

In order to achieve this, however, the school administration must decide to stop the merry-go-round on which its professional persons have been spinning for decades. New job descriptions and goals are needed to replace those that cannot prove productive in programs for children with brain dysfunction.

School administrators also frequently decry a lack of funds for the special one-to-one help that children with brain dysfunction sometimes need. In some communities, however, innovative programs have been devised in which high-school students have been trained to teach swimming to children with brain dysfunction. The high-school students do this instead of taking gym. On a similar basis other high-school students have been trained to provide adaptive physical education services to these children. Some communities have extended such service into after-school hours, utilizing their teenagers to babysit for the parents. These communities report that their teenagers find gratification in such work, and the juvenile delinquency rate has decreased accordingly.

The service clubs within a community have also been utilized to provide direct service to children with brain dysfunction. These service clubs not only have raised funds for special equipment needed in the program, but they also have invested time under professional leadership to provide camping and other advantageous experiences for the children.

Hopefully, as school districts initiate programs for children who have brain dysfunction, their administrative policy will see the school as responsible for total-life planning for these children. To be effective such planning requires a close alliance with the community's professional resources. In conjunction with a well-baby clinic or a hospital's pediatric department, preschool identification and preventive programs can become a reality. For those who have not been identified until junior

24

high or senior high, classes can be established with prevocational readiness as their main goal. Then, in conjunction with vocational schools and the community's business people, these children can be trained to become proficient in a specific trade. As these children feel useful and worthwhile, they are less likely to act out their frustrations in antisocial ways. The social and economic value of such a program can readily be demonstrated to the community's police, lawyers, judges, and business people.

There is a legion of persons in a community who can help make a habilitative program effective if they are given an opportunity to play a constructive role in it. This requires preplanning and a communication campaign. It necessitates evaluating the resources of a community and spending the time and effort to contact people, to convince them of the importance of their contribution, and to show them the role they can play in the program. Inherent in the habilitative program that is in actuality, not mere lip service, the joint effort of the school and the community is the likelihood of success.

REFERENCES

Dapper, Gloria. *Public Relations for Educators.* New York: Macmillan, 1964.

Johnson, R. H., and Kartman, W. *The School Board and Public Relations.* New York: Exposition Press, 1964.

Kindred, L. W. *School Public Relations.* Englewood Cliffs: Prentice-Hall, 1957.

_____. *How to Tell the School Story.* Englewood Cliffs: Prentice-Hall, 1960.

Sumption, M. R., and Engstrom, Yvonne. *School-Community Relations.* New York: McGraw-Hill, 1966.

III. Preparing the School

Only after the school district has decided upon its policies for the establishment of classes for children who have brain dysfunction should the schools which will have those classes be selected. In part, the selection of schools will depend on the number of children requiring these classes. A rural community may have only enough to fill several classes, and these might be housed in a special-education center, along with classes for children who have other exceptionalities. In communities that have no special-education center, classes for children with brain dysfunction might be added to a school in which classes for the retarded or for another handicap already exist. However, before the decision is made to place classes for children with brain dysfunction in such a school, the principal's experience with the already existing classes for the handicapped and his or her resultant attitude toward the prospect of additional special classes would have to be carefully evaluated.

Those communities that already have a special-education center, or are contemplating building one, should consider the disadvantages of that center for the child with brain dysfunction. Unlike other handicapped children in that center, this child, in general, when identified young enough, can be expected to return to regular class where he then can succeed. To be with children, such as the crippled or the blind, who have no hope of overcoming their disabilities and must adjust their self-expectations to their handicaps, can be harmful to this child's developing a positive concept of himself. Moreover, there is usually much to be gained by providing the opportunity to be in a regular class, even for a small portion of the school day, once he is able to succeed there.

Because transportation is costly, time-consuming, and does not contribute to the child's educational growth, many school systems, when establishing classes for the child with brain dysfunction, try to make such a class available in each of its schools. In spite of the difficulties inherent in transporting children to schools outside their neighborhoods—difficulties even more appreciable for children who are hyperactive and impulse-ridden—they are far outweighed by having a cluster of classes for children with brain dysfunction located in one school.

As will be discussed in Chapter IV, a teacher of these children needs to feel secure with them, to be an ego bank toward them, and to play an important role in changing their self-concept of being inadequate in a hostile, alien land. To accomplish this, the teacher must not have such a feeling herself. Unfortunately, that too often has been the case when only one class for children with brain dysfunction was placed in a school.

Unless initiation of such a class was preceded by careful preparation of both the principal and the faculty within the school, the faculty will have great difficulty in appreciating what problems these children present to the teacher. Because these children look normal, the other teachers expect them to behave normally. Other teachers resent the fact that the teacher of the class not only has a small number of children, but also the service of a teacher's aide. They resent the fact that the aide relieves the teacher for breaks at different times during the day. They resent the fact that the teacher eats lunch in the classroom with the children and thereby "avoids" lunchroom duty. They resent the fact that this teacher also "avoids" playground, study hall, and other duties. In short, they resent the fact that the teacher of children with brain dysfunction does not make those children do what is required of the school's other children. Of course, having a cluster of classes for these children in one school does not in itself guarantee that the other teachers will be less resentful. Nevertheless, their resentment and ignorance can be lived with more easily and in time corrected more positively when one teacher does not have to do so all alone.

27

A cluster of classes offers each teacher of these children additional advantages. First of all, there is the opportunity for communication; the sharing of ideas concerning materials, techniques, and behavioral management. Secondly, it affords better use of the supervisor's time, for two reasons. First, by discussing their own problems among themselves, whenever they have the opportunity, the teachers can crystallize the nature of their problems and have at least some tentative solutions to bring to the conference with the supervisor. Secondly, although children . with brain dysfunction do have many individual differences, frequently the kinds of problems with which one teacher needs help are the same as those with which the other teachers need help. Thus, group conferences with the supervisor are often feasible. Certainly the inservice training of teachers conducted by the supervisor can be accomplished more economically when several teachers are in one place than when they are dispersed.

As yet, no mention has been made of advantages that a cluster of classes offers to the children, only to the teachers. It is not an error of omission, but a point of emphasis. The teachers cannot provide adequately for the children unless they themselves are adequately provided for. The teacher cannot program successfully for the children when encumbered by myriad doubts, confusions, and isolation.

A cluster of classes benefits the children also. Because these children develop at unusual paces, often more disparity is present among the needs and skills of the class by mid-year than was present in September. A cluster of classes offers opportunities for regrouping the children, thereby providing programming for somewhat more homogeneous needs. Another advantage to the children is that by having a larger number of these children in one place permits activities that would not be possible were only six to eight children in the school. Still another advantage to the children is that the larger number makes them feel somewhat less alien to the other children in the school.

Regardless of the number of classes for children with brain dysfunction to be started in a given school, it is imperative to

28

their success that the principal of the school be receptive to them. It is also imperative that both the principal and the entire staff of the school be given a careful orientation before the classes begin. The children can derive little benefit from having classes in a school whose principal was forced to accept them. Even a talented and devoted teacher can do little to offset the attitude fostered by a rejecting principal. If the principal is of the opinion that these children need only "a good clout on the fanny," or that one of these children is more trouble than twenty of the regular students in the school, and these opinions cannot be dissuaded, the children will fare much better in a school whose principal is more receptive to them (Cruickshank, *et al.*, 1969). This usually holds true even when the children would have to travel appreciably longer each day.

When a principal is receptive to classes for children with brain dysfunction, orientation of that principal and the faculty of that school should not be attempted in one meeting—even in an all-day meeting. Both principal and faculty need to know the characteristics of this child and what to expect in their daily encounters with him. Both principal and faculty need to know what role each can play with this child in various situations that will arise within the school day. Those who have worked with children with brain dysfunction can readily anticipate the kinds of problems that will arise between this child and the principal or other faculty members. As an example, a child with brain dysfunction would have to use the regular toilet facilities, unless the special classroom was adapted to include these (which for some school districts may be too expensive to do). This child, on his way to the toilet, might deface or otherwise spoil a display prized by another teacher. Once in the toilet room, he might tease or get into a fight with other boys, thereby coming to the attention of the principal. Such problem situations can be posed in advance, so that the school personnel can see both the child's plight and how to help the child overcome his difficulty in that situation. All school personnel must also know that their encounters with these children cannot go uncommunicated. Each encounter must be communicated to the child's teacher, or to

29

someone else within the school designated to coordinate communication. Moreover, assurance must be given that communication will not be a one-way affair, that follow-up to that incident will be reported to the person who had the encounter with this child. The faculty also must be assured that when a child who has brain dysfunction is deemed by his teacher ready to move into a regular class, even for a part of the day, the teacher of the class will be consulted in advance. That teacher will be thoroughly prepared concerning what to expect of the child, how to handle him, and what to provide for him. Both the principal and the faculty must also know that the classes for children who have brain dysfunction will not be a top-secret mission: from the outset they will be informed of the progress and the problems of those classes, regardless of who does or does not have contact with these children.

Before such classes are begun in a given school, both the faculty and the parents of the children entering those classes need the opportunity to gain an understanding of the program these children will have. For example, both faculty and parents need to understand why a staggered admission has proven successful for these children; why the teacher requires time to get to know the needs of and to establish a relationship with each child in the class individually, before he is integrated into the group (Cruickshank, 1967, pp. 132-37). They also need to know what to expect concerning lunches, transportation, the conditions under which the child will be sent home when he cannot have a successful day in school, the frequency and time of conferences with parents, what communication is needed from the home, and similar topics. (For further discussion of some of these areas, see Cruickshank, 1967.)

One such topic that must be understood is class size. Before such a class is initiated, it is necessary to refer to the state law or school code, because in some states the size of this class is dictated by law. At any rate, both faculty and parents need an explanation of the size of the class: the teachers, so that they do not feel jealous of the teacher who has the smaller class, and the parents, to offset the false impression that their child would progress more rapidly if the teacher spent time only with him. This contention on the part of some parents springs from the same wishful thinking that leads them to give a child three teaspoons of medicine when the doctor prescribed one, believing it will make the child better three times as fast.

As part of their preparation for the establishment of these classes, parents also need the opportunity to work out their feelings that their child will be stigmatized by entering the class. Parents frequently hold this conviction regardless of the official label attached to these classes. The fear of stigma usually emanates from the anxiety of the parent, not from the child. These children almost universally feel relieved to know what is wrong with them and to learn that they can be helped. In fact, such relief is to be expected in view of their deep-seated feeling of inadequacy and long-standing conviction of being totally inept and rejected (to be discussed at length in Chapter IV). Within this context, to learn specifically what is the cause of all their failure and hardship and to be given assurance that their future will be different from their past can only bring them relief. When he entered The Pathway School and first learned of his brain dysfunction, an eight-year-old child voiced it so well: "I always thought that I was a basket case, that there was something so wrong with me that I'd never get a job, that nobody would ever want to marry me, and I'd always goof up everything I'd ever try in my whole life. Now that I know my brain got hurt, and this school can make it work right, and other kids got better and went back to regular school, maybe I can make it too."

When the school's policy is that parents must participate in the program for children with brain dysfunction, parents must know in advance what is expected of them. They must know how frequently they are to attend meetings, where, and with whom. Although they recognize the value of working with the parents of these children and of having the habilitative program extend into the home, many administrators fear that they cannot make the child's acceptance in the program contingent upon parental participation. Nevertheless, there are administrators who have set parental participaction and cooperation as a prerequisite for admission, and have stated this to parents as part of the preadmission evaluation. They have indicated to parents that all programs have certain requirements necessary to their successful operation; a biology class requires the dissection of a frog, a class for children with brain dysfunction requires parental participation. If the parents object to either, the child will not be in that class. By law, the school district can provide homebound instruction to those children whose parents refuse to participate. Although such a stand may seem harsh, parental cooperation *is* essential to this program, and there is no sense in setting up a class and at the same time setting up the odds against its success. Nevertheless, it is usually not necessary to take such a drastic step. If the need for parents to participate is clearly spelled out, and if their apparent uncooperative attitude is carefully indicated in a discussion with the parents, their cooperation usually can be attained.

Another common source of contention that needs to be clarified in advance concerns homework. Before a child who has brain dysfunction can succeed in such an independent activity, he must establish many skills. However, parents are accustomed to children having homework; they therefore need to know that while preacademic skills and other basic ego functions are being established, the child will have none. They also need to know that when he is being prepared for transition into regular class, homework will be a part of that readiness.

Another aspect of planning concerns supervision. Even when a cluster of classes is established in a school, the teachers need supervision. Ideally, supervision should bring the supervisor into the classroom for observation and for direct demonstration to the teacher. This should be followed by a problem-oriented conference between the teacher and the supervisor, focusing primarily on the learning and behavioral problems that arose during the supervisor's visit. If a full-time supervisor is not possible because of budget limitations, the director of special education or someone within that department should visit these classes for such observation and problem-oriented conference on a regular basis. Unless the school principal is trained to do so, such supervision is not the principal's job. The type of supervision that is meaningful to the teacher and helpful to the children requires expertise and successful experience with these children. If the director of special education or anyone within that office has not had adequate experience, that should be remedied before the inception of these classes.

Frequently a teacher who has demonstrated skill in working with these children is chosen to be the supervisor. Selection of the supervisor should not be made solely on this criterion. Some teachers skillful in working with these children do so intuitively and cannot analyze the factors responsible for their success. As a result, they cannot communicate these factors to others. Furthermore, such a teacher, if placed in a supervisory role, could not help other teachers analyze what they were doing in a specific situation or what they should do in that situation to be of greater help to a child. The supervisor not only needs expertise and successful experience with these children, but also the ability to teach teachers.

At times the school principal does have all the qualifications necessary to supervise teachers of children with brain dysfunction. That indeed is a happy coincidence, because the principal then can better relate the supervision to other responsibilities concerning these classes. Regardless of whether or not the principal supervises the teacher, the principal must fully realize the important role the school's chief administrator plays with these children. At the same time, children with brain dysfunction require a teacher who understands both their background and their current needs, they also frequently require the principal's authority to set behavioral limits for them while they are in the process of ego development. For instance, the principal's authority may be needed to let a child know that if he continues to disrupt the class, he will be sent home until he can control himself well enough not to deprive his classmates of their opportunity for learning. Such a setting of limits may have to come from the principal, in addition to the teacher, to be effective. As another example, the principal may have to

33

reinforce the teacher's authority in asserting that a child, although ready to succeed academically in a regular class, cannot enter that class until he learns to control his impulses well enough to raise his hand, rather than blurt out the answer to a question the teacher asked. (The important role of the principal will be discussed further in Chapter IX.)

During the planning phase, provision also should be made for inservice training of the teachers of these classes. Such training provides an opportunity to extend investigation of classroom problems and their solutions, to share information concerning techniques and materials found effective for specific needs, to share principles and practices concerning behavioral management, and to plan activities and outings beneficial to the children. It also provides the opportunity to bring in consultants who can help crystallize solutions to problem areas.

Inservice training also offers the other teachers on the faculty, by attending selected meetings, the opportunity to learn more about children with brain dysfunction and the problems they present to their teachers. It enables the other teachers to learn what happens to children who are not properly identified at an early age. Kindergarten teachers in particular can work with the teachers of children who have brain dysfunction, in specially planned meetings, to develop a program for the identification of such children during the kindergarten year. Such early identification is immeasurably valuable to the child, to the school, to the parents, and to the taxpayer.

When policy has made provision for the redeployment of psychologists and guidance counselors so that they have time to work with teachers and parents of children with brain dysfunction, these specialists also should be intimately involved in inservice training. For them, inservice training provides the clarification of the role of their service in relation to the role of the teacher. It also provides for the communication of how these different roles can most effectively meld to further the child's progress.

The type of planning outlined in this chapter cannot be accomplished in a day, a week, or a month. More likely a year

34

or more will be required for planning, if the program when launched is to function smoothly and successfully. Such a long period may seem a luxury, but it is not. The school board must understand this before it finalizes policy for the establishment of classes for children who have brain dysfunction. There is nothing more demoralizing or expensive than the initiation of a poorly thought-out and inadequately instrumented program. Patchwork is always more expensive than prevention. Moreover, the program that falters from the outset may incur such disdain both within the school system and within the community that it may never overcome the stigma, regardless of ultimate worth. Alexander Dumas said, "Nothing succeeds like success." A correlate to that might be, "Success requires planning." And, for the sake of the school's administrators, the child, the family, and the community, the program must be a success.

REFERENCES

Cruickshank, W. M. *The Brain-Injured Child in Home, School, and Community*. Syracuse: Syracuse University Press, 1967.

Cruickshank, W. M., Junkala, J. B., and Paul, J. L. *The Preparation of Teachers of Brain-Injured Children*. Syracuse: Syracuse University Press, 1968.

IV. A Conceptual Model

As part of the planning necessary to establish a successful educational program for children with brain dysfunction, a conceptual model should be adopted that will furnish that program with a basis for consistency. Such a model would synthesize all pertinent information available and make provision for the incorporation of new knowledge. It would also indicate the means for translating the information into everyday programming for the children. Opportunities for assessing and improving the effectiveness of the program are thereby provided. Within the above frame of reference, a conceptual model presents a system of postulates and descriptions that help in visualizing that which has not been or cannot be directly observed. It provides a logical starting point for launching the program, as well as a reference point against which the operation of the program can be evaluated. To present such a conceptual model is the intent of this chapter.

Because the focus of this conceptual model is on the education of the child, it emphasizes, hopefully, what will prove most useful to the educator; namely, a framework within which a child's daily performance can be assessed and translated into educational programming. Therefore, it bypasses any attempt at mathematical quantification of the key factors involved in learning, and it makes no attempt at a comprehensive statement of what is presently known about the interrelationship of neurophysiology and learning. Nevertheless, the mathematical and neurophysiological concepts that have been expressed by many scientists (such as in Rosenblith, 1961, or by Penfield and Roberts, 1959) form the tacit undergirding of the present model.

As applied to the child with brain dysfunction, this model indicates first, for those who are inexperienced with this child, what he is like at school age and which factors contributed to the picture he presents. An understanding of this picture can perhaps best be achieved by contrasting his development with that of the normal child.

In the normal child, the primary guarantees of his adaptation are built in at conception. Just as genetic coding* tells certain cells to become differentiated into specific tissues and organs, it tells those organs what their functions should be. It also indicates the means by which those functions will become practiced, refined, and organized to prepare the organism for what will be demanded of it through successive stages of development. Actually the exploratory practice, refinement, and organization of the various basic functions begins during intrauterine development, to ready the fetus to cope with its emergence into its new, extrauterine environment. Similarly, after birth the child goes through a series of developmental stages in preparation for the increasing demands for self-sufficiency that life will make upon him. During both the intrauterine and extrauterine development of the organism, what is being practiced, refined, and organized are the basic tools by which the child's ego is fashioned.

The ego, of course, is the central directing force of the mind. It is to the mind what the executive branch of the government is to the country. No child is born with an intact ego, only with the potential for developing one. Whether or not the child will develop an adequate ego is contingent on whether or not all aspects of his central nervous system (biochemical and otherwise) are intact. Only then does the child have the inborn capacity to develop, through growth, experience, and learning,

*Deoxyribonucleic acid (DNA) is the genetic material that contains the biochemical blueprints according to which proteins, the basic building materials of life, are synthesized. These blueprints determine the form and function of each living organism and of all organs within an organism. Ribonucleic acid (RNA) translates the genetic blueprints into building activities by guiding the manufacture of prescribed amino acids and their predetermined configurations to create a specific protein.

37

the primary skills of the ego. These include such important basics as motility, perception, concept formation, and language. Furthermore, no child is born with awareness of others, impulse control, frustration tolerance, or ability to mediate between biological drives on the one hand and environmental demands on the other. Such higher ego skills are developed as an outgrowth of the more basic ego functions. Thus, simply by virtue of being born with an intact central nervous system, the average child has the inherent opportunity to develop all such ego functions in the usual course of growing up.

Initially, cephalocaudal and other aspects of neural maturation provide the child with the opportunity to use and gain gratification from exploratory activity. For example, the child thereby has the opportunity to derive satisfaction from learning to control his generalized motoric responses. He wants and needs that gratification to be able to go on to higher levels of development. If observed while practicing control of his motoric responses through exploratory movement, the infant seems compelled to exercise the same movements over and over again. Even such a rudimentary attempt to gain mastery over one aspect of himself is designed to help him develop what will become a basic, vital tool of his ego.

With further neural maturation, cortical inhibition takes place, thereby allowing the child the opportunity for voluntary practice; in turn, providing him with greater opportunity for mastery and the resultant gratification of self-esteem. The first few years of life—during which the child learns such skills as walking, talking, feeding himself, and being toilet trained—provide him with literally hundreds of opportunities a day for being pleased with himself, for the budding of a positive identity that later will bloom into the conviction, "I am one who can."

While this goes on *within* the child, his strivings are appealing and a source of great pride to his mother, stimulating her normal maternal responses so that she provides him with an *external* source of gratification as well. This, in turn, gives the child the approval, encouragement, and stimulation he needs to achieve still greater mastery and self-esteem. As a result of both

38

the child's inner feelings about his accomplishments and the environment's approval of him, his self-worth is nurtured.

If his parents are not too encumbered by neurosis, and if his environment is reasonably wholesome, his primal feelings about his experiences in this world will be positive. From this base he can establish healthy identifications with his parents and other key figures in his life; and he can interact successfully with other people and the environment so that his higher ego functions, such as frustration tolerance and consideration for others, become established and then strengthened. Because so much of the child's life is focused on school, academic success fosters self-esteem and strengthens higher ego functions to an even greater degree.

In marked contrast to the experiences of that child are the experiences of the child who has brain dysfunction. This seems to be true regardless of the etiology of the child's brain dysfunction: whether his condition resulted from poor nutrition or lack of proper prenatal care; whether it resulted from birth injury, such as the fetus' head being too large for the size of the mother's pelvic opening, or a lack of proper oxygen at birth, or because the protein synthesis responsible for brain development was stopped too early during a critical period of the central nervous system's growth, in response to a premature birth (Schain, et al., 1967). This seems to be true whether it resulted from a high fever or disease in infancy, or from some accident or trauma in childhood. Regardless of cause, the common factor seems to be that there is some resultant interference with the function of the brain.

Because the brain—via the functions of the ego—is the primary organ of adaptation, when its functions are disrupted, the child's total development is disrupted. The electrochemical and biochemical bases for brain functions do not support normal development. They do not provide the hardware that enables the child to explore, interpret, and achieve a sense of mastery in relation to his environment. In turn, the primary tools needed by the ego to function appropriately do not develop properly. Then the higher ego functions, which develop from the child's interactions with his environment, but are rooted in the primary tools of ego function, do not develop properly. Therefore, brain dysfunction itself robs the child of the inherent opportunity to develop effective ego functions in the usual course of growing up. His attempts at mastery result not in success, but in frustration; not in self-esteem, but in self-derision; not in a sense of "I am one who can," but in a sense of "I am one who can *not*."

This child is also robbed of the ability to stimulate his mother's normal maternal responses. Instead of pride and love, he evokes in her anxiety and frustration. As an example, a mother expects to find gratification in feeding her infant. When, as a part of his generalized motor insufficiency, each feeding is a harassment of alternate screaming and falling asleep, she obviously reacts to him differently than she would to a more cooperative child. Conversely, his experience in being fed is very different from that of the other child. He feels his mother's tension and rejection. He feels the nipple being jammed into his mouth with the fervent hope that he will go to sleep and stop bothering her for the rest of the night. As a result, he cannot feel the world to be secure and benign in its giving.

The feelings of frustration and inadequacy within himself and the feelings of tension and rejection he gets from the environment form the nonverbal matrix in which he will mold his basic concepts of himself and the outside world. Within himself, he is frustrated because his whole biology commands him to try, to do, to master; and he either can not, or at best can achieve only arduously, without facility. At the same time, his mother reacts in an unstimulating fashion, if not in an actively rejecting or defensively smothering way. Thus, his introduction to this world is not a pleasant one, but one that fosters feelings of frustration and rejection.

In many instances, when the child does belatedly achieve a skill, such as motility, he tends to use it continuously, as if to make up for lost time and to inundate himself with previously unattainable gratification (Rappaport, 1961). Such a surge of activity is usually met by heightened dismay, anxiety, and

40

resentment on mother's part, because she usually has had no one to help her with such feelings. It is very difficult for a mother to live with anxieties about her child, whom she feels is different, knowing she cannot get help with or relief from her anxieties. When she turns to her husband, she gets no relief. Rare indeed would be the father of a newborn son who would even entertain the possibility that there is something wrong with his child. She then goes to her pediatrician. Because there is such a shortage of pediatricians today, the pediatrician does not have the time to sit and listen to her problem, to try to relieve her anxiety. She is thereby forced to live with her anxieties as best she can.

Because she does not get the necessary help, her reactions to her own child often only stimulate his difficulties. Often there ensues a power struggle between mother and child that may last a lifetime. Take, for example, the child who is delighted that at last he has achieved motility, and as a substitute for mastery, he practices it continuously and in double time. Up at 5:00 a.m., he arouses everyone else by 5:05, has thoroughly mixed the sugar and flour and pots and pans on the kitchen floor by 5:15, is gleefully tramping on them by 5:18, and moves on to conquer such new horizons as living room drapes by 5:20. Not understanding his motives, his mother is convinced that his sole purpose in life is to torment her and to deprive her of her last vestige of sanity.

Often, in desperation, she feels driven to beat her child into submission, to lock him in his room, or to otherwise make him capitulate to her will. In this way she tries to preserve some semblance of her own identity and self-respect.

The child, however, is only beginning to have some rudiments of positive identity; to pride himself on being a lamp-knocker-over, or a drapery-climber, or a sugar-spiller, or one who beats all others getting up in the morning. These things he now *can* do. These are triumphs he wants to share with his mother. These he regards as first steps to her love and affection. But she does not "read" his intentions; so she does not praise him for his long-awaited and hard-won skills, nor does she help

41

him to channel them into socially acceptable activities. She comes instead with stern thou-shalt-nots, and the child feels his budding identity to be in mortal danger. As Erikson (1950, p. 212) pointed out, if a child has no identity, he has no life, and so he often will fight harder to preserve his identity than to preserve life itself.

This youngster, therefore, in the true sense of the word, is a deprived child. Even though he may come from a family whose income is $100,000 a year, he is no less deprived than a child who comes from a slum area. He is deprived in his *internal* environment. In a sense, his deprivation is even more harmful to his development than is the deprivation of the child from the slum area. Because the child with brain dysfunction usually has the intelligence to know what he wants to do in response to his adequate environment, but cannot make himself do it, his frustration and sense of ineptitude continuously mount. Moreover, in his first experience with what he regards as success, he met only derision and obstruction. Therefore, he must fight back. He must do something that will give him some recognition, that will enable him in some way to be somebody who can. At the same time, because she cannot understand him or live harmoniously with him, his mother must try to subjugate him. Through the years, this interaction spirals with ever increasing velocity, viciousness, and futility. In so doing, it continuously reinforces the child's concepts that he is alone in an enemy land whose purpose is to torment him by constantly hurting his pride, if not by extinguishing his identity altogether. That concept is further reinforced because his congenital skill deficiencies continually make him "odd man out," creating bitter jealousy of the success he sees other children achieve and of the admiration and affection the adults lavish on them.

Because he has a dysfunction of his primary organ of adaptation, his brain, he can be expected to try to be "somebody who can" in a way that is maladaptive. He does this, for example, by being a lamp-knocker-over, or the one person in the family who can make mother scream every thirty seconds. The skill deficiencies he showed at six months of age, or at one year of age, or all during his first five years of life do not simply remain as developmental gaps later to be filled in by some well-intentioned person. Because life is a dynamic process, the child fills in the gaps himself. A gap can no more exist in a child's development than a hole can exist in the ocean, and for the same reason: both are by their very nature dynamic and in a state of constant change. And, as already stated, because this child has brain dysfunction, he is maladaptive in filling the gaps. The teacher must then help him to learn how to undo the maladaptive ways in which he has been functioning, as well as to build the real skills he needs.

By school age, the experiences that have comprised this child's microcosm have been very different from those of average children. Such experiences have fashioned him an ego very different from theirs. To be of genuine help to him, the teacher must be aware of this child's concepts of his inner and outer worlds, because such concepts will pervade and dominate every contact with him. The teacher must expect to be regarded by him as an enemy; enemies are all he has known. The teacher must expect to have to be proven trustworthy; his life experiences give him no reason to trust others. The teacher must expect to be tested out in all different ways, because the child fears that the teacher will grow angry and reject him and further hurt his pride; no one has passed his tests yet. The teacher must expect it to take a long time to be trusted by him and for him to stop the contest of wills; his psychic life is at stake. The teacher must expect to be needed to help him control his impulses, no matter how much he protests that he does not want such help; as yet he has not had the opportunity to develop the ego functions necessary for self-control. In brief, the teacher must expect to be reacted to with all the habitual attitudes and maladaptive coping patterns this child has devised over the years.

If the teacher understands all such aspects of the child who has brain dysfunction, the teacher will be an ego bank that provides the child the wherewithal for genuine achievement and for a sense of mastery still unknown to him—an ego bank that

43

provides the opportunity to have others respond to him with approbation, not condemnation; an ego bank that provides limitless love, not in the sense of pitying him or of molly-coddling him, but by facing his difficulties with him, by helping him to understand why he does those irksome things, and by letting him know that he will be helped constantly until he is able to respond in a fashion pleasing both to himself and to others. The teacher will be an ego bank with patience, because the child will require months or years to be able to perform voluntarily what society demands of him.

Such self-expectancies can be instrumented more easily when the teacher remembers that the ego *does* have an extrauterine development just as the fetus has an intrauterine one. The ego must evolve through an orderly progression of stages of growth precisely as the fetus must. Neither is capable of hurrying through those stages in kaleidoscopic fashion simply because one wishes it. All the teacher's talents, time, and armamentarium of techniques and materials must be dedicated to the promotion of those stages of growth, or this child cannot achieve true maturity or ego autonomy. Certainly he cannot achieve these by himself. By school age the deviation is too much for normal development to overcome. His skill deficiencies, his supersensitive and vulnerable pride, his painful experiences with others, and his maladaptive means of coping with all of these are so entrenched that his ego cannot proceed for long without being enslaved by demands either from his inner or outer worlds. If he does not receive the help he needs, then his patterns of response continue to be maladaptive, and by the time he is a teenager, they become increasingly antisocial. This child cannot be expected to outgrow the maladaptations he has spent most of his life practicing. He can only be expected to outgrow his clothes.

Hopefully, the intent of the school is not simply to provide mother a respite by babysitting with her child. If the intent is to enable this child to become self-supporting and self-respecting, the teacher's responsibility is to begin the teacher-pupil relationship where the child is at that time, not where the teacher or principal or parent may wish him to be. It is the teacher's responsibility to communicate to the child an under-standing of what the child is now struggling with and has been for years. The teacher must convey an attitude that indicates neither fear of, nor demand for abandonment of, the habitual response patterns and skill deficiencies this child has been practicing for most of his life. This attitude must convey that he is not expected to give up either the defensive patterns or the skill deficiencies, which by now have become habituated and therefore comfortable, until he can replace them with the genuine success the teacher will help him to achieve. It is also the teacher's responsibility to cope with his maladaptations and deficiencies, because he cannot do so for himself, until he can replace them with truly gratifying ways of responding. Because he is unable to handle either his inner drives or the demands and stimulations of the outside world, the teacher and other adults helping him must provide him with a total-life structure that enables him to cope with both successfully. The core of that total-life structure is the ability to relate with him in a fashion that says: "I am here to help you, not to hurt you or to have a contest of wills with you; to help you recognize your problems and limitations and suffering so that you can overcome them and begin to use effectively and joyously the assets I know you have."

When the *relationship* communicates that, the child will begin to recognize that others *can* feel good about him, that others *do* want him to feel good about himself. He will begin to perceive a difference between what the teacher represents and the hurt that the world has always meant to him. If that difference persists long enough and is evident in enough persons who are important to him, he will have a sufficiently consistent basis for comparison to be able to discriminate between his present world and that of his past, so as to form the realization that the whole world is not the way he had previously conceived it. If the relationship does *not* communicate that to him, he cannot be taught; he cannot be helped to build skills; he cannot be aided to achieve more adaptive behavior; and, in time, even coexistence with him becomes impossible. In twenty years of

45

working with these children, this writer has not found one who was helped by a battle with an adult who did not understand him. Even when the child won such a battle, he actually lost. He lost the opportunity to change a maladaptation into what could become genuinely constructive and pleasing.

There are two reasons why the child who has brain dysfunction must be understood as a totality and why the aforementioned relationship is so important to his habilitation. First of all, fear and anger neurologically and psychologically militate against the learning that becomes a truly internalized and integrated part of the child, as well as against any other taking-in process. Secondly, his ultimate weapon is "You can't *make* me learn!" From infancy, when he first had a bottle jammed into his mouth with the fervent hope that he would go to sleep and stop bothering everybody, he has practiced refusing to take anything others offered him except under his own terms. Certainly that pattern cannot be expected suddenly to reverse itself when he walks into a classroom.

When properly structured, relationships form the nucleus from which all other structuring emanates. A properly structured relationship eventually allows the child the opportunity to identify with the teacher and other adults in his life, internalizing their goals and expectations for him. Then he *wants* to please them. Then he is motivated to let them help him learn those skills he should have acquired as a normal part of his ego's development. Whatever his skill deficiencies, a properly structured relationship provides both the child and the teacher the opportunity to develop in him skills that otherwise would have remained only nascent.

Relationship structure is defined as the ability of an adult to understand a child sufficiently well at any given moment, through observation of the child's performance (which includes his feelings and behavior, as well as how he uses his skills and deficits), and to relate to him in a way that aids the child's development of his ego's functions. *Educational structure* is defined as the careful planning and control of time, space, materials, and techniques according to the developmental needs

46

of each youngster, in order to provide him the opportunity to succeed where he previously failed. Expanding those concepts, the key to successful learning may be defined as a highly structured, methodical presentation of tasks appropriate for the child to learn at his current stage of development, in a relationship that enables him to feel supportive understanding, one that allows him to borrow from the adult's inner strength and goals until his own inner controls and motivations and skills can be established.

The first part of the conceptual model presented in this chapter, then, acknowledges the child's emergent functions at any given stage of growth to be the product: (1) of their interaction with all other related functions present at that time; (2) of the adequacy of precursory skills; and (3) of the child's experiences with both his precursory and emerging skills. The child is seen as a three-dimensional dynamic totality, with the dimension of current skill complexes, previous skill complexes, and the dimension of what he experiences as a result of both earlier and current skill complexes. This conceptual model indicates that no specific skill deficiency can be assessed or remedied without taking into account all the child's other deficiencies and skills, his experiences with and feelings about all his skills and deficits, and the patterns he has erected in the past to compensate for those deficits. Within this framework, the child is also viewed with regard to the interwoven effects of all biological and experiential factors on his emerging ego. The child's dysfunctions, therefore, are not viewed in isolation, but in terms of his psychobiological totality.

This suggests that the habilitative program designed for this child should involve a well-trained teacher, who is but one member of the interdisciplinary habilitative team that addresses its collective talents to providing him the opportunity to develop effective functions within himself and his family, and as a responsible member of society. It has the further implication that if the opportunity to habilitate this child is not seized when he is still a child, too often that opportunity will be lost when he is an adolescent. Currently, age seems to be the greatest enemy of good prognosis. Even when the child is completely understood as a totality and is given an appropriate habilitative program, complete with relationship and educational structure, the same habilitative goals cannot be achieved in adolescence that can be achieved during earlier years.

The aspect of the conceptual model already presented has two purposes. The first purpose is to provide guidelines by which a relationship structure with the child both at school and at home can be built. The second purpose is to pave the way for educational structure. This can enable the teacher to evaluate the child's performance more accurately—that is, all aspects of him that are involved in how he goes about arriving at an answer. Then the second aspect of the conceptual model, which will be presented next, can help the teacher to evaluate specifically what a given task asks of the child *and* how that can be related to the child's current needs. Armed with such understanding, the teacher can effect the necessary merging of the child's performance with appropriate opportunities for learning.

Whereas the first aspect of the conceptual model addressed itself to the child with brain dysfunction as a totality and included an overview of his development, the second aspect of this conceptual model is, in a sense, a microscopic enlargement of one aspect of the total child: the functional systems through which he learns. For all children learning takes place through these systems, so they are important; but for the child who has brain dysfunction, these functional systems are of critical importance.

Before setting forth the second part of the conceptual model, the current status of learning theories, especially as they apply to children with brain dysfunction, should be examined briefly. Data rapidly accruing in various biochemical laboratories make it increasingly clear that learning consists of a number of inordinately complex processes. This is simply and concisely spelled out in "The Chemistry of Learning," recently published by IDEA Information Office, P. O. Box 446, Melbourne, Florida. A few points made in that pamphlet will be cited.

Dr. David Krech of the University of California found in experiments with rats that the experience of learning literally caused chemical and anatomical changes in the brain. Experiments made by Professor Holger Hyden at the University of Goteborg lead him to believe that learning causes a change in the way the brain synthesizes protein, including RNA. Research being conducted in several universities suggests that learning is not a unitary act, but is a set of enormously complicated processes, such as acquiring information, integrating information, establishing that information in memory, selectively retrieving that information, and so forth. Moreover, according to Dr. Heinz Von Foerster, professor of electrical engineering at the University of Illinois (reported in *Science News*, May 18, 1968, p. 473), learning is such a highly dynamic phenomenon that the protein molecules on the neuron change their shape and molecular structure in response to an electrical charge that results from an experience. Because the structure of the neuron changes, the next time it is called upon to respond, its function will be different. Without citing more extensively from the laboratory, even those few points already indicated make it obvious that learning can no longer be regarded as a simple relationship between a stimulus and a response, and that learning cannot be achieved merely by reinforcing a given response when it occurs (which is the basis of operant conditioning).

Learning, and especially learning disorders, must be approached with a clear understanding of the child's total organismic functioning. Toward that end, the present attempt to clarify the processes and components of the organism's functional totality is undertaken in segments without any intent to imply segmentation. It should also be recognized that this model represents a learning activity that may encompass a half hour of time in the earliest stages of infancy or 0.001 of a second in the later stages of childhood.

Current knowledge permits focus on three aspects of the inordinately complex process by which a child becomes a learning, performing individual. These are: (1) the information processing (or input) modes, (2) the integrative system, and (3)

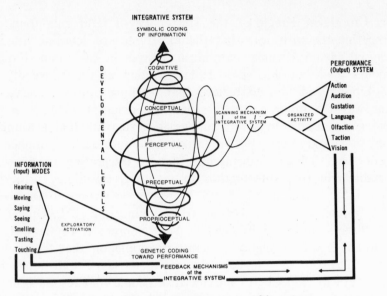

Figure 1. The functional systems of learning

the performance (or output) system. These are graphically represented in Figure 1.

The manner in which the information processing modes are listed in Figure 1 does not imply a developmental sequence of emergence, only an attempt to identify them. These include hearing, moving, saying, seeing, smelling, tasting, and touching. The information processing modes provide the child with the basic data or ingredients necessary for learning to take place. However, as every cook knows, merely having the ingredients in the cupboard does not produce a cake. The ingredients first have to be identified as those specifically required by the recipe for that cake. Then they must be accurately measured out, properly blended, and exposed to certain other elements, such as heat, in a prescribed sequence. The "baking" process is accomplished by the integrative system, which will be discussed shortly.

Today there are few means of directly measuring the adequacy of the information processing modes. In most instances, inferences concerning their adequacy are drawn through observation of the child's performance. "Seeing" is the only information processing mode that can be measured and appraised directly. Even the measurement of hearing acuity, by means of an audiometer, depends on the child's reactions. On the other hand, seeing can be measured directly by means of the pupilary response to light, by noting whether the eyes team properly while moving to follow a target, and by means of a retinoscope, which indicates such refractive errors as myopia or astigmatism, while the eyes carry out the functions for which they were designed—to gather and transmit light.

The fact that the eyes can be so readily assessed has in some respects hindered a better understanding of the role of seeing and its end result, vision, in the learning process. Too often when the eyes have been found to be "normal in all respects," the interpretation has been made that the information carried into those eyes on light waves therefore would result in equally normal performance. Likewise, when the eyes have been found to be distorted in any way, too often the assumption has been made that performance would be equally distorted.

Regardless of which information mode is being evaluated, when performance is found to be poor, the accompanying sensory organ can not automatically be blamed. By the same token, when the accompanying sensory organ is found to be "normal," but performance poor, the integrative and performance systems must be carefully evaluated.

If one or more of the information processing modes is not intact, the child may receive no data, inadequate data, or incorrect data that could give him misleading cues. As a result, the learning process itself will be hindered, as can be observed in the child's performance of the task to be learned. In that case, one part of the teacher's job is to help the child to develop information processing modes capable of providing him with more accurate data. Usually the teacher can not accomplish this alone, but must seek the help of appropriate specialists, such as an audiologist, an optometrist, an expert in speech and language, or an expert in adaptive physical education. If the origin of a faulty information processing mode is organic rather than functional in nature, then help will be required from appropriate medical specialists, such as an otologist, an ophthalmologist, or a physiatrist.

An explanation is required concerning the reason for including "moving" and "saying" in the information processing modes, since it is customary to include there only the five sensory organs and their accompanying functions.

That the genetic plan anticipates highly practiced, organized, and refined actions is evidenced in the fact that the infant is boned, muscled, and nerved in a beautifully articulated manner that designs him not only for movement, but for getting information from moving as well. From birth on the infant can be observed to move in thrust and stretch and relaxation. Moving makes him aware that he has mobility. It also makes him aware of gravity, with which he will contend throughout his life. Because the infant is heliotropic, his movements also attempt to bring him into alignment with brightness and high contrasts of light. Moving also gives him information concerning the use of hearing for the purpose of localizing the source of a sound. Finally, moving enables touching to be meaningful, for pressure alone cannot provide information about texture, shape, size, or weight. These sources of information, both in their rudimentary as well as in their organized state, are important to the process of learning.

The infant's babbling, his coos, gurgles, and chortles of pleasure and comfort, and his cries of discomfort, provide him with considerable information. They help him to differentiate sounds that emanate from him and sounds that come from others. They further aid in his individuation by providing information concerning the response of others to the sounds he makes. His own sounds also give him information concerning the use of his hearing for the purpose of monitoring speech.

Although each of the information processing modes begins its operation as a primitive reflex, it must quickly achieve a degree of organization sufficient to foster the child's development. First, the infant discovers each of his information processing modes. Then he must learn their purposes and how to use them. His vehicle to such learning is labeled "exploratory activation."

52

(See Figure 1.) Through exploration of each of his information processing modes, he learns to activate its genetically intended purpose and ready utility.

Once the data are received by the information processing modes, these are encoded as signals to be neurologically transmitted for meaningful integration and effective performance. Through the integrative system the information processing modes develop a reciprocity and interweaving that brings them to unity and makes them an effective component of the child's learning process. Only then can the child organize and sequence all the data available to him from his external and internal environments. Only then can he effect a dynamic suppression of irrelevant data and a dynamic attention to pertinent data. Only then can the cacophony of all the signals constantly bombarding the child be transmitted into information that is harmonious to his intended performance. To carry the metaphor one step further, the integrative system orchestrates the incoming and outgoing signals so that the result is in harmony with adaptation.

The first level of the integrative system used by the infant is labeled "proprioceptual." (See Figure 1.) Here, primarily, he practices organizing the signals that come from within his own body, so that he develops awareness and knowledge of his own body positions and movements in response to both internal and external signals. The infant explores the types of movements he is capable of making and the results of each of these movements. He probably "plays" with his body articulations and musculature, just as later he will spend time playing with the objects of his outside world.

When a signal from the outer environment is received by the information modes, it instigates a movement, which in turn produces a certain set of internal, proprioceptual, signals. The next time that external signal comes, the internal (proprioceptual) signals are more ready to respond, and the resultant movement is somewhat less erratic and primitive. After some more exchanges, the proprioceptual signals alert the information modes and set them to receive those data that are pertinent to a more effective reaction.

These interchanges at the proprioceptual level contribute to a sense of selfness, which in turn creates a sense of whereness. Out of selfness emerges the self-concept, which is an essential component of the ego. Out of whereness emerges the egocentric locus, that point in space occupied by "me," which serves as the reference point for all spatial judgments made by that person. Just as the infant must move an arm or leg to know for sure where that extremity really is, he must also move himself and make decisions about his own movements to know where he is in space. All learning involves movement at some level and to some degree.

Before leaving the proprioceptual level of the integrative system, it should be emphasized that the child does not function at that level only once in his lifetime. Proprioceptual activity begins before birth, and it never stops. The proprioceptual level is *emphasized* early in the child's development, and then he moves on to practice, refine, and organize the other levels of the integrative system. What he learns at each level prepares him to utilize skills to be made available to him at the next level. However, as an adult there will be times when his higher-order skills will not be adequate to cope with an unfamiliar situation, so that he will again rely primarily on lower-order skills, even on those at the proprioceptual level. The interrelationship and interchange among the levels of the integrative system are represented by the vertical spiral in Figure 1. The spiral is meant to underscore the fact that there is no sudden or distinct shift from one level to the next. The infant slowly but progressively gains mastery over one level so that he *can* turn his attention to achieving mastery over the next level. Nevertheless, in that process he maintains some degree of reliance on the level already mastered.

The integrative system's next level of development is designated "preceptual." (See Figure 1.) Here the child primarily focuses his attention on each information mode, what information is available from it, and how it can be used most effectively. He practices and refines the precept, or working principle, of each mode that contributes to his learning. For example, he learns to listen to what he hears, to look at what he sees, to feel what he touches. In so doing, he *earns* his senses, which were not a nicely packaged and beribboned gift awaiting him at birth. He obtains practice in refining each information mode as it relates to the performance required of him either by the external or the internal environments.

It is probably at this level that the integrative system's feedback mechanisms receive their first abundant exercise. The feedback mechanisms, which will be discussed later in this chapter, are instrumental in refining the purpose for and use of the information modes, in order to respond to the environment more adaptively. It is also likely that the integrative system's neurologically based internal scanning mechanism becomes practiced at this level. This too will be discussed later in this chapter. For now, it will suffice to indicate that the internal scanning mechanism is different from the external scanning that is an integral part of vision.

Although no information mode operates in isolation, each mode must become accomplished in its own skills and criteria of operation if it is to contribute as intended by genetic precept to the organism's total functioning. In his progression through the preceptual developmental level, the child primarily practices one mode, then another, and still another. In so doing, he compares and contrasts each with another, so that each becomes better understood and more effective. If, for any reason—such as faulty genetic coding, injury, illness, or deprivation—a mode fails to process the information it should, that source of contact with the outside world will be incomplete. The expected result would be an incomplete, or to-some-degree maladaptive, relationship with the outside world.

At the preceptual level, the child is not yet ready to sort and organize all the information reaching him. Instead, he is still learning to receive the information and to refine the information modes. As each of these modes is refined by the child, all modes become better available to him, and his storehouse of information increases.

The integrative system's third level of development is indicated as the "perceptual" level. (See Figure 1.) Here the child primarily explores and practices the ways in which

55

information obtained from the various modes is similar and different, and how that information can be interwoven to attain a more efficient and discriminatory means of learning. For example, he learns to taste what he is looking at, to see what he is listening to, to say what he is looking at or listening to or tasting or feeling. At this level, the child discovers how the information modes can support, validate, and interweave with each other. He finds that these modes are all an integral part of him and that in combination they provide him with more information than any one of them could provide by itself.

When functioning at this level, the child's performance shows that he is responding to more than the external information signals he receives. Even though the information cue emphasizes one mode, his performance indicates that he has also drawn from stored information gained through other modes. In this way two or more modes are used in combination to derive an enhanced understanding of the situation at hand. Moreover, as he analyzes the information being received and compares it with information already stored, the child finds that he can interchange information as if he were substituting one mode for another. This is why he can taste what he is looking at, or see what he is listening to. At this level of his development, he not only collects and contrasts data from various information modes, but also compares these data with already stored information that he acquired at this and previous levels of development. By means of the contrasting, the assessment of similarities and differences among the various data collected, the child develops a percept, or mental image, of persons, objects, places, and experiences that have become important aspects of either his internal or external worlds. These images represent a myriad of data in organized, or at least partially organized, form. These images thereby enable the child to manipulate information more economically and efficiently than ever before. The result is increasingly improved perceptual discrimination and further reduction of the number of cues necessary for appropriate performance.

When children are observed while in the process of building their *own* perceptions—instead of those imposed on them by well-intentioned adults—they do not appear to derive real perception from only one information mode. They do not seem to have what could genuinely be called "visual" perception, or "auditory" perception, et cetera. Instead, they seem to achieve *perception*, which is an emergent of the developing integrative system and is achieved by the process of melding two or more information modes, as was described in the preceding paragraphs. Although perception can be initiated by any of the information modes, it contains contributions from all those modes. Perception also has the potential to become further practiced, refined, and organized so that the next level of development can emerge.

At this point, perhaps it would be helpful to pause long enough to indicate that the above description of perception is not antagonistic to previously espoused theories of perception, such as those of Hebb (1949), Werner and Wapner (1952), Allport (1955), Strauss and Kephart (1955), Bruner, *et al.* (1957), Kephart (1960), Solley and Murphy (1960), and Erickson, Piaget, and Sears, as discussed by Maier (1965). The interested reader will find in those works a wealth of information that is helpful in clarifying the complex process of perception and its relationship to the equally complex processes of learning and cognition. What has been set forth as perception thus far in this chapter omits the important roles of motivation, identity, and expectation in the perceptual process. These are discussed in detail in the works of Bruner and Solley and Murphy just cited. The roles of motivation, identity, and expectation, as they relate to the child with brain dysfunction, have been alluded to earlier in this chapter and will be discussed further later.

When the child is at the perceptual level of development, it is critically important that his thus-far-developed integrative system as a whole is intact and reliable. Firstly, an insufficient or unreliable information mode cannot make its intended and required contribution at the proprioceptual level. Secondly, any inadequacy within that primary level of the integrative system deprives the child of the frames of reference required for two important aspects of ego development: self-concept and spatial orientation. Thirdly, those inadequacies lead to even greater inadequacies and maladaptations at the perceptual level. Fourthly, when an insufficient or unreliable information mode is allowed to remain, it produces "static" on the neurological line. This interferes with the functions of the integrative system, resulting in a lowered or inadequate performance that may be misconstrued as the product of mental retardation or other equally irrelevant causes. "Static" on the neurological line may also cause the child to "turn off" an information mode and instead practice substitute solutions that lead to maladaptations, which to some degree deteriorate all aspects of the child's performance.

In Figure 1, as the vertical spiral reaches the perceptual level, it begins to narrow toward its apex. This narrowing represents the integrative system's coming within reach of its ultimate and genetically blueprinted goal. The route to that goal is via the development of the integrative system's conceptual level. Here the percepts of the previous level become further refined, organized, and abstracted for greater ease and economy of manipulation. The child's internal and external worlds become further ordered as he learns to think of them in terms of different systems of classification, categorization, and serial arrangement. The child is thereby better equipped than ever before to explore and practice the many ways in which an actual or vicarious experience can be expressed in action, in language, or in other abstract symbols. He is also better able to explore the relationship between such experiences. Then the child can translate his own actions and experiences into symbols, or symbols into his own actions and experiences. Obviously, the child must gain facility at this level of development if he is to achieve academically. Otherwise, reading, arithmetic, and other school subjects cannot be mastered. Edwards (1968) phrased it so well: "At eight months, or a year, he has begun to grasp the shorthand which allows him to hold in his head the whole of reality and to manipulate it, to solve the problems it sets him through mental operations. Until he is five or six or older, the chief intellectual task of his life will be the creation of a symbolic vocabulary, or several of them (words, numbers, images, musical notes), which become the medium of his life as a human being."

The apex of the spiral of development (see Figure 1) is reached when the child gains the skills and facilities of the integrative system's "cognitive" level. Here a single word, or any other cue from any of the integrative system's developmental levels, can retrieve from the storehouse of memory all related, pertinent information accrued by the child up to that moment in time and can make that information available in the service of optimal performance. If some phase of the symbolic cue is indistinct or incomplete, each developmental level can be quickly probed and reviewed for the information necessary to clarify or complete the cue. Thus, the cognitive level represents comprehensively knowing and realizing (which literally means "to make real") the symbolic coding of all past experiences and information in order to achieve optimal efficiency in fulfilling the organism's genetically blueprinted quest for adaptation.

Within this level of the integrative system's development, the symbolic coding and correlation of all information stored in memory facilitates the work of a neurologically-based internal scanning mechanism (represented by the horizontal spiral in Figure 1). This scanning mechanism is in keeping with the organism's extreme parsimony; that is, its intent to accomplish any task with the least expenditure of energy. Thus, each situation that challenges the organism to perform activates an automatic scanning and redintegration of all already learned and codified responses, accrued at any of the integrative system's developmental levels, to determine which of them is applicable to the current situation.* That scanning takes place within 0.1

*Dr. W. Ross Adey of the Brain Research Institute of the University of California, in Los Angeles, has conducted research (reported in *Science News*, Vol. 91, p. 572, June to 0.001 of a second. As all previously stored information is scanned and assessed, signals are sent via the feedback mechanisms, which may not involve the cerebral cortex or other parts of the brain, both to the information modes and to the performance system to provide further refinement of incoming information and to effect optimal performance.

The neurologically-based feedback mechanisms serve as a symphony conductor to accomplish the integrative system's task of orchestration. They signal the information modes concerning which information should be amplified or facilitated at any given moment and which should be suppressed or opposed. They also signal the performance system as to which response components should be augmented or inhibited. Again, the feedback mechanisms are in the service of optimal performance, according to the organism's genetically blueprinted quest for the easiest, most efficient, and most economical means of adaptation.

The more often the internal scanning and redintegration occur, and the more practiced are the feedback mechanisms, the greater is the proficiency and economy in retrieving essential information. As the retrieving becomes more organized and practiced, all performances become more efficient and facile. Optimal performance is represented in Figure 1 by the apex of the horizontal spiral, which is labeled "organized activity."

Recognizing that the child with brain dysfunction is typically described as lacking in spatial orientation, direction, and adequate body image, his awareness of himself in relation to his spatial world becomes critically important to his ability to achieve organized activity. A child must know *where* an object is before he can know *what* it is. Spatial judgments must be accurate and reliable before he can make adequate interpreta-

---

17, 1967) indicating that protein molecules, called mucopolysaccharides and mucoproteins, together with the neuron itself, constitute the information core of the brain. The protein molecules are packed along the surface of the cell membrane and in the space between the neurons. Studying brain waves by means of computers, Dr. Adey also found that when a wave closely resembled the one present when the information was originally stored, the new wave supposedly recalled the original experience. This would be an electrochemical "match" or "best fit."

tions concerning the details of an object. For example, if a child does not know that an object is a certain distance away, its size could mislead his judgment of what that object is. Out of knowledge of spatial orientations come size, distance, direction, and other constancies that he can rely upon for further judgments. Unless a child knew the relationship between his own egocentric position and the spatial world surrounding him, a picture could not have a three-dimensional perspective for him. Likewise, he could not make accurate judgments of where sounds were coming from, or whether or not he could reach out and touch an object without changing his position in space. Moreover, his language would be withered, because there would be an absence of both words and gestures that reflect size, shape, distance, and direction, which are the symbols of spatial appreciation.

A child must build an awareness and appreciation of the space that lies in front, behind, and to each side of him if he is to achieve mastery over his environment. Only when he has space packaged well enough to know where he is and where his environment is can he translate and interweave his performance into an effective and efficient whole. Only then can his activities achieve the level of organization that produces optimal intellectual performance with the least cue and with maximal economy.

Appreciation of space relies heavily on vision. The works of Hebb (1937), Held (1959), Riesen (1947), Smith and Smith (1962), and Stratton (1896), among others, indicate that vision is the ultimate judge and evaluator of surrounding space and one's position in it. At the proprioceptual level of the integrative system's development, the internal signals that arise during movement cannot be fully interpreted and utilized unless there are external signals with which the internal signals can be compared. One can have no sense of selfness unless he has a sense of the space he occupies, in which he can function as a whole. This space volume can be most directly and fully appraised by the light-gathering and light-transmitting mode, which, through the work of the integrative system, becomes vision.

Vision is first and last a guidance and monitoring system (Getman, in Rappaport, 1966, pp. 58-83). It guides and monitors actions in relation to balance and ease of movement around the body's vertical and horizontal gravitational axes. It also guides movement through space and monitors interactions with other persons and objects while moving through space. To manipulate the environment successfully, the child must know where he has been, where he is going, and how such changes in spatial relationships en route should influence his actions. He needs such information whether his actions are self-initiated or in reaction to objects or persons. As a guidance and monitoring mechanism for the organism's interactions with the environment, the visual system has no peer. However, it achieves this superiority only through the abstraction, elaboration, and refinement of the functions of guidance and monitoring. Thus, the child needs opportunities not only to see and to learn to look at what he sees, but also to use vision for the self-initiated decision-making that will bring about the needed abstraction, elaboration, and refinement of visual guidance and monitoring. By recognizing the important role of visual guidance and monitoring in organized activity, the teacher is better able to understand vision in proper perspective to the total child and his performance.

As organized activity becomes increasingly practiced and refined, it merges into the performance system. The performance system itself, like the integrative system, cannot be observed, but its resultant skills can be. These performance skills, as listed in Figure 1, are: *action*, the economically and effortlessly balanced, graceful, and poised movement prerequired for instantaneous readiness to act in any given situation; *audition*, the facility for locating, identifying, and interpreting sounds that emanate from the environment (giving added dimension to and complementing the visual space volume, the "out-thereness," that the child builds for himself); *gustation* and *olfaction*, the practiced differentiation of that which is pleasurable and healthful from that which is noxious; *language*, the facility for

62

verbal and nonverbal expression and comprehension of cognitive symbols exchanged with other persons; *taction*, the ease of ready interpretation of temperature, texture, weight, size, shape, distance, and direction; *vision*, the accurate interpretation of color, shadow, dimension, and details of objects in order to obtain more subtle clues than are available through taction (or, at times, audition) concerning size, shape, and distance, so as to fulfill its purpose of spatial guidance and monitoring.

The performance system is more than the total of its collective skills. The performance system is the integrated, economical, and facile expression of all which the organism knows. Regardless of which performance skill is called upon to take the lead in a given situation, all other performance skills—and, indeed, the whole of the functional systems—support the expression of that skill. Just as the integrative system has as its prime purpose the codified and correlated storage of information, so that it can be readily retrieved for effectual use, the performance system has as its prime purpose the integrated, economical, effective instrumentation of what needs to be done.

However, it should be remembered that for the child, optimal performance is developed only after many years of appropriate opportunity and it cannot occur at the same age in all skills. It should also be remembered that performance can only be optimal when there is intactness in all aspects of and within all developmental levels of the functional systems and their organic substrata. Otherwise, there is "noise" on the performance line.

Ultimately, optimal performance requires not only economic integration with the least expenditure of effort and effective response based on the fewest cues, but also a symbolic representation of the entire activity to be performed. For example, the olympic pole vaulter has achieved optimal performance not only when his entire activity has been properly and economically integrated, but when he can practice that activity mentally, or symbolically, without the need to run through it each time on the field. Similarly, optimal performance in reading

63

takes place only when the mechanics of reading and the content of what is being read combine in a facility that provides the reader with a clear, fluent imagery of meaning.

As the teacher evaluates the child's performance, it must be remembered that more than the performance system is involved in whatever the child is doing. Before the teacher makes the judgment that a child's performance has improved, there should also be noticeable refinement in the functioning of the information modes. If that is not the case, the integrative system and its feedback mechanisms probably have not been able to do their work properly. Therefore, the teacher can doubt the validity of the "improved" performance, which most likely reflects rote, imitative behavior. On an imitative basis, a child can complete a particular act with apparent skill without having learned what is needed to support or validate other developmentally related activities. Such an unintegrated "splinter" skill can best be avoided by being sure that apparent improvement in performance is accompanied by improved skill in information processing. A splinter skill looks good on the surface, but the child cannot use it as a tool for adaptation.

This conceptual model has several additional direct applications for the teacher in everyday educational programming. Firstly, because most current tests are centered on the perceptual and conceptual levels of development, a child's inadequate performance on them indicates that educational programming should begin either at the preceptual or proprioceptual levels. Secondly, by observing the child's performance from the standpoint of this conceptual model, the teacher can discern more specific information concerning the educational program and at which of those two developmental levels it should begin. Thirdly, the teacher can discern whether the program should emphasize the informational, integrative, or performance aspects of the child's total functioning.

From a slightly different vantage point, this conceptual model helps to define the relevant factors in the educational environment. These are represented in Figure 2. One part of this is what the *child* brings to the educational environment; namely,

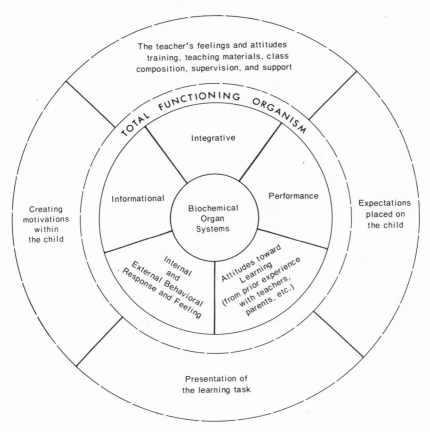

Figure 2. The educational environment
Part I: The child's ego   Part II: The learning situation

all his ego functions. It will be recalled that the child who has brain dysfunction cannot be expected to develop his functional systems in the same way, according to the same timetable, with the same feeling responses, and with the same responses from the environment as a child who does not have a brain dysfunction. Therefore, the teacher can expect to find some inadequacies or insufficiencies within this child's information processing modes and within his integrative and performance systems. The teacher can expect him to have had insufficient opportunity for proper development at the proprioceptual and preceptual stages, with resultant inadequacies or inconsistencies apparent at the perceptual, conceptual, and cognitive stages. It is becoming increasingly clear that these functional systems are not separate little black boxes locked in the reaches of the inner space within the child's skull. Each function does not develop along its own dimension, as though it moved on independent tracks. All functions are interrelated parts of the pryamid of growth. If there is a deficit in any aspect of the functional systems, some degree of deficit can be expected in all other aspects of the functional systems. This, plus the child's maladaptive attempts to adjust to his skill deficiencies, account for the ego insufficiencies and deviations that are quite apparent by school age.

To understand this conceptual model is to appreciate that even though there is a biochemical-organic nucleus to this child's problems, today, the primary mode of habilitation for him is education. This remains true in spite of the fact that important assists come from psychotherapy and other specialized services, including, at times, medication and neurosurgery. The very fact that the primary responsibility for habilitation rests on education emphasizes how essential it is that the educator understand all aspects of what this child brings to the learning situation. The teacher and everyone else concerned with habilitating this child must devote full time and energy to the understanding of this child's development and functioning, rather than to dissipate the time and energy of the adults and the child in a perennial pursuit of cure-alls. Although we are on the threshold of vastly greater knowledge than has ever before been achieved by man concerning the interaction between brain and learning, in our present state of ignorance there is no panacea, no magic. Within that context, it should be remembered that because this child brings to his teacher his accumulated experiences, plus his feelings about them, plus what he has devised to cope with those feelings and experiences, the teacher cannot simply give a ten-year-old what he missed when he was six months old and expect a more adequate performance to result. His deficit does not produce a hiatus that goes begging until at age ten somebody manipulates his body in infantile movements and thus solves all his problems. The child who has a deficit cannot cope with the world until that deficit is remedied. Instead, he must cope with that deficit as best he can, and because he has a brain dysfunction, he can be expected to cope with it maladaptively. Therefore, he brings to the teacher his maladaptive attempts to adapt to the holes in his development. He does not bring the holes.

The other aspect of the educational environment for which this conceptual model offers guidelines is the learning situation itself. (See Figure 2.) This concerns not what the child brings to the teacher, but what the teacher brings to the child. First of all, it indicates the importance of the teacher's guarding against preconceived notions concerning what will be motivating to a given child. The teacher must know what is happening in the child's life and what has been put into his storage banks from previous experiences before deciding what kinds of tasks to present to him. Only then can the teacher realistically attempt to create motivations within this child that are meaningful to him. Some teachers may feel: "Oh, it doesn't matter what the child has been like or what experiences he has had. All that matters is that he is here in my class now. I'll simply give him candy until he can do whatever I want him to do." That teacher must ask if, 5,000,000 pieces of candy later, that child will be able to emerge into the world of reality and encroaching automation and, without the help of candy, take his rightful place in the sun. He must question whether such an approach will genuinely enable this child to internalize his expectations of him so that they become the child's permanent self-expectations. He must evaluate whether such motivation genuinely reinforces the integration of performance skills so that they may be used with optimal effectualness in all required situations. Finally, that teacher must question whether or not believing that a piece of candy will "make the child learn" is a substitute for genuine understanding of that child's functional systems.

If a teacher does understand the child's past and his maladaptive attempts at adaptation that are now firmly fixed in his storage banks, and if a teacher does understand something about relationship structure and what the materials intrinsically have to offer this particular child, then the teacher's next problem is how to present the learning task to him meaningfully so that the child can have a successful experience, rather than another frustrating experience or failure.

How the teacher presents the task to this child is determined partly by the teacher's own past experiences with children and the resultant generalities present in her own storage system. It is easy to conclude that Johnny is just like Tommy solely because Johnny had characteristic A, which the teacher had previously found Tommy to have. She can easily reach the conviction: "I've got it made. I don't have to have any anxiety about Johnny. I'll program for him the same way I did for Tommy, and he will succeed like Tommy did." Such a conviction should be tempered by still another conviction: one swallow does not make a summer. Although Johnny had characteristic A in common with Tommy, and although the teacher did an excellent job with Tommy, what happens if the similarity stops there? What happens if the teacher finds after getting to know Johnny that there is greater difference between the two boys than similarity? What happens if the teacher finds after nine months that Johnny is not really like Tommy at all? A year has been wasted for the child and equally harmful feelings of ineptitude and guilt have been created for the teacher. The result would be that a failure experience has been set up for both. Since teachers are not machines, they need a feeling of success, of gratification, of accomplishment. Therefore, it is important that they not set up failure situations either for themselves or for the children.

Task presentation will be most successful, both for the teacher and for the children, when it is a part of prescriptive teaching: teaching that is cognizant of what each child needs, why he needs it, and how to program for all his special needs at their appropriate levels of development. Prescriptive teaching cannot be accomplished if the teacher judges what the child needs solely on the basis of the child's productions; that is, on the basis of what he has drawn on paper, or on the basis of what test scores he has achieved. Instead, prescriptive teaching must be aimed, as Piaget has so aptly indicated, at revealing the process by which a child arrives at a particular reply to the question presented to him.

Prescriptive teaching can be accomplished only when the teacher assiduously applies two principles: (1) to make judgments about the child's developmental levels and needs primarily from observation of the child's performance; and (2) to make expectations about the child's performance only after the task he is to perform has been accurately analyzed in terms of what it requires of the child, in terms of what questions it asks of the child, and in terms of the developmental levels at which those questions are asked. Unless both principles are applied constantly, the learning situation for this child can be little more than a farce, and the educational opportunities offered to him little more than an approximation of the teacher's vagaries. If the educational environment is based on anything short of these principles, the opportunities presented to this child will not be for successful learning, but for continuing failure and repeated hurt pride.

The application of these two principles is antithetical to the obsolete educational concepts that successful learning is inherent in the teaching materials and that a child's progress can be accurately measured simply by knowing the end product of what he has done. When dealing with a dysfunction of this magnitude, the teacher cannot afford to base the primary mode of habilitation, education, on obsolete concepts.

The purpose of this chapter has been to supply a conceptual model that would help educators to understand the child with brain dysfunction as a totality. Therefore, its intent was to provide guidelines for setting up the classroom, for establishing an appropriate educational program, and for evaluating the effectiveness of all which is done to habilitate this child. This particular conceptual model was chosen for presentation because its use during recent years has indicated it to be a promising framework for the successful habilitation of children with

69

learning and behavioral disorders due to brain dysfunction. To those schools that choose to use it, a word of caution. Administrators and others within the school system who are indirectly connected with this child and his program should be familiar with this model. The supervisors, teachers, and other school personnel who work directly with this child should have the concepts of this model so well integrated as to have them at the cognitive level—readily available for facile application. Otherwise they will derive no benefit from it, and moreover, they will not know it well enough to evaluate its merit or create a better conceptual model with which to replace it.

I sincerely hope that within the near future the present model is replaced by a better one. It will indicate progress in understanding the complexities of this child's problems and of the process of learning in general. If the present model serves as a stepping-stone to that goal, by helping others to see its weaknesses and thereby to create a superior model, it will have been worthwhile. In the meantime, it has proven of value to educational programming, and it encompasses the most comprehensive understanding of this child currently available. In seeking to replace it with a better conceptual model, we can be guided by the words of the ancient Persian philosopher, Lukman: "I learned wisdom from the blind, who advance not their feet until they have tried the ground."

REFERENCES

Allport, F. H. *Theories of Perception and the Concept of Structure.* New York: Wiley, 1955.

Bruner, J. S. *et al. Contemporary Approaches to Cognition.* Cambridge: Harvard University Press, 1957.

Edwards, E. P. "Kindergarten is Too Late," *Saturday Review* (June 15, 1968), 68.

Erickson, E. *Childhood and Society.* New York: Norton, 1950.

Hebb, D. O. "The innate organization of visual activity: I. Perception of figures by rats reared in total darkness," *Journal of Genetic Psychology*, LI (1937), 101-26.

_____. "The innate organization of visual activity: II. Transfer of response in the discrimination of brightness and size by rats reared in total darkness," *Journal of Comparative Psychology*, XXIV (1937), 277-99.

_____. *The Organization of Behavior.* New York: Wiley, 1949.

Held, R., and White, D. "Sensory Deprivation and Visual Speed: An Analysis," *Science*, CXXX (1959), 860.

Kephart, N. C. *The Slow Learner in the Classroom.* Columbus: Merrill, 1960.

Maier, H. W. *Three Theories of Child Development.* New York: Harper & Row, 1965.

Penfield, W., and Roberts, L. *Speech and Brain-Mechanisms.* Princeton: Princeton University Press, 1959.

Rappaport, S. R. "Behavior Disorder and Ego Development in a Brain-Injured Child," *Psychoanalytic Study of the Child*, XVI (1961), 423-50.

_____ (ed.). *Childhood Aphasia and Brain Damage: Volume III, Habilitation.* Norristown: The Pathway School, 1966.

Riesen, A. H. "The development of visual perception in man and chimpanzee," *Science*, CVI (1947), 107-8.

_____. "Arrested vision," *Scientific American*, CLXXXIII (1950), 16-19.

Stratton, G. M. "Vision Without Inversion of Retinal Image," *Psychological Review*, IV (1897), 341.

Schain, R. J., Carver, M. J., and Copenhaver, J. H. "Protein Metabolism in the Developing Brain: Influence of Birth and Gestational Age," *Science*, CLVI (1967), 984-85.

Smith, K. U., and Smith, W. M. *Perception and Motion: An Analysis of Space-Structured Behavior.* Philadelphia and London: W. B. Saunders, 1962.

Solley, C. M., and Murphy, G. *Development of the Perceptual World.* New York: Basic Books, 1960.

Strauss, A. A., and Kephart, N. C. *Psychopathology and Education of the Brain-Injured Child.* New York: Grune and Stratton, 1955.

Werner, H., and Wapner, S. "Toward a General Theory of Perception," *Psychological Review*, LIX (1952), 324-38.

V. The Classroom

Before discussing those aspects of the classroom that are specific to the child with brain dysfunction, an overview will be presented of those factors that are in general conducive to learning. As stated in Chapter IV, the functional systems by which all children learn are especially important to the child with brain dysfunction. Therefore, environmental factors that help the functional systems to operate more efficiently can be of critical importance in this child's learning ability. These factors mainly concern lighting, variations in brightness, the working surfaces, and the effect of the relative height of chair and desk on the balanced relationship between visual and postural alignments to a task. Investigations of how such aspects of the classroom relate to the child's ability to learn and to his general well-being have been made primarily by Dr. D. B. Harmon (1942, 1945, 1946, 1949). His conclusions and recommendations will be discussed presently. However, before doing so, it should be mentioned that Dr. Charles B. Huelsman, Jr. (in Robinson, 1953, pp. 149-55) did a small study that was related to, but not directly equivalent to, Harmon's work, and found different results. Whereas Harmon based his conclusions on the study of more than 160,000 elementary-school children and on a later study of 396 children in grades one through five, Huelsman studied 57 fifth-graders (31 in an experimental class and 26 in a control class). Moreover, it would appear that Huelsman's project focused on the factor of lighting, whereas Harmon's placed equal emphasis on all environmental factors that influence the functional systems. Many studies of the effect of increased lighting on learning or visual well-being have shown that up to a certain point, increasing the amount of light enhances recognition of detail. However, Tinker (1939) and others have shown that when lighting is increased to more than approximately fifty-five footcandles, reading is interfered with because emphasis of letter detail obscures the recognition of words and phrases as a whole. Therefore, under those conditions, comprehension is diminished. Even though Huelsman's criticism of the statistics used by Harmon may be justified, Harmon's findings are sufficiently impressive to warrant some attention here.

The principles set forth by Harmon indicate that a child learns through all activities, not only through symbolic experiences with printed words. As a result, while learning, a child cannot be expected to stay in one fixed position, or to have only one surface on which he focuses visually. As a child changes activities, his visual and spatial orientations also change, as does his orientation to his vertical and horizontal gravitational axes. Therefore, a child needs a classroom that does more than simply provide adequate illumination of his desk top or the chalkboard. The classroom's lighting should facilitate his performance of all types of visually centered tasks any place within that room. The classroom's structural lines, where objects within the classroom are positioned, and the light-reflecting qualities of the materials making up the classroom, all should help to define the boundaries of the space within which the child performs. They should also provide a background that contributes both to the clear definition of the task to be performed and to the accurate location of that task in the child's three-dimensional spatial world. It is equally important that the classroom's desks and chairs help the child to come into proper balance with gravity and the visually centered task he is to perform. From the conceptual model presented in Chapter IV, it can be readily appreciated that the classroom's lighting, its reflectances, and its furniture can enhance the operation of the child's functional systems. Each of these three factors will now be discussed separately.

Lighting. Most school districts accept the need for a minimum of thirty footcandles of illumination on desk tops and chalkboards, while some have minimums of twenty to forty footcandles. However, adequate light on the surface of the chalkboard or the desk does not provide all that the child needs to facilitate his learning.

The human eye has difficulty adapting to marked contrasts of light and shadow. If the differences of brightness within a classroom are too great, details both of the task at hand and of its surroundings will be lost through glare or shadow. Under such conditions, it also becomes very difficult to interpret the task clearly in relationship to its surroundings. Therefore, such conditions interfere with the purpose of vision: to guide and appraise the child's movements so that he can perform his task effectively and efficiently. Vision best fulfills its role as a guidance and appraisal mechanism when it is free to scan the surroundings without encountering marked contrasts of brightness. Conversely, glare, wide discrepancies in brightness, mirror-like reflections from background surfaces, and strong light coming from a single direction contribute to inaccurate visual interpretations, physical stress, and fatigue.

Harmon's work indicates that for tasks such as reading and writing, the visual target (in this case the page in the book or the paper on the desk) should not be more than three times brighter than the desk top or the overall brightness of the rest of the room. For tasks such as building with blocks, or other activities involving three-dimensional materials, the brightest area of the visual target should not be more than seven times brighter than the darkest area of shadow created by the contour of the object. Ideally, this ratio should be 4.5 to 1, and should not exceed 7 to 1. The added contrast on the object is needed to produce the soft modeling shadows required for the accurate interpretation of the object's depth, form, size, and location in space. On the other hand, if the 7 to 1 brightness ratio is exceeded, harsh shadows will result, which adversely affect the child's interpretation of the object's depth, form, size, and location in space.

The primary source of illumination in most classrooms is daylight. Because both the quantity and quality of daylight vary with the time of day (being best at noon), as well as with the season of the year and the geographic location, daylight must be controlled if it is to aid in the learning process. Uncontrolled daylight entering through clear-glass windows causes an unbalanced distribution of light, not only for children seated farthest from the windows, but also for those seated closest to the windows. For the latter, the brightness of light entering the child's eye nearest the window is many times greater than the brightness of light entering his other eye. Harmon (1949, p. 13) cites the established ophthalmological principle that when light entering one eye is 12 per cent brighter than the light entering the other eye, vision will be suspended in one eye. When daylight is controlled only by the use of window shades, glare is reduced, but adequate and evenly distributed illumination does not result.

For the proper control of daylight, Harmon recommends light diffusers or optically designed glass panels, extending over the entire length of the window wall, both redirecting about 70 per cent of the daylight upward, toward and across the ceiling of the classroom, with the remainder of the daylight being diffused obliquely downward. The light-diffusers or optical glass sections reach from six feet to the ceiling. A vision strip, starting at three feet and going to six feet, provides eye contact with the outside and also illuminates the wall opposite the windows. An outside opaque hood at a height of six feet shields the vision strip from intense brightness. In addition, however, artificial lighting must be provided, even in classrooms used only during daylight hours. The artificial lighting keeps illumination at the required standard on overcast days, and it promotes the even distribution of light throughout the classroom. The amount of artificial lighting used should be sufficient to enable the desk tops along the wall opposite the windows to have almost the same footcandles of illumination as do the desk tops adjacent to the windows. For artificially lighting classrooms, Harmon recommends luminous ceilings, or rows of plastic-enclosed, large-area light fixtures with fluorescent lamps, wired to at least two switches—one switch controlling the light farthest from the windows. All lights would be used at night, of course.

Reflectances. To help keep the variation of brightness within the desired limits, the walls and other background surfaces of the classroom should reflect most of the light that strikes them back into the room. Harmon recommends that those portions of wall surface within the child's line of vision should reflect 55 to 70 per cent of the light that reaches them. Such reflectances would be equal to the amount of light reflected by a book or piece of paper in such tasks as reading or writing (i.e., 55 to 70 per cent). Because the function of the portions of the walls that are above the chalkboard, as well as the ceiling, is primarily to distribute light, their reflectances should be at least 85 per cent. If dadoes are used, although they are not necessary, these lower portions of the walls should have reflectances of 45 to 55 per cent. The exception is the wall area beneath the light strip, which should have a reflectance of 70 per cent, to minimize the brightness contrast between it and the light strip. Floors are recommended to have reflectances ranging from 20 to 30 per cent.

Of obvious importance is the amount of light reflected by the surface that forms the background of the task on which the child focuses his attention. Harmon indicates that a near-space visual task (one that is approximately within the reach of one's arm) reflexly focuses the child's vision wherever there is maximal *contrast* of brightness. Thus, the customary dark-finished desk, which typically has a reflectance of only 13 per cent, would make the child focus between the edge of the book he is to read and the desk, thereby competing with his focus on the printed page. Equally difficult for the child would be a light-finished desk with a reflectance approximating that of the task, causing the child a conflict in focusing between the edge of the desk and the floor and in focusing on the printed page. Both desk tops would interfere with the child's freedom of visual movement over the printed page. Therefore, Harmon recommends a desk top whose reflectance approaches but does not equal that of the task and which has distributed over its surface a light but discernible asymmetrical pattern that would differentiate the desk top from the floor. Such a surface could be a natural wood with an asymmetrical grain, such as birch, or a similarly grained synthetic material.

The closer a task is to the child's eyes, the more his performance is affected by the difference in brightness between his task and its background. Therefore, Harmon suggests that the reflectance of the desk top be neither less than half the reflectance of the task nor greater than the reflectance of the task. This would permit the desk top's reflectances to range from 30 to 55 per cent. The same reasoning would not apply to reading what is written on the chalkboard, because that would be a visual task in far space (the space approximately from the end of one's arm to infinity). However, so that the brightness contrast of the chalkboard area would not interfere with other tasks, Harmon recommends that its reflectance not be less than one-third the reflectance of the surrounding wall. Thus, the green chalkboard, with reflectances of 25 to 30 per cent, when chalked-in for use, would be better than the conventional blackboard, which has reflectances of 5 to 8 per cent.

The information cited above on footcandles and reflectances can readily be applied by lighting engineers who, hopefully, would be consulted by the school's administrator. However, the conscientious teacher will want to evaluate personally at least the critical factor of brightness contrast. That can be accomplished by means of the usual light meter, or preferably by one that is graduated on a scale of footcandles. (For example, General Electric's light meter, model 213, measures footcandles of illumination; it also measures reflectances in foot-lamberts, which are units of brightness. This instrument can be purchased for less than $25 at an electrical equipment and supply company.)

The role of color will be discussed in Chapter VIII, but Harmon's suggestions concerning the paint used in the classroom can be summarized as follows: the paint should be desaturated, or grayed; warm pastel colors (such as beiges or sandalwoods, with a touch of cream) should be used in classrooms on the northern, northeastern, and northwestern sides of the school; cool colors (the greenish blues) should be used in classrooms on

77

the southern, southeastern, and southwestern sides of the school; and the wall surfaces should have a matte finish.

Furniture. The child, as a totality, brings all of himself to each learning situation. He does not use only his eyes for a visual task, for example. To continue the example, a sustained visual task requires the child's two eyes to team properly. In turn, to be able to team properly, the two eyes require the head, neck, and trunk to come into an alignment that will aid the eyes in accomplishing their purpose. When the task also requires the manipulation of objects (tasks such as writing or building a block tower), the eye's supporting structures—the head, neck, and trunk—must not only hold the eyes in a position best suited to that task, but they must also support and balance the arms and hands in a fashion that best suits these to work harmoniously with the eyes to accomplish the task most effectively and efficiently. That a visual task requires the use of more of the body than the eyes is further indicated by the fact that one of the neurologically based feedback mechanisms goes directly from the retina to certain muscles of the neck, as do connections from the trunk. That feedback mechanism signals those muscles to action; it also signals their readjustment when this is required to maintain the body in a balanced alignment with both gravity and the visual task. Therefore, no matter how adequate the lighting is and no matter how well controlled the variations in brightness are, the child also needs furniture that further helps him to maintain a balanced relationship between his gravitational and visual mechanisms.

Harmon studied the relationship of eyes, head, and trunk to the desk top while children were engaged in various visual activities when seated. He found that the child reflexly tilts his head and trunk slightly forward and raises his forearms approximately 20 degrees from the horizontal, to assume a position of physiologically balanced readiness to cope with a sustained near-space visual task. In that position the least possible energy is expended because the eyes are on a plane parallel to the book he is reading; then each eye is the same distance from the task, allowing equal retinal stimulation in each eye, so that the result

78

will be a fused, single image. Moreover, that position is physiologically and functionally efficient, because in it there is a matching of proprioceptual signals that the child gets from the evenly distributed actions of supportive muscles on both sides of his body and of the visual signals he gets from the proper alignment of his eyes to the task. In that position, the child's

Figure 3. Readiness position

eyes also are the proper distance from the visual task, which again facilitates the matching of proprioceptual and visual signals.

As can be seen in Figure 3, when in the readiness position, the three points consisting of the midpoint between the eyes, the elbow, and the knuckle at the base of the middle finger approximate a right triangle. The base of that triangle points toward the child's center of gravity and is parallel to the plane of his face, while the perpendicular of the triangle forms the line of sight between the eyes and the visual task. Thus, if the child is seated with his back rigidly straight or with it bent over so that his eyes are too close to the task, he cannot maintain the proper balance between postural and visual signals.

Seated at the usual flat or near-flat school desk, the child is forced forward into an off-balance position in a reflex effort to bring his face parallel to his visual task. That off-balance posture causes extra pressure on his back in an effort to support his trunk against gravity, thereby inducing stress and fatigue, which detracts from his attention to his task. To reduce the pressure on his back, the child tends to support part of the weight of his trunk on one elbow, thereby twisting his head and trunk, so that his eyes then are not equidistant from the task, causing a difference in focus between the two eyes. If this twisted position were maintained throughout the performance of the task, perceptual distortion could result. Moreover, when the head tilts to one side more than 20 degrees from the plane parallel to the task, the light entering one eye is 12 per cent less than the light entering the other eye, leading to suspended vision in one eye. Thus, improper furniture can be just as detrimental to learning as improperly controlled lighting or variation in brightness.

The teacher can protect the child from such impediments to learning by providing him with a properly inclined desk top and by being sure that his eyes are the proper distance from the visual task. As illustrated in Figure 3, the distance a child's eyes should be from his task is approximately equal to the distance between his elbow and the knuckle at the base of his middle finger (as measured on the outer side of his forearm). The child should remain approximately this distance from near-space visual tasks, regardless of the nature of the task. However, to a certain limit, the degree to which the desk top is slanted can vary with the task.

For reading activities, the child can best maintain his eyes parallel to the book and at the proper distance from the book when his desk top is sloped 20 degrees from the horizontal. When reading from a book that lies flat against a horizontal desk top, the two sides of the triangle shown in Figure 3 cannot be equal. That is possible only when the desk top is sloped 20 degrees. If the signals from his back posture and from his visual alignment do not match, stress and fatigue result, and comprehension will decrease.

The movements of writing and drawing are most comfortable and efficient when they pivot from the elbow and the shoulder. The child can maintain the movements with greater freedom and with an ease of balance between postural and visual signals when the desk top slants 20 degrees from the horizontal. Some specialists prefer the desk top to be slanted 10 degrees for writing tasks. At that slope, the paper does not tend to slide off the desk top. However, Harmon suggests the 20-degree slope so that the child has the least tension in the upper and lower arm when doing fine movements. At the 10-degree position, the child's writing or drawing movements could not be as well controlled.

When the child engages in construction activity with three-dimensional material, his visual and postural alignments shift. At the same time, the movements required for construction activities are more discrete, centering about the wrists and elbows. To provide proper freedom for such activities, the forearms are horizontal, instead of inclined at approximately 20 degrees from the horizontal as they are in reading and writing activities. Therefore, the desk top should be flat only for construction activities.

The child's chair should also aid in the freedom of movement and the balance of postural and visual alignment that are required by the task. The chair should allow him to have his feet on the floor, with a slight space between his thighs and the seat of the chair. It should also swivel, so he can readily rotate his trunk to bring his preferred hand into a suitable position for effective use, counterbalanced by his other hand. Because the child, by reflex, tries to maintain the same distance between his eyes and the task in all near-space visual activities, as his line of sight changes from one activity to another (or from the bottom of the block tower he is building to the top of that tower, and vice versa), by reflex, he moves his head and trunk position either forward or backward. Therefore, the chair should be free to move forward and backward to accommodate the child's change in the curvature of his back and in his center of gravity, as he shifts his position in accordance with the requirements of the task. When the child's chair is in a fixed position, he is

Figure 4. Adjustable desk and chair

likely to feel pressure under his thighs, which causes a distraction from the task and results in increased wriggling and distraction.

Once the child is in the proper chair, the desired height of his desk will be that point at which his elbows barely brush the edge of the desk top.

Figure 4 illustrates the chair and adjustable desk found to be best suited to the children at The Pathway School. These are manufactured by the Scholar Craft School Furniture Division of the Southeastern Metals Company, Birmingham, Alabama. Although this desk does not have all the inherent flexibility required, the top can be readily adapted to slope at the 10- and 20-degree positions by means of a "lift lock" mechanism made by Garrett Tubular Products, Inc., Garrett, Indiana, and a continuous hinge measuring 1 1/16 inches by 30 inches, which is

Figure 5. Adjustable lift lock and hinge

available in any hardware store. The "lift lock" and hinge are shown in Figure 5. Of all desks currently available, the Scholar Craft desk was found to be the easiest and least expensive to adapt. One note of caution for those who intend to order them. The storage bin for a "right hand" desk is on the right side of the desk, whereas for proper postural balance and movement a right-handed child needs the storage bin on the left side of the desk. Therefore, a "left hand" desk should be ordered for a right-handed child.

Lastly, Harmon suggests that the child's desk be placed so that neither the side of his face is parallel to the windows nor his back to the windows. Both desk positions cast varying degrees of shadow on the book or paper with which the child is working. Instead, Harmon recommends that the desk be positioned so that the angle between the child's line of vision and

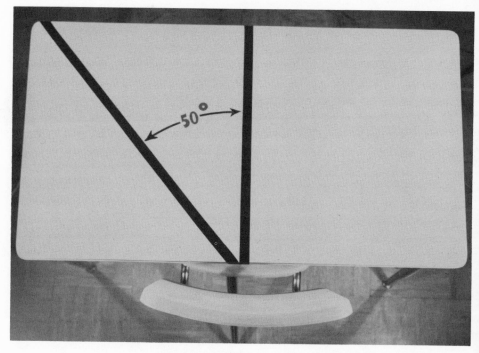

Figure 6. Desk top template

84

the front margin of the window is 50 degrees. The teacher can readily establish the proper desk placement by putting a template cut at a 50-degree angle on the desk surface. This is illustrated in Figure 6. This placement of the desk will cast a shadow over the child's right shoulder.

Carrels, which Cruickshank (1961, p. 16; and 1967, 120-23) calls "cubicles," or any other aspect of the classroom designed especially for the child with brain dysfunction should, in my opinion, be used only in ways that do not conflict with Harmon's recommendations. My opinion is based on Harmon's (1942, 1949) findings that improper attention to lighting, to variations in brightness, and to furniture created postural, dental, and visual problems in large numbers of school children, as well as interference with their learning efficiency. It seems obvious that one should safeguard against the risk of such complications when trying to overcome the complex and difficult problems of children with brain dysfunction. Additional classroom factors that should be considered in relation to the specific needs of children with brain dysfunction are size, stimulus control, the activities to be carried out, and the furnishings most likely to insure the success of those activities.

Cruickshank (1961 and 1967) feels that the classroom should be smaller than the customary size called for in architectural or state plans and that the size should be dictated by the psychological characteristics of the children who will use it. Flexibility is necessary in architectural planning, and environmental flexibility is mandatory for these children.

Work that has been done at The Pathway School suggests that the size of the room is not the main determinant of the child's learning to monitor extraneous stimuli or of his learning the boundaries of his spatial world and how to organize himself within those boundaries. A determinant more cogent than the size of the room seems to be the activities presented to this child and his developmental readiness to use those activities successfully. Actually, a classroom whose size is approximately 18 feet by 20 feet has proven too small to provide this child with all the activities he needs for the development of real skills.

Conversely, a standard-size classroom (which is 850 square feet, or approximately 21 feet by 40 feet) that housed many activities that were separated by dividers proved helpful to this child's skill development. Thus, size in itself seems only relevant when considered in conjunction with all other factors that relate to the child's development of requisite skills.

For the sake of clarity, the classroom that currently seems best suited to the needs of the child with brain dysfunction will now be described. As will be seen, this classroom is not at variance with Cruickshank's recommendations, but it does include modifications of his suggestions, together with innovations that are in keeping with the conceptual model presented in Chapter IV. Therefore, what Cruickshank (1961, 1967) has already set forth so well will not be repeated here. Only the modifications of his suggestions will be discussed.

In recognition of the diversity of developmental needs shown by this child and of the fact that his needs change as he acquires some genuine skills, a classroom should have sufficient inherent flexibility to program for his variegated and changing needs. At the same time, complete flexibility is too expensive for most public schools, architecturally, so a workable compromise is necessary. That compromise can begin by altering a standard classroom in keeping with Harmon's suggestions. When the classroom is designated for children who have marked ego insufficiencies, the light strip Harmon recommends can be replaced by translucent glass, so that outside activity does not produce a distraction. Secondly, the floors should be carpeted to further reduce distraction and to lend the room a sense of quietude otherwise unavailable. The new synthetic carpets have proven durable and less expensive to maintain than floor tile. In addition to soundproofed ceilings, walls and other structures can be effectively and inexpensively soundproofed by means of standard non-tempered pegboard, which has proven to be highly sound absorbent. If the children to be placed in that classroom are expected to be impulse-ridden and as yet not to have achieved any real degree of impulse control, obviously the holes in the pegboard would be too tempting to put pegboard where the children would spend most of their working time. On the other hand, it could well be used in that portion of the room devoted to eye-hand coordination and similar skills. In areas utilized for such activities, the holes in the pegboards would not be an attractive hazard, whereas they would be on the walls of the carrel. Moreover, the fact that the holes are symmetrically one inch apart lends a textured quality to the pegboard, at a distance; then the holes are no longer seen individually.

Work done at The Pathway School indicates that this child profits most when the majority of the activities he needs can be carried out in the classroom, rather than elsewhere in the school. The latter tends to fragment the child rather than offer him a program that provides him with the continuity he needs. For many children, continuity of program within the classroom is more effective than individual help from a number of specialized educational experts in areas such as reading, mathematics, and adaptive physical education. Nevertheless, some children do need such individual help in addition to continuity of program within the classroom. Even then, however, team teaching by the specialist and the teacher within the classroom may hold more promise than having the child go out of the classroom for such individual help.

Through the use of dividers, areas of the classroom can be designated for language activity, or adaptive physical education, or a "motor-math" program. These dividers should not be more than 4 feet to 6 feet tall, so that they do not upset the controlled lighting and brightness contrast. They should be sturdily built, painted to match the walls, and on castors, so that they can be moved easily. These dividers provide the child with the spatial boundaries he needs to perform a given task. As activities shift and as a child needs to expand his spatial perimeter, these dividers can serve the purpose. For children who have not as yet gained sufficient control to refrain from pushing the dividers around, dividers can be used that do not have castors, but instead are fixed to the floor. These can be moved fairly readily if a different arrangement of activity space is required during the course of the school year.

Dividers should not be regarded as substitutes for carrels, however. The purpose of the dividers is to help the child perceive the spatial attributes of an activity, so that he can better organize himself within that activity. The purpose of the carrel is reduction of distracting stimuli, when optimal attention and concentration are required for a sustained near-space visual activity. The carrel is also effective when a child, in the process of gaining greater ego skills, feels in real danger of not being able to cope with an activity and needs the added structure and security of the confines of the carrel.

The carrels found most effective at Pathway (see Figure 7) have walls that are 4 feet high and 3 feet wide, with a 4-foot space inside the walls. The walls that form the carrel are fastened securely to the walls of the classroom. The space thus provided enables the desk and chair appropriate to the child to be placed within that carrel. Experience at Pathway has indicated that the movable desk and chair do not contribute to distractibility or hyperactivity, except, in some cases, during the initial period of adjustment to them. To the contrary, there is indication that the enhancement of physiological readiness for near-space tasks significantly reduces distractibility and hyper-activity.

Current observations at Pathway suggest that a child should be faced into the carrel only when he has a basic comprehension of the task to be performed and can complete the task independently. This enables him to concentrate on the integration of the task with the fewest possible distractions. However, he should remain in that position only for the duration of that task. Otherwise, the required freedom to shift his gaze from near space to far space is restricted. When the child repeatedly requires help from the teacher, frequently calling or signaling to the teacher for such help, it seems better for him to face the side of the carrel. Then the auditory signals he gets from the teacher and the visual signals he gets from the materials he is working with are localized. For the teacher to give him information while behind him could cause confusion, because he could not localize the auditory and visual signals he was

Figure 7. Study carrel

receiving, and they might compete with each other for his attention. This factor could be especially important to a child functioning at the proprioceptual or even at the preceptual level of development. As the child is better able to monitor extraneous stimuli, he can be placed with his face to the class. That would be an intermediate step to working outside the

89

carrel altogether, returning to it only when he felt a real need to do so.

So that the teacher can better supervise and help with the activities going on within the carrels, they should be located within one area of the classroom. The needs of the children within the class would determine the areas of the classroom designated for other activities. Before discussing possible activity areas within the classroom, chalkboards should be mentioned, because these would be present in all classrooms. In keeping with the levels of development of the child's integrative system discussed in Chapter IV, chalkboard activities are prerequisite to adequacy in desk work. Therefore, their absence in any classroom would be a major error.

Especially for children who have the spatial problems attendant to brain dysfunction, the chalkboard should not be flat against the wall. Instead, it should be slanted with its base 15 degrees away from the vertical. When a child is asked to draw a vertical line on a chalkboard that is on a vertical plane, he reaches forward and presses harder on the chalk as he moves the chalk down the surface. Thus, his proprioceptual signals tell him that "down" is "away" from his trunk. In contrast, when he draws a vertical line on paper at his desk, "down" is "toward" his trunk. By slanting the chalkboard 15 degrees, the translation from the vertical plane to the horizontal plane is made easier. The slant enables the child to get more nearly equal proprioceptual signals of posture and of pressure on the chalk at any point on the chalkboard, thereby more closely approximating the proprioceptual signals he gets when working at his desk. The slanted chalkboard also allows the child more freedom of movement from the shoulder; that is, he does not have to reach and extend his arm as far from the shoulder, thereby throwing himself off balance, as he would if the board were in a vertical position. This again facilitates a balance between postural and visual cues.

One activity area within the classroom might be needed for speech and language development, complete with tape recorder, headphones, and other required equipment. Another area might be needed for adaptive physical education, having in it such equipment as walking beams, jump boards, and the Eye-Hand Coordination Exercises (published by Teaching Resources Inc., Boston, Mass.). Still another area might be designated for basic experiments in the various sciences. In some classes, children could perform activities within those areas only under constant supervision. In other classes, where the children had achieved greater ego growth, they could go to such areas for independent activity, which they would regard as an earned and cherished privilege.

In some classrooms, the program would require no carrels or desks, because the emphasis would be on skills that are precursory to academic work. (This will be discussed further in Chapter VII.) At other times outdoor activities can be structured more meaningfully and beneficially than classroom activity. Both the teacher and the administrator must realize that there is no single "right" classroom for all children who have brain dysfunction. They must also realize that there is no magic in any physical structure. Whatever magic there may be is within the child's own development. The teacher's satisfaction comes from an accurate understanding of the processes involved in the child's development and from being able to prescribe a program appropriate to the child's needs. A helpful classroom is one that enhances opportunities for learning and has the inherent flexibility to facilitate programming for the child's varied and changing needs.

REFERENCES

Cruickshank, W. M. *et al. A Teaching Method for Brain-Injured and Hyperactive Children*. Syracuse: Syracuse University Press, 1961.

Cruickshank, W. M. *The Brain-Injured Child in Home, School, and Community*. Syracuse: Syracuse University Press, 1967.

Gesell, Arnold, *et al. Vision, Its Development in Infant and Child*. New York: Paul Hoeber, Inc., 1949.

Harmon, D. B. "Some Preliminary Observations on the Developmental Problems of 160,000 Elementary School Children," *Medical Woman's Journal*, XLIX (1942), 75-82.

_____. "Lighting and Child Development," *Illuminating Engineering*, XL (1945), 199-233.

_____. "Light on Growing Children," *Architectural Record*, XCIX (1946), 78-90.

_____. *The Coordinated Classroom*. Grand Rapids: American Seating Co., 1949.

Robinson, Helen M. (ed.). *Clinical Studies in Reading, II.* ("Supplementary Educational Monograph #77") Chicago: University of Chicago Press, 1953.

Tinker, Miles A. "The Effect of Illumination Intensities Upon Speed of Perception and Upon Fatigue in Reading," *Journal of Educational Psychology*, XXX (1939), 561-71.

VI. Educational Programming

For an educational program to be appropriate for a class, it should begin with planning, prior to the arrival of the class itself. The planning stage gives the teacher an opportunity to study diagnostic findings on each child's constellation of skills and deficits, past experiences, home life, and other topics pertinent to what each child will bring with him to the learning situation. Hopefully, the group of children selected for a given class will have been chosen mainly through the judgments of an administrator who is both knowledgeable and skillful with children who have brain dysfunction. When the diagnostic committee or administrator responsible for class grouping is not expert with these children, it would be wise to have each teacher cooperate in choosing his or her own class. However, this is only second best to having the class grouping done by an able supervisor who knows both the teachers and the children well.

An able supervisor, working closely with the teachers and the children, can judge which teachers are by temperament and experience best suited to work with acting-out children or with passive-resistant children, with younger or older children, with children first entering the program or with those being readied to return to regular class. That supervisor also knows which children have done well with a certain type of teacher and need more experience with the same or same type of teacher, and which have done well but now need to experience working with a different type of teacher. For those children who have not done well, the supervisor would know why, and whether the child did poorly for reasons related or totally unrelated to the skill and personality of his teacher. The able supervisor would also know which children have similar needs and which children work well together, or at least do not detonate open warfare at the mere sight of each other. Obviously, no one teacher or group of teachers could assess all of the above (and other) variables as well as an effective supervisor could. This is especially true, because such assessment would require the teacher to make a candid self-assessment, which is difficult indeed.

After the composition of the class has been decided, and after the teacher has had an opportunity to learn what others have found out about the children who will be in that class, plans need to be made for the physical setup of the classrooms. As discussed in Chapter V, dividers for certain activity areas might be needed, or the usual furnishings may not be needed at all for a program that will be preacademic rather than academic in nature. Plans are also needed for acquiring or having access to the equipment and materials the supervisor and teacher antici- pate needing for a particular class. Moreover, if a youngster to be included in the class has a history of excessive illness, the teacher or supervisor will want to establish contact with and seek advice from that child's pediatrician. If another child is receiving psychotherapy, contact should be made with the doctor or agency involved (with the parents' consent, of course). Similar contact should be made when a child has had seizures that only recently have been controlled by medication, and in a variety of other cases. Such initial contacts can become major avenues of communication concerning a child's habilitation. Plans can also be made for the teacher to work with a consultant in certain specialized educational areas in which a child shows obvious need. That consultant's time may not be available if requested some weeks after the class begins. After the completion of such planning, the teacher is ready to spend time individually, with each new student in the class.

The staggered admission, in which each new child is integrated into the class on an individual basis, has been carefully spelled out by Cruickshank (1967, pp. 132-37). What needs to be clarified is how the teacher initially evaluates the child's current constellation of skills and deficiencies, to know at

94

which level of development to begin working with him. At the outset, the teacher should explore, with the child, why the child believes he is in that class. The teacher then should establish that he or she will help the child overcome (within realistic limits) the problems for which he came to that class. These concepts will be discussed further in Chapter IX.

From the first contact with a child, the teacher should assiduously apply the two basic principles of prescriptive teaching discussed in Chapter IV: (1) to make judgments about the child's developmental levels and needs primarily from observation of the child's performance; and (2) to make expectations about the child's performance only after the task he is to perform has been accurately analyzed in terms of what it requires of the child, in terms of what questions it asks of the child, and in terms of the developmental levels at which those questions are asked. It is extremely difficult for most teachers to apply those two principles comfortably and continuously, because their training and experience have not prepared them to do so. When the teacher's training and experience are geared to the expectation that the teaching materials and techniques will accomplish the goal, it is difficult to learn how to observe the child's performance and how to analyze the task to be presented to the child. But these skills can be learned, and, fortunately, as they are practiced, they become easier to apply, both comfortably and continuously.

As an example of how the teacher can apply the two basic principles of prescriptive teaching during the first contact with a child, let us explore the initial interaction between a teacher and child. The child is 11 years old. On the Weschler Intelligence Scale for Children, he achieved a verbal IQ of 77, a nonverbal IQ of 79, and a full-scale IQ of 76, although he indicated having a normal intellectual potential. He had spent two years in each of the first, second, and third grades, becoming increasingly fearful of competition. The child also was terrified of water. His instructional level in reading was at the primer level, and in arithmetic at the beginning first-grade level. His physical and neurological examinations were negative, except for an unsteady gait and uncoordinated movements. During his first visit with his teacher, she observed that his arms did not swing while he walked. He could jump, but had much difficulty in trying to hop and skip. He could jump rope backward, but not forward. He could draw his previous school only after he first pictured it with his eyes closed. To place forms accurately in a form board, the child had to run his fingers over the forms. When presented with a form board, in which each shape to be placed into its appropriate recess in the board was split into two pieces, he could not see the relationship between the two halves of a form. From this meager information, the teacher could begin an educational program for this youngster.

His walking without the use of his arms, his difficulty in skipping and jumping, and his inability to see the relationship between the two halves of a form indicated that he had not as yet learned how to use the two sides of his body in synchrony. He was still a two-sided being, as is the infant. When he had not yet learned to utilize his proprioceptual signals well enough to unify his body, certainly higher levels of developmental function of his integrative system could not be expected. It is small wonder, then, that he was terrified of water. He could not synchronize his body parts and movements in the environment he lived in for eleven years, so he certainly could not cope with the added demands of a strange environment, water. Moreover, he apparently was overly reliant on current cues from the information mode of seeing, because these cues interfered with performance such as visual recall and jumping rope. He could muster fairly adequate visual recall only when he shut out the current cues being received through seeing. When attempting to jump rope forward, he failed because the necessary visual judgments concerning where the rope was in space and how far it was from the ground, when he saw it, interfered with his jumping, an action not yet well organized and refined. But, when he jumped rope backward, there was no "noise on the line" in the feedback mechanisms from his inadequate visual judgments, so he could concentrate on the movement involved in jumping over the rope, as well as on the proprioceptual signals he received concerning where the rope was in space. He also showed reliance on tactual information when he had to feel the solid forms before he could "see" in which recess each belonged.

Thus, this youngster's performance told the teacher that he had certain basic, strong needs at the proprioceptual level of development and that even though he relied at times on proprioceptual information, that information was not as yet well organized, refined, and practiced. Therefore, she would not begin the educational program for his skill deficiencies with pencil-and-paper tasks and formalized reading activities, which require integrative skills at the perceptual and conceptual levels. Instead, his performance dictated that he needed her help, first of all, in becoming aware of the muscles that moved his body.

The teacher would then begin to program for him activities such as having him lie supine on the floor and tighten his whole body, to feel the difference between tensed and relaxed muscles. Then he would be helped to become aware of tensed and relaxed muscles in his arms, legs, trunk, and neck. He would learn where he feels sitting up from a supine position, so that he could better organize the proprioceptual signals involved in the action of sitting up, and so that he could learn about angles from the proprioceptual signals within his own body. While standing, he would learn where he felt bending over and what effect bending over had on his actions in relation to his gravitational axes, which would also further his information about angles. He would learn what it felt like to walk when both his legs and arms moved slowly and exaggeratedly, like a wooden soldier, so that he could become aware of contrasting proprioceptual signals. He would learn what it felt like to twist his body by driving one arm through space, and then the other. As each arm made a thrust, he would become aware that to maintain his balance, his other arm would have to make a counterthrusting movement. Of course, his teacher would do none of these tasks with him before knowing herself, through the proprioceptual signals she received from her own body, what each task asked of him. Before presenting each task to him, she would analyze it not only at the proprioceptual level, but at all levels. Her analysis of each task would also tell her the different developmental levels that could be emphasized through the task, as well as how she could increase the complexity of a given task as the child showed apparent mastery of it, to help him further organize, refine, and practice his performance of it.

As this child's performance indicated better organization of skills at the proprioceptual level, his teacher would work with him on tasks that emphasize the preceptual level of development. However, in emphasizing the preceptual level, she would also see to it that he had many opportunities to refer back to the proprioceptual level, to check the skill he was in the process of learning against the frame of reference already developed at the proprioceptual level, and to enable him to facilitate the functions of his neurologically based scanning and feedback mechanisms. For example, after having him identify the shape of objects by touch, with his eyes closed, the teacher would have him walk the shape of that object. This activity gives him the opportunity to realize that the information he is getting from feeling the roundness of a circle, for example, matches with the proprioceptual information he gets by walking a circle. To promote further integration she could also have him draw the form on the chalkboard, trace it in the air, and etch it in the sandbox with his toe.

Continuing to work with this child at the preceptual level, his teacher would help him to make discriminatory judgments, one at a time, in tasks that emphasize each information mode that shows inadequacy. At this level the child also needs opportunities to experience how one mode reenforces the information obtained through another mode. Shadow play is a good example of an activity that can help this child become aware of such reenforcement. In shadow play he can see his shadow move as he himself feels the movement, thereby making him more aware of the parts of his body that he is moving. At this level, chalkboard activities would also be helpful for this child. (Chalkboard activities are carefully spelled out in *Developing Learning Readiness*, by Getman, Kane, Halgren, and McKee, a kit of teaching materials and activities published by McGraw Hill, 1968.) Then his teacher would help him to refine his awareness of direction and control of movement by means of appropriate paper-and-pencil work, in which he would have to change direction, judge distance and size, and so on. Before moving on to activities that emphasize this child's perceptual level of development, his teacher would be sure that each information mode in which he had shown deficiency was sufficiently organized and refined to contribute accurately and efficiently to his performance. Otherwise, his performances that relied heavily on the perceptual level of development would not be adequate.

At the perceptual level of development, this youngster would benefit from activities such as listening to a story and translating what he heard into pantomime and into a picture he would draw. In such activities, the information he gets through hearing is translated into movement, so that he again refers back to his proprioceptual and preceptual frames of reference for clarification and further integration. He would also be helped by asking him to judge the size of the doorway across the gym, how many steps he would take to get from the chalkboard to the door of the classroom, and the directions from school to his home. When indicated, he would check those judgments by actually moving through space to find the accurate answer. There he would be clarifying his percepts of space and his percepts of movements through space.

When ready for activities that emphasized his conceptual level of development, the skills he had been working on could be further refined by his learning to read and write words that referred to movement and spatial judgment, words which by this time would be concrete representations of the skills he had been organizing and refining.

In this youngster's case, the sequence of only one aspect of his educational program has been briefly sketched: that which concerns the skill deficiencies observed by his teacher in her initial contact with him. In devising his educational program, the teacher also began to help him organize and refine other skills at

99

whatever developmental levels he could succeed. Thus, even initially, she had programmed for this particular child at the proprioceptual level in those areas already discussed, at the preceptual level in auditory discrimination and memory, and at the conceptual level in understanding the cause-and-effect relationships involved in placing events in their proper sequence.* Applying the conceptual model in this fashion is quite remote from repetitiously giving each child 10 minutes per day of one activity and 12 minutes per day of another activity, regardless of his constellation of skills and deficits.

As another example of how the teacher can discern where to start a child's educational program, let us imagine that no prior information on him was available to the teacher. Unfortunately, in many school districts such an instance would be commonplace rather than hypothetical. Nevertheless, let us suppose that a nine-year-old boy, about whom the teacher has no prior useful information, enters the classroom. He looks at various objects without making a comment, until he sees an eight-inch rubber ball. At that point he exclaims, "I hate to play ball!" Rather than ignore the exclamation or reply with an insipid, "That's nice," the teacher uses this opportunity to demonstrate to the child that she is a helping person, one who *does care* about him and who will aid him to overcome his difficulties. Therefore, her reply is: "There are things you can do with a ball that are fun. We'll find out what those things are so that later I can help you play ball as the other boys do. Then you will really be proud of yourself." With that, she rolls the ball on the floor to the child and asks him to catch it. He does so without difficulty, and rolls it back to her upon request. As this activity continues for a few minutes, the teacher observes that he has no difficulty judging how fast the ball travels the distance between them and that he has no difficulty in placing both hands on it as it comes to him. She also notes that he can accurately aim it at her and can

---

*The reader may wonder about the relationship of this child's educational program to his academic growth. After nine months this child was reading at the second level of second grade and was mastering basic arithmetical skills and concepts at the second grade level.

easily propel it to her with his right arm and hand, while his left arm and the rest of his body cooperate in accomplishing the movement. Having commented on how well he could do that with a ball, she explores whether or not he can catch the ball when it is lobbed to him. With arms extended ready for the ball, he catches it on his forehead, and has another utter defeat. After sympathizing with him briefly and making sure he is not hurt (to demonstrate again that she truly cares about him), she says, "Let's see if this ball will be easier to catch." Then she lobs a large whiffle ball to him. This time, he gets his hands to the ball just in time to bat it to one side, but not catch it. The teacher exclaims with pleasure: "You almost caught that one. We're getting closer to helping you learn how to catch." Next she throws a balloon to him. As he catches it with awkward apprehension, he breaks into a big smile; and the teacher has begun to program for what is to this youngster an important area of deficit.

By observing the child's performance in the few simple tasks she presented to him, the teacher learned that he could use his body in a unified fashion, that his vision could steer his movements, but that his vision could not make accurate judgments about an object's trajectory through space. Therefore, the teacher provided him with the opportunity to make such visual judgments when she slowed down that trajectory, first by using a whiffle ball and then by using a balloon. Obviously, the teacher would have to learn why this boy could not make such judgments when playing with a regular ball, and she probably would need the help of a vision specialist to do so, but she did accomplish the foundation for a good, trusting relationship with this youngster. Moreover, by demonstrating to him that she could help him overcome a deficit that was fearful and disturbing to him, she had given him the precious gift of realistic hope.

Whether or not a teacher has educationally meaningful prior information on a child, it is not possible to prescribe at the outset an entire educational program for him. All the teacher should expect initially is to establish the beginning of a trusting and understanding relationship with the child, identify some

101

major areas of need, and know the developmental levels and activities that will help him to start building skills in those areas. To do that is quite an accomplishment. From there on, each child's program is built day by day in accord with his development and his needs. This does not mean, however, that a teacher should not structure each child's day by means of long-range goals and daily planning. Through observation of the child's performance and through knowledge of what each activity requires of that child, the teacher should set realistic goals for the child's accomplishment of given skills, and each day he should plan activities for the next day that would help to implement those goals.

In doing his daily planning, the teacher must be cognizant of the range of skills and deficiencies encompassed by the entire class. When the needs of each child are well understood, activities can be planned that, in most cases, will enable each child to participate in that activity at his own developmental level. For example, a "motor" activity might involve one child, who could not accurately judge the ball's trajectory in space, having a whiffle-ball catch with another child, who was refining balance and the interweaving of body movements by playing catch, while the latter was on a balance board. Two other children in the class could be refining skills at their level through the use of the Eye-Hand Coordination Exercises, while several other children further organized their movements through shadow play. As another example, a "reading" activity might involve one child, who reads at the fourth-grade level, reading a story to the class "written" (dictated to the teacher and typed by the secretary) by another child, who is a nonreader, about a trip the class had taken. Another child who needed practice in visual recall could enumerate all the things he saw at a specific place mentioned in the story. Still another child, who needed practice in inferential thinking, could answer what-would-have-happened-if questions, in connection with various events cited in the story. In both examples, each child would be participating in the activity at his own level of skill development.

102

Group activities can also be profitable for children who have not as yet achieved any academic skills, but instead have achieved a high degree of proficiency in hyperactivity, hyper-distractibility, and similar behavior. Activities for these children will be discussed further in Chapter VII.

No class can be so homogeneous that all the children have the same developmental needs in all skill areas. At the same time, each child can gain a great deal by working on his skill development through interaction with other children in his group. To participate in the group helps him to realize that he is not hopeless, that he is not the only one in the whole world who has difficulty. Each child can derive considerable support from witnessing and often helping his classmates in their struggle to overcome their difficulties. A child can derive great pleasure in helping a classmate overcome a problem in an area different from his own problem, or one in which he has already made substantial progress. Frequently, children seek opportunities to help their classmates. In turn, the child who needs help with a particular problem often accepts help from another child more willingly than from an adult. This does not mean that a child can substitute for a trained teacher, but that he can be a catalyst to or assist in what the teacher is trying to accomplish. Furthermore, the creative teacher, who also understands the developmental level at which each child needs help in building adequate skills, can originate activities in which the class has fun. Group activities usually lend themselves to being more enjoyable than activities done by the child while alone in his carrel. Learning *should* be fun. Enjoyment is nature's built-in motivation, its guarantee of the organism's striving for development.

Initially, some youngsters will not be able to participate in group activity, no matter how well planned and implemented. For them individual work is needed while the others in the class participate in the group activity. Here the aide can be particularly helpful, working with this child while the teacher helps the group. However, the youngster who cannot as yet participate in group activity need not always do individual work in his carrel. He may be comfortable on the fringe of the group, doing the same activity, but on a one-to-one basis. Moreover, this child should be encouraged that the day will come when he will be able to play with the other children, and then he will be very pleased with himself. Until then, he will learn things that will help him get ready for that day.

Once the teacher knows each child well enough to set realistic goals for his accomplishment of skills, a daily plan of activities can be devised. In parceling the school day to provide time for all required activities, several factors should be kept in mind. Firstly, although most children with brain dysfunction do need consistency, the activity schedule should not be rigid. Instead, it should have the flexibility to accommodate the child's changing and variegated needs. If a child is upset when he enters the class because he was teased on the bus, it will not help him to insist that he does work requiring great concentration. If a child is on the brink of gaining a skill, it will not help him to change his activity at that moment. If an activity evolves as a natural outgrowth of an assigned task, to ignore that opportunity will not help the child. Secondly, the class needs a variety of activities throughout the day. A morning of desk work or an afternoon of movement activity will not promote optimal learning. Thirdly, because the children can concentrate best in the morning, before fatigue begins to take its toll on attention and behavior, the day's first activities should focus on a child's area of greatest difficulty. This does not necessarily mean desk work. It could mean movement activities to help him become aware of his proprioceptual signals, or chalkboard work to help his directionality. Some youngsters require a warm up activity, to get into the frame of mind required for learning. Such an activity can be of short duration and can be geared to lead naturally into the area of greatest difficulty.

The teacher should also regard the activity schedule itself as subject to evaluation and change. An activity schedule that well answers the class's needs for a two-week period in September might be inappropriate for the same class in January or April. When a schedule needs to be changed, the children can be told in advance of the change, and the reason for the change. That also gives the teacher an opportunity to review with the children their progress thus far and to state what expectations will be made of them in the next phase of their growth. Such a discussion helps each child to see himself more realistically, in terms of his recent gains rather than in terms of his obsolete but habituated self-image. It also helps him to prepare himself for what he must still achieve, and he can do that more easily when his recent gains are periodically reviewed and acknowledged.

Because of the paucity of experienced teachers of children with brain dysfunction, most classes that are started for these children will be taught by neophytes. To safeguard the appropriateness of the educational program and to promote the teachers' competencies, effective supervision is mandatory. Effective supervision cannot be provided by an itinerant special-education supervisor responsible for all exceptional children within the school district. No matter how well-meaning or knowledgeable that person may be, the harassment attendant to the impossibility of knowing all the teachers and children for which he or she is responsible would preclude effective supervision. A principal, who is a strict disciplinarian, is equally incapable of providing the necessary supervision. The erudite or would-be expert college professor, who cannot see either the teacher or the child as a person, but mechanically sees only a method, is singularly unqualified to perform effective supervision. The expert, self-professed or actual, who is oblivious to the everyday needs and struggles of the teacher, and who is intent only on the glorification of a technique, also cannot supervise adequately. Effective supervision requires a person who respects teachers as human beings, who understands what they are struggling with, who is experienced with these children and can meaningfully transmit that experience to others, and who is responsible for a small enough group of teachers to know them and their classroom problems thoroughly. For the school district to content itself with a lesser supervisor is a misappropriation of public funds, for under those conditions the program and the children have little chance for success.

The effective supervisor visits each class to observe firsthand the problems and progress of both the children and the teacher. The classroom visit is then followed by a problem-oriented conference with the teacher. The purpose of the conference is to help the teacher to understand more clearly, in a given problem, the child's developmental needs, his maladaptations, and tasks that would help him to build genuine skills. The visits should be sufficiently frequent to provide continuity to the educational program of both the children and the teacher.

Another responsibility of the able supervisor is to provide inservice training that is meaningful to the teachers. Such a training program basically consists of a cohesive series of opportunities to explore in depth what is learned in the problem-oriented conferences. It provides the teachers with the opportunity to understand the developmental sequence involved in programming for a child who has a particular problem. It helps the teacher to see how one task can be increased in the complexity of what it requires of a child, so that he is sure to integrate his emerging skill optimally. It shows the teachers how to devise an activity for a class composed of children who are "completely different." It also reassures the teachers that their own learning is developmental in nature and cannot be instantaneous. This type of inservice training is not accomplished by lecturing at the teachers. It is accomplished by the teachers discussing problems that are of vital concern to them in their everyday work, the discussion being guided by the supervisor. This type of inservice will not be met with resistive yawns, sullen silences, or protests of being too tired after a hard day's work.

The foregoing discussion on educational programming emphasizes the teacher's responsibility to understand the principles and the application of prescriptive teaching. Because of the current reality of the scarcity of teachers experienced with children who have brain dysfunction, it also emphasizes the school district's

106

responsibility to provide effective supervision. Until colleges of education provide prospective teachers with a genuine and applicable understanding of child development and with a genuine and applicable understanding of the principles of prescriptive teaching, the school district cannot realistically expect the teacher to be responsible for devising an educational program that truly promotes this child's habilitation.

REFERENCE

Cruickshank, W. M. *The Brain-Injured Child in Home, School, and Community.* Syracuse: Syracuse University Press, 1967.

VII. Readiness Development

The child who has learning and behavioral disorders due to brain dysfunction can perhaps be best described from an educational standpoint as unintegrated. Usually his integrative system (discussed in Chapter IV) has never functioned adequately, and it continues to malfunction throughout its levels of development. Therefore, what "skills" he has learned often are not sufficiently interwoven and correlated with him as a totality to be used effectively and efficiently whenever needed. The teacher's job is to help this segmented and fragmented child learn how to make his integrative system operate in accord with its natural design, so that he can be a unified and effective being. To accomplish that the teacher must help him organize, refine, and practice his integrative system first at its proprioceptual level of development, thereby providing a stable frame of reference for the further development of the integrative system at each of its successively higher levels. In this way the teacher is readying him to succeed not only in academic tasks, but also in life itself.

Many children with brain dysfunction are at the three- to six-year-old level of development, with commensurate social ages, and with abundant hyperactivity and hyperdistractibility. For them, the classroom described in Chapter V or the educational program discussed in Chapter VI would not be entirely appropriate. Instead, they need more abundant opportunities to organize themselves at the proprioceptual and preceptual levels of development in relation to their environment. At The Pathway School, these needs are best met in a classroom that has no carrels or usual furniture, because these tend to interfere with the child's learning the relationship between himself, with his own body as his egocentric locus, and the objects that occupy his spatial world. Once he knows these relationships, he has a matrix in which to process information more readily, store it in memory more meaningfully, and retrieve it for more effective performance.

A large number of these children are still two-sided (Ayres, 1965), not yet able to use their body parts cooperatively for unified movement. Among the needed activities this class provides for these children is "horizontal play," in which they can learn about directional changes in space and the time required to get from one place to another. For this purpose the children engage in play such as making tracks in a sandbox with a toy car, "driving" a toy truck across the floor to the gasoline station, or propelling by hands and feet a small, three-wheeled dolly along a painted line while lying prone on it.

An equally large number of these children have not learned to make accurate judgments concerning the size of objects that are at various distances from them. Judgments about the size of an object are based on cues from other vertical objects. The child develops his awareness of vertical cues primarily through "vertical play," such as stacking boxes, going up and down stairs, and climbing. To judge size, the child also must learn that an object, such as a chair, is really the same size whether it is six feet away or twenty feet away. If not, he would be like the young child who cried bitterly after his father's airplane took off, "because it got too small to hold Daddy." Opportunities for learning to relate vertical cues to size judgment and for learning size constancy are also abundant in this class.

Outdoor activity helps these children. Even children who panic in a large space, such as a gym or an auditorium, usually can be comfortable and can learn outdoors. Often the child who panics in a large space does so because he has not as yet learned to make accurate judgments concerning near space, which he needs as a frame of reference before he can judge far space. When within a fenced area, however, he can touch the fence and thereby establish the boundaries of the activity area. As he learns to deal with spatial cues within that perimeter, he then can learn to deal with larger spaces, getting vertical cues about size and distance from telephone poles, trees, and other aspects of the landscape. Outdoor activities for these children do not include the use of swings. While swinging, the child would find it difficult to establish stable far-space boundaries of his activity. On the other hand, the child could make far-space judgments about size while coming down a sliding board, with his teacher standing near the bottom of the slide as a fixed point of reference. The seesaw also helps the child to make size judgments, because the child at the other end serves as a consistent point of reference for making spatial judgments. To pull and push a wagon or doll carriage aids in learning about the space that is in front of and behind the child. Vehicles that can be ridden over the ground are also helpful. These assist the child to judge distance, direction, and how long it takes to get from one point in space to another. The sandbox is also useful for those reasons, as well as to provide an opportunity for the child to verify a scene he sees in a picture by building it in miniature. This facilitates his ability to translate what he sees in a picture into real life, and vice versa, thereby making pictures and other symbols more meaningful for him. Frequently, teachers of hyperactive children worry about sand being kicked or thrown into a child's eyes. As a precaution against that, the sand can be kept slightly moist. Moreover, as a child finds real gratification in the activity, he is less likely to use the sand for maladaptive purposes.

Outdoor activity also provides these youngsters with opportunities to organize the auditory aspects of their environment. They can identify and localize common sounds. They can auditorily identify to whom footsteps belong, as well as how far away the owner is. Similarly, during a trip through the neighborhood or to a park, they can readily explore touching, tasting, and smelling. The teacher also can help them to put into words the information derived from such explorations.

The educational program for the class being discussed usually begins with the exploration of the characteristics of an object introduced either by one of the children or by the teacher. Seated in a circle on the floor, each child has the opportunity to discover and verbalize the characteristics of the object, informa-

110

tion which is then reinforced by being systematically called to each child's attention by the teacher. Here each child can use his various information modes one at a time, thereby refining and practicing his integrative system's preceptual level of development. The advantage of being seated on the floor rather than at tables is that the latter, when drawn into a circle, have all sorts of angles that could be confusing to a child who is at this level of development. Furthermore, the circle of children provides its own perimeter for the activity.

In another activity, each child selects from specified shelves a toy he wishes to use for his activity. These toys include large, unpainted wooden blocks of different sizes and shapes, wooden trains and sections of track that can be put together, variously sized cars and trucks, a variety of easily manipulated building materials, and items that can be used only one way, such as a nest of cubes that can fit one into the other only in one sequence. Each child uses his selected toy for an activity of his own choosing, which he is allowed to do as long as the toy is used appropriately. When the teacher finds that a child has not been spontaneously selecting the activity he needs, the teacher then guides the child's selection. During that activity time, both the teacher and aide circulate among the children, participating in each child's activity and helping him to develop whatever skills are related to that activity. This could include helping a child learn what "under" or "over" meant, and, when the child was ready for it, their word symbols.

Whether the class's activity is one already described, or eating lunch, or swimming, the primary focus is on skill development at the proprioceptual and preceptual levels. When the child is ready for activities that will help him develop skills at a higher level, much emphasis is placed on providing him many opportunities to check each emerging skill against information available at the preceptual and proprioceptual level, information which has been proven through his prior experience to be valid and reliable.

When cutting and pasting, the children in this class do so mainly on the floor. In such activities, the teacher is not concerned about the children being in a position of balanced physiological readiness for the task (discussed in Chapter V), because their gravitational and visual axes are continually changing as they crawl around the paper they are cutting. This freedom of movement in connection with cutting out large, simple shapes provides repeated opportunity to bring the postural and visual signals into balance with the task. At this level of development, it is relatively easy for the child to crawl around the circle he is cutting out, but he is far from being able to use vision to guide and plan the movements required to cut in an arc. Only later, when he has achieved the skills of visual guidance and planning, and he can use them for sustained near-space activity, will it be important for him to be in a position of balanced physiological readiness.

Other activities at the proprioceptual and preceptual levels that are important to this class concern breathing and other motor aspects of speech. Diaphragmatic breathing helps a child to become aware of the process of breathing and aids breath control. This can be taught to a child quite readily by having him place one hand on his chest, while his other is on his stomach. His goal is to move his bottom hand in and out while his top hand remains still. He can practice breath control not only by moving his bottom hand slowly, but also by gently blowing on a paper tissue, held by the teacher in front of his mouth, so that it remains an inch or so away. Later, he can see how long he can make the tissue stay out there by blowing on it slowly and steadily. In other related activities, the child could explore making sounds with his throat, with his teeth together, through his nose, with his head tilted forward, and with it tilted backward. Such activities provide experience in the relationship between body movements and the quality of sound a child can produce. In particular, children who are developing postural warps often have a harsh or strained sound to their voice because their head is tilted backward, and they are oblivious to the cause of that sound. (This type of postural warp is frequently associated with visual problems, and so might require the attention of a vision specialist who is familiar with the interrelation of the visual and gravitational aspects of the child's functional systems.) Tongue movements can also be explored. Initially, the child may not be able to imitate a tongue position shown to him by his teacher. Instead, a dab of peanut butter may have to be put on his upper lip, or on the left corner of his mouth, for example, so that he extends his tongue to get to it. This or tracing the perimeter of a cookie with his tongue, or tracing with his tongue a shape made by a cheese spread (a can of Nabisco's Cheese Mate spreads cheese easily from a nozzle and requires no refrigeration) provides practice in tongue movements. All such explorations help the children gain better control of breath and voice, readying them for academic and social requirements.

Chalkboard activity is also important for this class. This type of activity helps to refine the proprioceptual signals and organize visually guided movement skills at the preceptual level. The entire class can work simultaneously at chalkboard activities, each child trying to improve his own work. As the children learn to represent shapes on the sloped chalkboard, they can do so next on large paper, and then on the usual size of paper, at a desk.

If one of these children feels the need to get away from the rest of the class, he can do so by entering a two-story chalet made to children's proportions. As he chooses to reenter the group, he can do so gradually by first venturing out on the balcony. The balcony also serves the purpose of giving the children a different visual perspective of their surroundings; one which they enjoy exploring, incidentally.

At this point it should be clear that the purpose of this class is not movement for movement's sake. Its purpose is to organize and refine the child's performance at the basic levels of development, so that he has an adequate frame of reference for further development of his integrative system. In each activity the child moves for a purpose: to make judgments, to discern similarities and differences and constancies. He also practices all information processing modes, and he learns to verbalize his observations and judgments of his environment. His learning size

113

discrimination and the vocabulary associated with size, for example, are not left to a workbook, in which he might learn only the pattern to be followed so that he can complete the page correctly, while still not able to make size discriminations in real life. To continue the example, when size is genuinely understood by the child, because he has learned it through his own visually guided and appraised movements through space, words related to it will naturally appear in the child's vocabulary. Then he is ready to learn the label or symbol associated with that word. Thus, the children in such a class have a greater opportunity to process, store, and retrieve information that is meaningful and useful to them. This was exemplified by a report from the father of one of the children in this type of class at Pathway. The father reported that whereas his son never had talked about what he did in school, since being in this class, he talked about his school activities a great deal. It would seem that for this child his experiences in school were now meaningful.

Other children who have brain dysfunction may have less severe or more variegated developmental needs than do the children in the aforementioned class. However, they would need equal opportunity to develop a firm foundation for their integrative system, although through somewhat different activities. These activities would have as their prime purpose to help each child achieve a balanced relationship between his postural and visual alignments to the task he was performing. Those activities, therefore, would not be rote movement for movement's sake, or calisthenics for the principal's sake, or action that would increase the size of his muscles but would not enhance the child's performance, or competitive games that would further hurt this child's pride because he does not have the skills required to compete in them successfully.

Cratty (all three references, 1967), who certainly has emphasized that movement activity is no panacea for all academic ills, equally emphasizes the importance of a balanced relationship between the postural and visual signals the child receives. In a study of neurologically handicapped children, Cratty (1964)

114

found that their score in balance best predicted their total score in a number of visuomotor skills. He also noted that 15 to 20 per cent of those children did better in static balance (while standing still) when their eyes were closed than when open. Because the visual information concerning their spatial world was so confusing, they did better by shutting off the visual information and relying on proprioceptual information. Cratty has suggested activity sequences that can aid the child to develop better balance. These sequences will now be described.

If the child cannot balance on one foot, his activity sequence should begin with him on a mat. First he is asked to balance on his side. He next balances in a sitting position, and his amount of sway is observed. His sway is more likely to be forward and backward than from side to side. Only children with rather severe neurological involvement would show difficulty in either of those two positions. Next the child positions himself on his hands and knees, and is asked to raise his feet, so that he balances only on hands and knees. Then he is asked to raise a hand or knee, so that he balances on only three points. Next he is asked to balance on two contralateral points, such as his left hand and right knee. After that, he is asked to balance on two ipsilateral points, such as his right hand and knee. Then comes balancing only on his two knees. Finally, he learns to balance on an ipsilateral foot and knee.

In an activity sequence such as the one just described, the teacher begins wherever the child can succeed. The next, more complex task in the sequence is introduced only when the teacher believes the child is ready to learn it. The increasing complexity of the task facilitates the integration of the skill.

The next activity sequence for improving balance is done while the child is standing. He begins with the most stable static position, his two feet as wide apart as his shoulders, with the toe of his rear foot even with the heel of his forward foot. Next, he puts both feet on a line parallel to each other, still at shoulders' width apart. After that, he brings his feet together. Only those children with rather severe neurological involvement will have difficulty thus far. Next, he puts one foot in front of the other, heel to toe. To complicate the task further, he is asked to balance on his preferred foot while using his arms to aid in balancing, then to balance on his preferred foot with his arms folded across his chest, then while using his arms but with his eyes closed, then without the use of arms or vision, and finally on his non-preferred foot with arms folded and eyes closed. Static balance then would be further improved by having the child perform a series of increasingly complex activities while on a balance beam.

The child's dynamic balance (while moving) can be improved through the use of a balance beam, which usually is made from 12 to 20 feet long, 4 inches wide, and stands 2 to 6 inches off the floor. For a general discussion of the use of the balance beam (or walking board), see Kephart (1960) and Getman, et al. (1968). To increase the complexity of the task, in order to insure the integration of the postural and visual signals, the child must make decisions while on the balance beam. The variations of complexity and their aid to the emergence of academic skills are limited only by the extent of the teacher's creativity. While walking the beam, he might be asked to step over a stick, or under one, or through a hoop, so that his center of gravity changes as he steps both over and under its rim. He could be asked to do so while walking forward, or backward, to explore space behind him, or while walking sideways, to refine the synchronous use of both sides of his body. The child can be asked to walk half way on the beam and step off to his left, or three-quarters of the way and step off to his right. He can be asked to reach a certain point, pick up an object on the floor, and continue walking the beam. Any task can be further complicated by narrowing the width of the beam, by tilting it so that one end is higher than the other, and by raising it higher from the floor (such as from two inches to six inches). The teacher will frequently find that as the task is made progressively more complex, the hyperactive and hyperdistractible child will show an increasing attention span, which usually carries over into other activities. Whatever sequence of tasks the teacher sets for the child, it is always imperative that the teacher know what that task asks of the child and whether it is at a level of difficulty commensurate with the child's current stage of development, so that he can succeed at the task.

Cratty also studied the child's awareness of himself in space and made suggestions (at the 1967 Pathway Institute) concerning the child's sequence of development in that area. His work was based on two concepts: (1) that the body image is formed as the child alternates between learning a little bit about his body and a little bit about his relation to things in space, thereby gradually learning more details alternately about his body and about space; and (2) that the child learns not only static but dynamic relationships between himself and his environment. Therefore certain sequences can be expected in the child's relationship between himself and his environment.

Cratty found that in step one the child learns about the big planes of his body. He learns about the front, the back, and the sides. He does not initially learn which side is which, or even the fact that they have different names. He also learns that things are near his head or near his feet. Therefore, the child's first spatial awareness is of front, back, sides, top, and bottom.

In steps two and three, the child relates objects to these body planes and, conversely, these body planes to objects. He recognizes that he is moving his back, front, or side toward something. He can also turn and move himself in various ways: lie down with his feet nearest the teacher, or put his side nearest the wall. Concurrently, while he is in a relatively fixed position, he should be able to indicate, "The wall is in front of me," "The chair is to my side."

In step four, the child learns to identify and move his arms and legs and other body parts.

At the fifth step, the child begins to learn about body movements, relative to his body planes and body parts. However, he has not yet learned to differentiate between his left arm and right arm, between his left side and right side. Left-right discrimination concerning his body and space does not fully develop in the normal child until he is around seven. As part of step five, the child learns that his body can bend

117

forward, backward, to the front, and to the side. He learns that his total body can move to the side, jump up, or go down. He learns that his limbs can bend and straighten and perform various acts. In this way the child gets ready for step six, when he determines the differences between his left and right, and between the leftness and rightness of all things.

Any kind of body-image training must involve transfer. Children too frequently can demonstrate only what they have been specifically taught. For example, they can slide their arms beautifully across the floor while lying correctly on their backs, but when asked to perform the same movement while standing, they become confused. Therefore, when helping the child to differentiate between his left and his right, the teacher should use all available tactile, visual, and movement experiences. To accomplish this, the teacher might have him turn and jump to his left, and to his right. The teacher might put him on his back, trace around his body, and have him cut out his own form and paste it on contrasting paper.

In step seven, the child learns about the relationship of his left-right components. He learns that all body parts have a left and right side. He knows where these are located. He knows that the left arm and leg truly spring from the left side of the body, and that above them is the left ear.

In step eight, the child relates his knowledge of left and right to stationary environmental objects around him. To aid him at this stage of development, he is asked to turn his left side toward the wall, or move his right side nearest to the desk. While standing still, he is asked to arrange things to his left, or to identify what is to his right.

In step nine, the child relates left and right to moving objects. To aid in this development, one child could walk around another, and the child standing still could indicate when the child walking is nearest his left side.

In step ten, the child relates left and right objects while he himself is moving. Two chairs can be placed four or five feet apart, and the child can be asked to walk around them in a figure eight and indicate when his left or his right side is next to the nearest chair.

In step eleven, the child learns to discriminate the left and right of objects relative to himself as a personal reference system. He learns that the desk or the book in front of him has a left and a right side.

Step twelve, in which the child begins to relate left and right to another person's reference system approaches what a normal eight- or nine-year-old can be expected to do fairly well. Normal four-year-olds begin to know about the body planes and how planes of the body relate to objects. Five-year-olds learn more about the body and the movements of the body. They also learn that the sides of the body are different, that one is called left and the other is called right, but they usually cannot identify which is which. At six and seven they begin to get a cognitive grasp of the leftness and rightness of their bodies. At about age eight they begin to move into another's reference system.

When the child moves into another person's reference system, he learns that others also have a left and right, that they see things in a different way than he does from where he is standing, and that they see things arranged differently than he sees them. Many workers suggest that a child is not healthy unless he can, at a reasonable age, break out of his egocentric reference system and know that other people can be other places than he is and see things differently than he sees them.

Many other types of readiness activity can be used by the teacher in the classroom or in an enclosed outdoor play area. Suggestions can be gotten from Mosston (1965, 1966) and Humphrey and Moore (1960), among others. In each sequence of activity, however, the teacher must again know what the task asks of the child and whether his level of development will enable him to succeed at it. As an example, the teacher might place on the floor (with chalk or tape) a 15-foot zig-zag line with a circle, square, and triangle juxtaposed at various positions along that line. By means of this, the teacher could hope to give a child experience in visually guided balance, by walking the line, in agility, by having him jump into the circle and over the square, and in auditory memory, by having him remember those three directions in sequence. Before presenting such a task to the child, however, the teacher should know if the child has the proprioceptual development to walk the zig-zag line, first of all, and whether it is sufficiently organized and refined to do it while concentrating on remembering the sequence of directions. The teacher should also know whether the child is capable of retaining a series of three directions, and whether he truly knows what "into" and "over" mean in terms of his body movements through space. The teacher can afford to give a child no task, no matter how innovative it is, without such prior analysis both of the task and of the child's developmental readiness for it.

To help children become ready for mathematics, Mrs. West of The Pathway School has devised what she calls a "motor-math" program. In this program, for example, she helps them to learn about size by doing tasks through which they can answer questions such as: How many people are in this room? How many big people? How big are they? How many small people? How small are they? How big can you make yourself? How small can you make yourself? Whether the motor-math program addresses itself to size, form, substance, or position in space, the teacher using it must know what each task asks of the child and what his ability to answer it successfully is at that point in his development.

Still another aspect of readiness development involves helping the child who enters the class with postural warps that, if allowed to persist, will lead to permanent structural deviations in the child's posture and will interfere with learning and social adjustment. To illustrate what can be done to help such a child, Miss Leonardo of The Pathway School worked with a twelve-year-old girl, whom we shall call Jane, thirty minutes a day, for a total of ten days. Miss Leonardo's goal was to help Jane discover herself anatomically, physiologically, and psychologically. Despite Jane's obvious postural deviations and poor self-image, Miss Leonardo related to Jane in a manner that encouraged Jane to see herself as capable of developing normally, beginning with the rudimentary skills she had at that time.

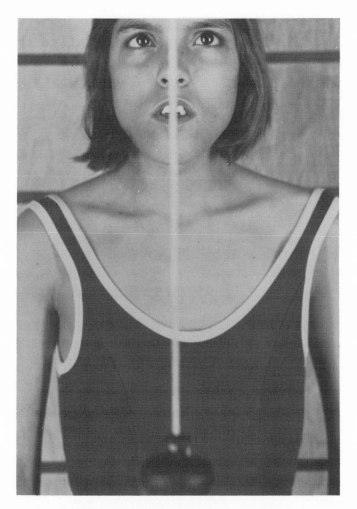

Figure 8. Before the program started

Figure 8, in which Jane is approximately twelve inches away from a plumb line, shows her appearance at the outset of Miss Leonardo's work with her. Note that Jane's eyes are not coordinated while she is sighting the plumb line. Her right eye has converged, and her left eye seems to be viewing the plumb

121

line off of center. Due to Jane's many and severe postural deficiencies, she had much difficulty in using her eyes as a team and in using her vision to guide and appraise her movements through space. Notice also that Jane's mouth is in a dropped position, which further detracted from her appearance. It is little wonder that Jane had a mutilated self-image, that she saw

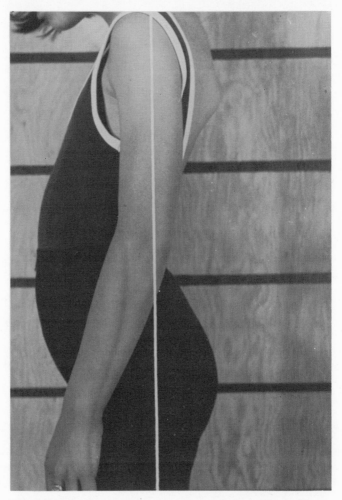

Figure 9. Postural imbalance before the program

herself as one who could not achieve, and that she communicated this to her family and to everyone who attempted to help her.

Figure 9 shows the excessive curvature of the upper and lower portions of her spine, known respectively as kyphosis and lordosis. Her sunken chest indicated tightened, or shortened, chest muscles. Her lowered rib cage in turn caused displacement of her vertebral column. It also interfered with breathing and circulation, because the heart and the lungs were not able to function in their normal position within the body. While her chest muscles were shortened, the muscles of her upper back, including the trapezius and the rhomboid muscles, were overly stretched. Therefore, corrective exercises were needed to shorten those muscles and to stretch the chest, or pectoral, muscles.

Further down her body, Jane shows a distended abdominal wall, with the likelihood of a concomitant displacement of the visceral organs, including the diaphragm, liver, intestines, stomach, and reproductive organs. To correct this condition, Jane needed exercises to shorten or tighten the oblique muscles in the abdominal area.

Figure 10, taken ten days later, shows improved postural alignment with her vertical axis, the plumb line now centering more toward her ear, shoulder girdle, and the center of her hips. Through the help of appropriate exercises, Jane was by that time able to respond to verbal commands to rotate her shoulders into proper position, contract her abdominal and gluteal muscles, and rotate her pelvic girdle into proper alignment, which lessened both of her excessive spinal curvatures and her hollowed chest. Quite obviously, she still needed to improve her postural alignment, but when compared with her posture shown in Figure 8, her posture after the ten-day program represents a dramatic change.

Jane's intensive program consisted mainly of helping her to become aware of her muscles, the proprioceptual signals obtained from them, and how to make them work for her to produce desired movements. At first Jane could not contract or relax her muscles, and so she had to be made aware of the

123

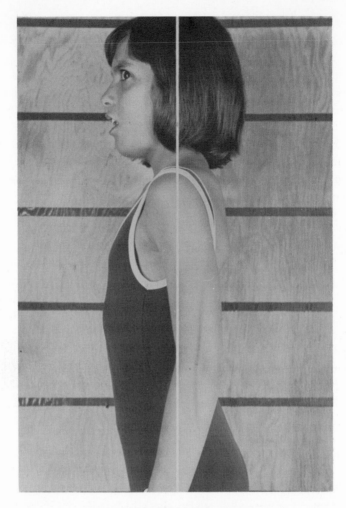

Figure 10. Posture after 10 days

proprioceptual signals involved in doing so. Toward that end, Miss Leonardo had Jane close her eyes, inhale, and hold her breath. Then Jane told her where she had felt "tight" while holding her breath. To help Jane become aware of the muscles involved in a particular movement, Miss Leonardo placed a resistive force against those muscles. For example, to help Jane

124

learn to move her head forward, Miss Leonardo placed her own hand against Jane's forehead as Jane tried to raise her head while in a supine position, so that Jane would feel the tension in her neck muscles. Similarly, to help Jane become aware of how to rotate her pelvis forward, Miss Leonardo first rotated Jane's pelvis for her, then placed Jane's hands on her own abdomen

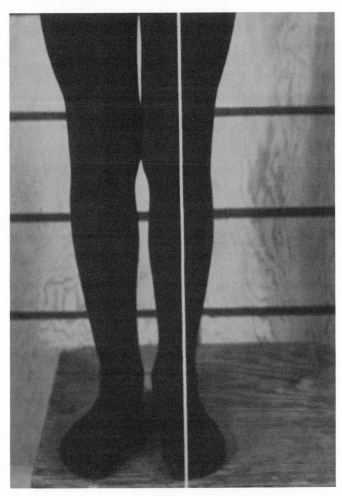

Figure 11. Lower extremities before the program

and back to feel the change in pelvic position. This type of procedure saved time in helping Jane to become aware of the proprioceptual signals involved in a given movement, because Jane could not become aware of the proprioceptual signals or the required movements simply by observation. This, of course, is true of most children with brain dysfunction.

Once Jane was able to be aware of her arms, legs, and various key muscles of her body, she benefited from the use of wall mirrors, ladders, balance beams, and other activities recommended by Dr. Getman (1967, 1968). The trampoline did not become useful until Jane was able to demonstrate her knowledge of body movement in simple walking and rhythm patterns. Then the trampoline appeared to be of great value to her in learning directionality and spatial orientation.

In Figure 11, taken at the outset of the program, the plumb line centered on Jane's kneecap and the heel of her foot. Note the extreme pronation of both feet and the overlapping of both knees. Poor postural alignment not only affected the upper portion of her body, but her lower extremities as well, because displacement of body weight affects the knees, ankles, and feet. In addition to the pronation of both feet, the arches were and are rather weak.

Figure 12 illustrates that as a result of appropriate exercises Jane could willfully rotate both feet and correct the pronation somewhat. Because Jane's knees had become somewhat flexed due to the abnormality of her posture, the muscles in the back of her legs had begun to shorten, requiring her to be given stretching exercises for those muscles. She was also given fairly standard foot exercises. Jane's hands, not seen in this picture, are clenched, showing the great effort she is expending to correct the position of her lower limbs. Nonetheless, the point is that by then she was aware of her body and how to begin to correct her body alignment.

Figure 13, taken at the outset of the program, shows the lateral deviation, or scoliosis, of Jane's vertebral column. This curvature caused certain muscles to become stretched, making the left side of her back appear much broader. The spinal curvature also caused the muscles on the right side of her back

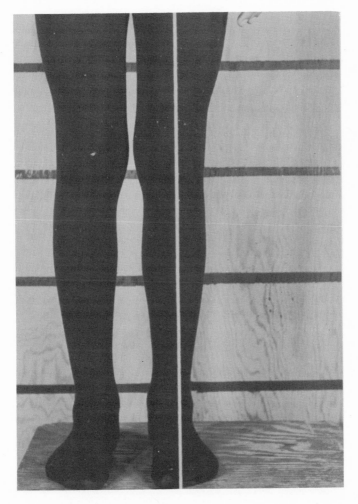

Figure 12. Lower extremities after 10 days

to shorten, making the right side of Jane's back appear to be smaller, or underdeveloped, as compared to the left side. Her right shoulder was also much lower than the left one. Notice also Jane's forward head position.

Figure 14, again taken on completion of the 10-day program, shows remarkable improvement. Jane was able to correct her body alignment far better than she could previously. Although

127

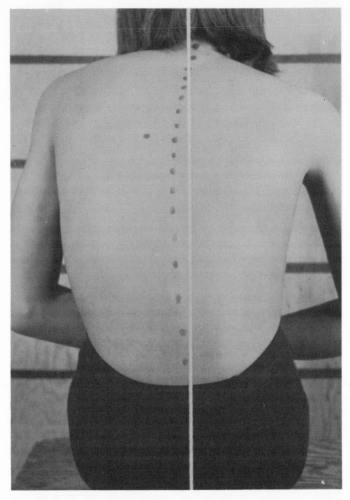

Figure 13. Spinal deviation before the program

she overcorrected somewhat, this is not alarming, because before fully correcting her body alignment, she can be expected to overreact, and then find a happy medium. Jane's progress in ten days illustrates the use of muscle-stimulating exercises as part of an overall program designed to help her learn to correct a

128

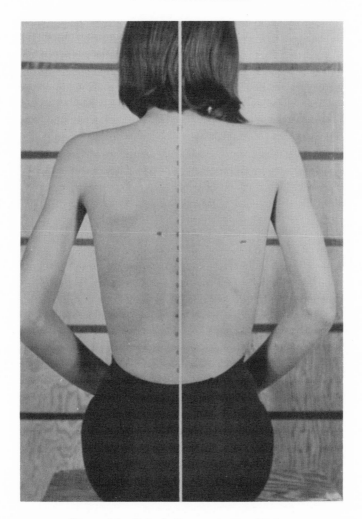

Figure 14. Spinal alignment after 10 days

deviant postural alignment, increase her body awareness, give her greater effectiveness in movement, and improve her self-concept.

The activities described in this chapter have as their goal the development of the child's readiness to succeed academically and socially. They particularly emphasize the proprioceptual and

129

preceptual developmental levels of the child's integrative system to provide him with a sound frame of reference for the building of perceptual and conceptual skills.

REFERENCES

Ayres, J. "Patterns of Perceptual-Motor Dysfunction in Children: A Factor Analysis Study," *Perceptual Motor Skills*, XX (1965), 335-68.

Cratty, B. J. *Movement Behavior and Motor Learning*. Philadelphia: Lea and Febiger, 1964. (2nd. Edition, 1967.)

_____. *Developmental Sequences of Perceptual-Motor Tasks*. New York: Educational Activities, 1967.

_____. *Social Dimensions of Physical Activity*. Englewood Cliffs: Prentice-Hall, 1967.

Getman, G. N. Eye-Hand Coordination Exercises. Boston: Teaching Resources, 1967.

Getman, G. N. *et al. Developing Learning Readinesses*. New York: McGraw-Hill, 1968.

Herrick, C. J. *The Evolution of Human Nature*. Austin: University of Texas Press, 1956.

Humphrey, J. H., and Moore, V. D. "Improving Reading Through Physical Education," *Education* (1960), 559-61.

Kephart, N. C. *The Slow Learner in the Classroom*. Columbus: Merrill, 1969.

Mosston, M. *Developmental Movement*. Columbus: Merrill, 1965.

_____. *Teaching Physical Education*. Columbus: Merrill, 1966.

VIII. Learning Materials

An obvious theme of this book is that most of today's teachers have not had the opportunity through collegiate training or guided experience to learn how to apply the two basic tenets of prescriptive teaching. Although all teachers should apply those two principles, to do so becomes of critical importance for the teacher of children with brain dysfunction. (See Chapter IV.) Those two tenets are: (1) to make judgments about the child's developmental levels and needs primarily from observing how the child goes about performing the task required of him; and (2) to make expectations about what the child should perform only after the task to be presented to him has been accurately analyzed in terms of what questions it asks of the child and in terms of the developmental level at which those questions are asked. Because the first of those two points was discussed at length in Chapters VI and VII, the second of those two points will be emphasized in this chapter.

If at this time the reader suspects, along with Charles Miner, ". . . thinks I, that man has an axe to grind," the suspicion is correct. Teachers are becoming painfully aware of their responsibilities, especially toward children who have inordinately complex learning problems as do those with brain dysfunction. This awareness is accompanied by a burgeoning dissatisfaction with the shallow material put out by some colleges of education and by some publishers of instructional materials. As special-education teachers use these recommended materials in the prescribed fashion and for their stated purpose, they repeatedly find that the materials do not in fact help the child to achieve the goal that the materials are purported to accomplish. Many such teachers across this country have become so disenchanted with instructional materials that they are loathe to use them and

131

are resorting more and more to improvising their own. That, however, will not answer their need either, for they will find that unless they apply to them the principles of prescriptive teaching, their own creations help the child no more than do the published materials. Rather than condemn all instructional materials, teachers can fulfill their awesome and burdensome responsibility to these children by being able to analyze *all* materials in terms of *all* the questions these set before the child.

To illustrate how a teacher can analyze materials to discern the questions it asks of the child, three types of materials commonly used in special education will be discussed: parquetry designs, peg boards, and readiness workbooks.

When using parquetry designs, most teachers believe that they are thereby providing the child with an opportunity to learn form recognition and spatial relationships. Regardless of what the teacher has been trained to believe, the issue is to identify the questions inherent in the materials themselves. Parquetry designs, as commonly used in special education, present to the child a variety of shapes, differently sized, variously and inconsistently colored, and juxtaposed in no set order. Moreover, the individual shapes themselves are inconstant; for example, the side of one cube is also perceived as a side of an adjoining cube. In addition, the use of color can heighten the inconstancy of form, even making the forms appear to be approaching or receding from the child. The confusing complexity with which the child can be confronted when he views a parquetry design is exemplified in Figure 15.

The design shown in Figure 15 asks the child to analyze an agglomeration of undulating forms and colors into the three shapes of blocks (triangle, square, and diamond) with which he is to reproduce the design. The questions asked by that design could not be answered by most well-integrated adults, and certainly not by a fragmented, unintegrated child who had brain dysfunction. Nevertheless, that specific design has been presented by trained and well-intentioned teachers to children with brain dysfunction for the purpose of helping them to learn form recognition and spatial relationships. The only reason those

132

Figure 15. A parquetry design in which color heightens the confusion

teachers presented that parquetry design to the children was because they had not questioned what that specific task asked of the child. Instead, they blithely assumed that it would be helpful to the children because parquetry designs are materials of choice for children with brain dysfunction. Such a naive assumption too frequently results in the child's continued frustration and failure and deprives him of the intended opportunity for a successful learning experience.

To prevent that type of inadvertency, the teacher should recognize that the usual parquetry design has two main variables with which the child must deal: color and form. Before considering the variable of form, which is more closely related to the materials' purported goal of helping the child with form discrimination and spatial relationships, let us evaluate the role of color.

Whether or not it is recognized, color plays an important role in which questions any materials ask, not only parquetry designs. Therefore, the teacher should be sufficiently knowledgeable about the role played by color in instructional materials to evaluate whether specific materials in fact employ color to aid or to hinder the child's opportunity for learning.

Harmon (1949) explains that the human eye, unlike the modern camera, is not color-corrected. This underlies the physiological and psychophysical reasons why colors seem to be warm or cool, stimulating or relaxing, approaching or receding. Because of the chromatic aberrations of the human eye, light of different wave lengths focuses at different points along an axis within the eye (see Figure 16). Some wavelengths have a greater luminosity than others; yellow-green (5500 to 5600 angstroms), which has the greatest luminosity and to which the retina has the greatest receptivity, focuses nearest the retina, with the shorter wavelengths focusing in front of it and the longer wavelengths behind it. Therefore, when the eye is adapted to light and at rest, it is most receptive to yellow-green, but it is nearsighted for the violets, blues, and greens and farsighted for the yellows, oranges, and reds. However, through his research, Harmon was the first to establish that when the eye is active in

133

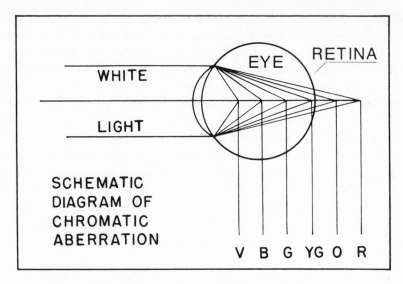

Figure 16. Schematic diagram of chromatic aberration
(adapted from Harmon, 1949)

a visual task, the child attempts to overcome those retinal displacements by projecting the colors so that they are displaced in the direction opposite to that indicated in Figure 16. As a result, in visual activities, when red, for example, is present among other colors, it appears to be closer and larger than the other colors. Similarly, violet then appears to be farther away and smaller than the other colors. When among other colors, each of the colors in between red and violet appears to be displaced accordingly (see Figure 17).

Harmon also indicates that when a colored object is placed against a large background area that is of a different color, another phenomenon occurs. The object's perimeter appears to move in accordance with the projected displacement of the background color, while the color of the object itself oscillates. For example, when placed against a red background, a blue square would appear as though its outline, or perimeter, were close to the child, while its blueness had punched a hole through

134

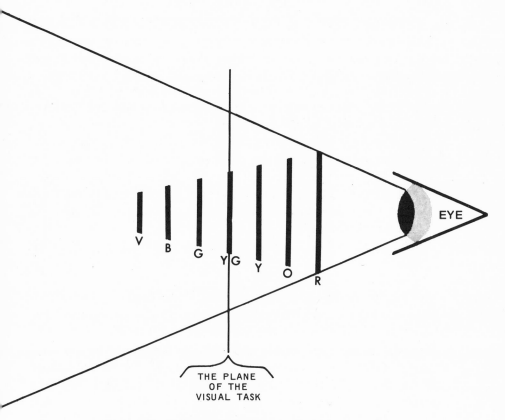

Figure 17. Schematic diagram of the projected
displacement of color

the red background and were behind it. That would cause visual
accommodation to oscillate. The oscillation would be less for
near-space activities than for far-space activities, but the child
would be under greater physiological stress in the near-space
activity and would try harder to overcome the oscillation in
visual accommodation. As a result, his head would move more
and his eyes would wander more through the task than would
occur in a like far-space activity. Therefore, when presented with
such a near-space task, the child's attention span would decrease.

Depending on the color of both the object and the background, on the lighting of the task, and on the distance of the object from the child, Harmon found marked changes in the apparent size of an object. In a near-space task, an object could appear to increase or decrease in size as much as 37 per cent. In a far-space task, an object could appear to increase or decrease in size as much as 67 per cent.

The teacher should apply these basic facts concerning color to the evaluation of all instructional materials, to be sure that the use of color promotes learning and does not nullify it. Not only color, but all variables involved in materials should be assessed from that standpoint to be sure that the materials are indeed *learning* materials.

The basic facts concerning color can be applied to parquetry designs. Figure 15 illustrates how easily color can abet inconstancy of form. In addition, even in a less confusing design, color could cause a child to become confused as he tries to reproduce the design. Depending on the color of a shape he was trying to fit into the design he was reproducing, its form could appear too large or too small for the space he thought it should occupy. Therefore, he would get opposing signals from the color and from his visual judgment, which would interfere with his performance of the task.

As another example of how color can interfere with the intended purpose of materials, color-cued rods of graduated lengths are commonly used to help these children learn number facts. If red is to represent a smaller quantity and blue a larger one, the red rod will look larger than the blue one as the child compares them. Thus the color indicates that the red rod is bigger than the blue one, while the actual length of the rods tells him the opposite.

Still another example of how color can interfere with learning is found in some reading materials. A given word in a sentence is colored for the purpose of giving it emphasis. However, the color actually causes that word to appear on a different visual plane than the other words. Therefore, the child must change his visual accommodation when he comes to it. The result is that he cannot perceive that word in context with the rest of the sentence. If different words are colored differently, or if each letter is color-cued, his learning to read meaningfully would be hampered even more. By the same token, the teacher should not instruct the child in cursive writing for the purpose of helping him to overcome disassociation and learn to write a word as a whole, while at the same time teaching him cursive writing through the use of two or more contrasting colors to form a single letter. By introducing color and thereby disrupting the child's visual process, the teacher defeats the purpose of the cursive writing and also interferes with his learning how to accomplish it.

In appraising the examples just cited, the teacher must remember that those distortions produced by color are much greater to the child than to the adult, because the child has not as yet learned to intellectualize away the distortions. For example, he has not as yet learned to be form-bound and size-bound. To the contrary, he is only in the process of learning form constancy and size constancy (see Chapter VII). Therefore, as a natural part of the flexibility inherent in his explorations of the world around him, he lets the variabilities and oscillations happen. As a result, when the teacher introduces distortions to him, he learns the distortions.

To resume the discussion of parquetry designs, the other main variable in addition to color is form. Before presenting the child with a given design, especially one that is colored, the teacher must know whether that child is able accurately to perceive the forms represented in that design. If a child has only recently learned to differentiate between a square, a triangle, and a diamond in the actual parquetry blocks, he should not be given a design that is colored. He also will not have a successful learning experience by being asked to reproduce a design that has a three-dimensional appearance (such as the one illustrated in Figure 18). In fact, he may not be ready to succeed even with simpler, uncolored parquetry designs. If that is the case, the teacher need not store the parquetry materials on a shelf or in the wastebasket. These, like most materials, can be used to

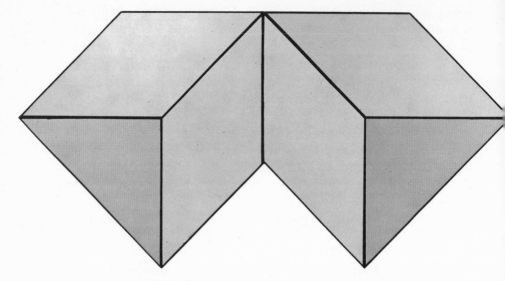

Figure 18. A three-dimensional parquetry design

provide the child with a successful opportunity for learning at whichever level of development he happens to be at that time, *if* the teacher knows what questions the materials ask of him. For children who are not ready for the perceptual level of experience, designs can be made that do not involve color, and all the parquetry blocks can be painted the same color.

When the teacher has observed that the child cannot differentiate between a square, a triangle, and a diamond, the teacher could begin by having the child walk out each shape, so that he obtains experience at the proprioceptual level (see Chapter IV). After a time, the teacher could hold up a parquetry form, and the child could duplicate it by walking it out.

If a child has some ability to recognize forms but has not as yet achieved facility in this, the teacher could use the parquetry blocks as a means of providing learning experiences at the preceptual level. Tactual information could be emphasized by having the child take from a paper bag the form held up by the teacher. Auditory information could be emphasized in the following manner. Each child has a square, triangle, and diamond on his desk. Standing behind the children or with hands hidden from their view, the teacher indicates what each of these forms sounds like as each corner of a form is tapped on the desk. The children then hold up the form that corresponds with what they heard. (No, the square and the diamond do not sound the same.) To emphasize visual information the children can play a variation of the card game, Go Fish. The object of the game is for each child to get all of one shape (the teacher designating which shape each child is to collect). Then in turn each child surveys which shapes the others have and asks for the shape that he needs. The child could also match those shapes to the teacher's pattern made of blocks, then to a pattern printed on a card, et cetera. Language, of course, can be introduced in any of the above tasks and in many other tasks as well.

When the child is ready for experience at the perceptual level, he should start with an uncolored design that is the juxtaposition of two and then three forms. In each sequence it is easier for the child to perceive each form of which the design is composed when only a corner of one form touches another form. Later in each sequence, the side of one form touches the side of another form. Color should not be added as a complicating factor until the child has achieved facility both in form discrimination and in spatial relationships. Before introducing increased complexity of form into the design, the teacher should be aware of whether or not the child has the ability to perceive space as a structured volume. Both Gesell (1949, 1952) and Piaget (1956, 1960) have discussed how the child learns the geometry of space. The application of this to learning materials will be touched on in the discussion of peg boards.

Because a prime purpose of parquetry designs is to help the child learn spatial relationships, rather than to introduce him to increasingly complex patterns in the parquetry designs, the teacher should help him to manipulate his perception of spatial relationships from different vantage points in space. Specifically, after a child can readily reproduce simple designs, he should be given each design again and asked to reproduce it when the design is rotated 90 and then 180 degress. After he has mastered that, he should be asked to reproduce each design, *as if* he were viewing it from different vantage points, such as, across the desk from him (which would be a visualized 180-degree rotation), or to the right of his desk (which would be a visualized 90-degree rotation). Such activities allow him to practice spatial orientations, which in turn helps him to make his spatial volume real and therefore capable of being manipulated. When that occurs, the child will not have reversal problems in academics, because reversals occur when the child does not have a real sense of the spatial volume in which he lives and cannot manipulate objects within it from different orientations. Similarly, to help insure the integration of the child's appreciation of the space volume in which he lives, three-dimensional parquetry designs can be used after he has mastered shifting his spatial orientation with two-dimensional designs. When the child can not only reproduce three-dimensional designs with parquetry blocks, but also reproduce in his own drawing the design he has made with those blocks, the teacher can be fairly sure that he will be able to apply those spatial judgments in everyday situations.

Pegboards are presented to the child with brain dysfunction probably more frequently than any other material. It is equally probable that most teachers using them are not aware of all the questions pegboards ask the child. When a teacher asks a child to reproduce a two-dimensional figure with pegs in a pegboard, the intended purposes are to aid the child to learn form recognition, to judge the size of the figure accurately, to place the figure on the board in the same position it occupies on the paper, and to enhance eye-hand coordination.

Here again, color often detracts from the intended purposes and value of the materials. For example, the child's form perception is not aided when each side of the triangle he is to form with pegs is a different color. It has long been recognized (see Strauss and Kephart, 1955, for example) that the child with brain dysfunction has difficulty perceiving wholes. To make each side of a triangle a different color detracts from his ability to perceive it as a whole, thereby hindering the child's

140

opportunity for learning and defeating the intended purpose of the task. A legitimate use of color to aid the child's development of form perception is in a task such as is illustrated in Figure 19. In that task, the color helps the child to perceive the form of each of the overlapping squares. Otherwise, in keeping with his perceptual difficulty, he would tend to see two discontinuous shapes, as is also illustrated in Figure 19. When the teacher uses color in such a task, however, colors that are at the opposite ends of the spectrum should be avoided, for the reasons discussed earlier in this chapter. Instead, the teacher should use two colors that are close together in the spectrum but still clearly discernible as different colors. Otherwise color

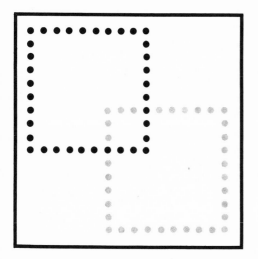

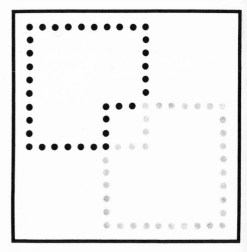

Figure 19. A legitimate use of color with
pegboards to aid form perception

does not fulfill the original purposes of the peg designs and need not be used until the child has acquired basic proficiencies. At that point color can be used to complicate the task, thereby helping to insure the integration of the skills being developed.

In assessing the questions that a design to be reproduced on the pegboard asks a child, the teacher must determine whether a given task asks the child only to match peg for dot by rote or to place the pegs purposefully as a result of judgments and decisions he is making. Convinced that they were helping the child, teachers have placed over a child's pegboard a template on which was drawn an intricate, colored design. Such a task required nothing more of the child than to match a colored peg with a hole encircled by a corresponding color. No judgment or decision-making was required. The task was purely one of rote matching. Teachers should realize that such a task does not help the child to learn form recognition or judgment of size, or spatial location. It only gives him an opportunity to practice finger dexterity. The task must require the child to make judgments and decisions before he can learn from it and then translate what he has learned, in an integrated fashion, into other activities. The teacher can promote integration by asking the child to evaluate the accuracy of his performance and to explain why he performed the task as he did. Integration can also be promoted by having the child draw the design he has just made with the pegs.

The child's performance of the task can tell the teacher when the child has been given a design that he can accomplish only through rote matching. In such an instance, the child first matches his pegs to the form of the design. Then he goes back over his peg design and corrects its error in size by matching the number of pegs with the number of dots. Then he goes back over his peg design and corrects its error in spatial positioning by matching the location of his pegs with the location of the dots. Finally he goes back over his pegs to match their color with that of the dots. Such a piecemeal, unintegrated, rote performance indicates to the teacher that the child has been given a task that is beyond his developmental level, thereby

142

defeating the intended purposes of that task. This signals the teacher that he needs a much simpler pegboard design.

When asked to do a simple task such as place pegs in the holes along the left-hand margin of the pegboard, the child may persevere and place pegs around the entire perimeter of the board. This performance signals the teacher that the child needs a task that asks a simpler question; namely, given only the exact number of pegs required, he is asked to place them in their specified position on the board.

The teacher might observe that the child can successfully place the pegs along the left-hand margin of the pegboard or in other simple arrangements, but that when asked to make somewhat more complex arrangements with the pegs, he errs in their size or location. Often that is because he has accomplished the simpler tasks by rote matching, whereas this task requires him to be able to count accurately. For example, a child could not readily and accurately reproduce the overlapping squares illustrated in Figure 19 without being able to count. Therefore, such a task is beyond the developmental level of a child who has no concept of numbers. When the teacher realizes that to reproduce the overlapping squares of Figure 19 with pegs asks the usual child with brain dysfucntion to perceive the form of the two squares involved, plus to perceive that they overlap to form a single figure, plus to count the dots to locate the exact point of overlap, the teacher does not automatically attribute the child's failure to a perceptual or visualization problem if at that time he has no concept of numbers. Moreover, if the child is to learn form recognition, size judgment, and spatial location in a meaningful and integrated way, so that he can apply them to other activities, he also must know how-many-ness. Otherwise he will have difficulty achieving the skill of visualization and making the judgments and decisions required of him by that type of task.

As the child learns the geometry of space, he becomes familiar with the horizontal and the vertical long before he knows what a diagonal is. Nevertheless, teachers ask the child to reproduce a diagonal on the pegboard, or even an X, which is

143

two diagonals, before he truly appreciates the horizontal and the vertical. If the teacher expects the child to learn from the task presented to him rather than to do rote matching, his level of development cannot be violated.

Readiness workbooks are another commonly used learning material. By adding to it the facts about color discussed earlier in this chapter, Cruickshank's (1967, pp. 161-65) suggestions concerning such materials are helpful. Before presenting readiness material to the child, the teacher should also keep in mind that the child should have developed readiness skills at the proprioceptual level and, in most skill areas, at the preceptual level prior to being expected to succeed at those paper-and-pencil tasks.

Another point to be remembered when giving material from a readiness workbook to the child is that what the exercise is headed may not really be the question it asks the child. For example, an exercise may be entitled "Spatial Orientation," but not actually require that of the child. To illustrate this, visualize a workbook page that has at the upper left a square, at the upper right a triangle, at the lower left a triangle, and at the lower right a square. The child is told to draw a line between the two squares, so that, supposedly, he discerns their relative relationship in space. Actually, the task is asking him to recognize that the squares are placed at different locations on the page. However, that workbook page *could* be used to help the child with spatial orientation. To use it for that purpose, the teacher would say to him: "Suppose you were standing there (on the upper-left square) facing that way (with his back to the lower-right square), where would the other square be?" As the child can learn to visualize that the other square is behind him and to his right, he is learning spatial orientation. No task helps a child to learn spatial orientation unless it designates *him* as the egocentric locus for spatial judgments and helps him to visualize where things are positioned in space in relationship to himself.

For a child to benefit from any readiness workbook, he must participate in the task and manipulate it in a fashion that makes it real to him. As an example, if a child is asked to draw the route through a maze, he must participate in that task as if he were actually moving through space. Otherwise the task offers him little opportunity for true learning. The maze drawn on paper is not real to the child, even when it has an ice-cream cone drawn at the end of it. The teacher can help him to make the task real by asking the child to tell how he would have to move to get through the maze. Doing that requires visualization and visual planning, which are the skills the mazes are intended to help the child to develop. Then, his drawing the indicated route reinforces his visualization and visual planning.

The teacher often notices that the child has a tight, white-knuckled grip while drawing a line through the path of a maze or while connecting dots, etc. Frequently that is because the child is not yet ready to work within the small space allotted to him by the task. Instead, he requires further work in large movements at the chalkboard and on large sheets of paper.

The teacher should also be aware that while the child is performing such a task, he may be so intent on following the dots accurately, or staying within the boundaries of the path accurately, that he is defeating the intended purpose of the task. That is, he is not practicing visually guided hand movements and visual planning. Instead, he is using vision only to appraise what he has already done. In that case, the teacher could erroneously assume that the task was not helping the child, or that he was not ready for it, whereas in fact the child was not performing the task as intended. To help him benefit from the task, the teacher could tell him that it was not important for him to stay exactly within the lines, but to get practice at steering his pencil where he was going and at figuring out the best way to get there. As he practiced visual steering and planning, he would naturally be better able to stay within the lines.

Recognizing that children with brain dysfunction classically have difficulty in discriminating a figure-ground relationship, teachers sometimes employ material from a readiness workbook that asks the child to identify an object when it is pictured within a totally alien background (such as a dinner plate hidden among ocean waves). Perhaps that practice arose because teachers misconstrued what was said by Strauss and Lehtinen (1947, Chapter III) and Strauss and Kephart (1955, pp. 58-61). In those books, drawings in which figure and background are incongruous were illustrated, but they were indicated to be *tests* for the purpose of identifying brain-injured children and of studying their performance in comparison with the performance of other youngsters. Strauss and Kephart clearly state that in real life any part of the background can become the foreground as one's attention is focused on it, and, in turn, that foreground can then become background as one's attention is redirected. Moreover, the figure and background are perceptually interdependent. They are not two separate entities. The unique characteristics of the figure are determined by its relationship with its background. Characteristics such as size, posture, position in space, and shape are recognized from the figure's relationship to its background. This can be readily observed by drawing a person on a piece of paper. The figure's size and other characteristics already mentioned are determined by and can change in accordance with the background that is drawn in relationship to the figure.

Rather than use such contrivances as objects hidden in alien backgrounds, which were not intended for teaching purposes, the teacher can better help the child to learn figure-ground discrimination by helping him to focus his attention on a specific object when it is within its natural context. That must be accomplished within the three-dimensionality of the classroom and the outdoors before it can be interpreted within the two-dimensionality of a workbook. After the child has established a basic skill in figure-ground relationship, this skill can be further refined and integrated through the child's work with realistic pictures. Here the child is asked to focus his attention on a particular object within a scene and to discuss its relationship with other objects therein. As his attention is shifted from one object to another, so is the figure-ground relationship.

As a last point on the use of workbooks, the teacher should remember that they were not designed with a specific child in

146

mind. Therefore, the teacher should not use them by having the child do page after page after page, even at different times on different days. Workbooks can be of value to the child only when they are used, as any other material, prescriptively to suit the then-existing needs of a given child. Even if a workbook has been accurately sequenced developmentally, a child may need more help in building a certain skill than he can get through the pages allotted to that skill in a workbook. Because it is tempting to rely on the sequence of the workbook to build the child's skill, the teacher should be especially careful to judge the child's acquisition of skill from his performance, not from the page he is at in the workbook.

The intention of this chapter was not to be a comprehensive evaluation of the effectiveness of all materials available to the teacher. Instead, it intended to provide the teacher with some illustrative guidelines of how all classroom materials can be analyzed in terms of the variables involved in them, in terms of all the questions they ask the child, and in terms of fitting their use to the child's existing level of development. Only such a complete assessment by the teacher insures their use as learning materials. When the teacher does assess available materials completely and accurately, then they can be used creatively to promote the child's growth.

Appropriate to this chapter is a statement made by Dr. G. N. Getman (in Rappaport, 1966, p. 82):

"Allow me to make one final plea to every adult who has responsibility for 'educating' children to live in today's cultural demands, be these social or academic. Let us constantly remember that there are *no* magical materials to motivate children to 'learn how to learn.' In fact, the very phrase, 'learn how to learn' is an unrealistic expression of the magic that materials and methods are supposed to contain. Children do not 'catch' learning by exposure, like they 'catch' measles. The children themselves are the magicians—they *make* the magic. They make it as every other magician does, by organizing and integrating their own action systems. Children must first *learn to act*, and when they have achieved magnitudes of skill in these

147

actions, they will *act to learn*. A more realistic expression, one that puts children into the learning process as active participants rather than passive recipients, would be: 'Learn to act, then act to learn.' In this fashion, materials will be fitted to the children, instead of to our adult perseverations and insistances that children fit the materials. All our efforts can thereby become increasingly relevant to the needs of children, instead of wishfully attempting to move children toward the goals determined by the 'needs' of adults."

REFERENCES

Cruickshank, W. C. *The Brain-Injured Child in Home, School, and Community*, Syracuse: Syracuse University Press, 1967.

Gesell, A. *et al. Vision, Its Development in Infant & Child.* New York: Harper, 1952.

Harmon, D. B. *The Coordinated Classroom.* Grand Rapids: American Seating Company, 1949.

Piaget, J., and Inhelder, B. *The Child's Conception of Space.* New York: Norton, 1956.

Piaget, J., Inhelder, B., and Szeninska, A. *The Child's Conception of Geometry.* New York: Basic Books, 1960.

Rappaport, S. R. (ed.) *Childhood Aphasia and Brain Damage: Volume III, Habilitation.* Norristown: The Pathway School, 1966.

Strauss, A. A., and Lehtinen, L. *Psychopathology and Education of the Brain-Injured Child.* New York: Grune and Stratton, 1947.

Strauss, A. A., and Kephart, N. *Psychopathology and Education of the Brain-Injured Child, Volume II: Progress in Theory and Clinic.* New York: Grune and Stratton, 1955.

IX. Behavioral Management

In keeping with the conceptual model presented in Chapter IV, the behavioral disorders of the child who has brain dysfunction should be treated not as independent entities, but as part of the total child. Firstly, a child's development of an adequate ego is contingent on the soundness of all aspects of his central nervous system (biochemically, electrochemically, etc.). Only then does he have the inborn capacity to develop, through growth, experience, and learning, the primary skills of the ego. These are the information processing modes of the functional systems of learning (see Figure 1), which, through the development of the integrative system, give rise to the child's performance skills. As an outgrowth of those basic ego skills, through the child's interactions with his environment, the higher ego skills, such as impulse control, frustration tolerance, awareness of others, and the ability to mediate between biological drives on the one hand and environmental demands on the other emerge. Secondly, because the brain, via the functions of the ego, is the primary organ of adaptation, when its functions are disrupted, it is disrupting to the child's total development. The result is that the child cannot achieve realistically gratifying ways of being "someone who can." Because he cannot exist as a psychic nonentity, and because he cannot expose himself to the constant pain of hurt pride that comes from daily frustration, failure, and rejection, he can be expected to find maladaptive means of trying to adapt to his environment. Therefore, the child's behavioral disorders must be viewed as a part of his psychobiological totality, which has the dimension of his constellation of present and past skills and deficiencies, the dimension of his feelings and experiences attendant to that skills complex, and the dimension of his maladaptive attempts to cope with both of those.

The longer his skill deficiencies and maladaptations continue without intervention, the less adequate he is in comparison with his peers, the more rejected he finds himself, and the more maladaptive are his attempts to cope with himself and others. If the ultimate goal of behavioral management, or psychotherapy, is to reverse that ever-increasing deviation of his ego development, it cannot focus solely on this child's behavior. Instead, it must address itself to all three dimensions of his psychobiological totality.

Where this child is concerned, psychotherapy cannot be an end unto itself, or a discipline unto itself, or a land unto itself, even though in its orthodoxy psychotherapy has for decades flown its own flag. The psychotherapist and the teacher and the parents and all others who work with this child have as a major objective to help him to develop a sufficiently intact ego to *manage his own behavior adaptively and gratifyingly*. To accomplish this, they must have as additional objectives to help him to develop effective functional systems of learning and to help him to replace his maladaptations with realistic means of accomplishing his own goals. Those objectives are in marked contrast to the goals of orthodox psychotherapy; namely, to delve into the child's fantasy life and dreams for the purpose of helping him to become aware of his instinctive drives and to resolve unconscious conflicts concerning those drives. Because the child with brain dysfunction usually has moderate to severe ego insufficiencies, orthodox psychotherapy, which of necessity breaks down part of the ego to get to the unconscious, results in greater ego insufficiency and worsens the child's behavior. For this reason, with the child who has brain dysfunction, the therapist should be much more directive and supportive than in performing orthodox treatment.

After winning the child's trust, the therapist must show the child his maladaptations in daily life, how they defeat his own goals, and the behavioral roles he could play instead to achieve his own goals more readily. Thus, the therapist also is an ego bank (see Chapter IV) with whom the child can identify and on whom he can depend for guiding concepts of conduct, for

150

strength, for insights, and for sustained support until he, the child, can internalize these into the better integrated and stronger ego he is building. The therapist must help the child to communicate his feelings and thoughts connected with his hurt pride, his rejections, and his failures, as well as those connected with his aspirations and goals.

Because the goal of psychotherapy with this child is to reverse the ever-increasing deviation in ego development and to overcome the ego insufficiencies, the therapist cannot accomplish this alone. He must work in tandem with the child's teacher and parents, so that at any point in time the child receives a consistency of structure and support, which serves as the matrix in which he can most readily and comfortably build his ego skills. Thus, the relationship structure (see Chapter IV) effected by teacher and parents complements what the psychotherapist does, and all these efforts must be carefully coordinated. This necessitates the therapist's direct communication with teacher and parents, or, when available, a parent counselor coordinates the relationship structure in the home with the work of the psychotherapist. Without such communication on a continuing basis, it is unrealistic to expect to provide the child with the matrix of consistency he needs for ego development. It is also unrealistic to expect busy people with hectic schedules to carry out that vital communication unless the time required for it is allocated in advance and is built into the program.

At The Pathway School the first 45 minutes of each school day, before classes begin, are allocated for team meetings. This provides daily opportunity for those working with a child to share ideas, anxieties, evaluations of progress, and plans. Such daily interactions foster respect for what each person is contributing to the child's overall development and result in a sharing of collective information, from which emerge plans better suited to the child's needs than could be made by any one person. The morning meetings also enhance consistency of approach to the child and reinforce what other team members are doing with the child. For this child to receive psychotherapy, regardless of how talented the therapist is, with no carry over into the classroom or home, erodes the benefits available from such treatment. On the other hand, when the therapist, the teacher, the parents, and all others working with the child take the same approach to him—not necessarily with the same words, because one person's words may not fit another person's mouth or personality—the child senses the solidarity of the adults working with him and feels that he can depend on their strength. To accomplish that requires sufficient communication time to understand why a particular approach is advocated, under what circumstances, at which stage of the child's development, and with what expected results. Ample time is also needed for the proposed approach to the child to be assimilated into each person's experience and personality, so that in each case the relationship with the child will be meaningful and appropriate. (For further elaboration of the importance of team collaboration, see Adamson in Cruickshank, 1966, Chapter 18.) Another means of communication used at Pathway is the crisis conference. This may be called at any time by any member of the child's team, by contacting the Educational Supervisor, to prevent or handle a crisis. Recommendations made there are also followed up at the morning meetings. In addition, at the end of each trimester each child's progress is reviewed from the interdisciplinary standpoint. Although public schools may not be able to schedule that much time for team communication, they cannot lose sight of its importance to the child's habilitative program, and they can adapt to their own needs the communication time Pathway has found effective.

Two major types of behavioral disorders are shown by children who have brain dysfunction: the acting-out and the passive-resistive. The first type is the one commonly described in the literature on brain injury: hyperactivity, hyperdistractibility, disinhibition, et cetera. The passive-resistive type of behavioral disorder appears to occur almost as frequently, however. This type of behavior is not actively destructive: the child does not run around the classroom or tear his classmates' papers. However, this child is adept at surreptitiously planting an elbow in another child's stomach or inobtrusively tripping a child down the stairs.

152

This child does not overtly intrude on others or directly call attention to himself. Instead, he dares the teacher to make him learn. He may do this by defiance; such as telling the teacher that he had all that junk before, or that he does not want to be treated like a baby. He may, on the other hand, defy the teacher by being all sweetness and light on the surface, but never accomplishing what is requested of him. Regardless of the maladaptive means he has acquired of avoiding further failure and hurt pride, he has mastered it to such a point of smoothness and efficiency that the teacher finds him very difficult to reach. Nevertheless, both the acting-out and passive-resistive types of youngsters want very much to relate to the teacher, parents, and other adults, but neither does so in a way that is genuinely gratifying to himself or to the adult. Unlike the autistic child, both the acting-out and passive-resistive children have a flight *into* relationship; but the mode of relating is maladaptive to their goal. This does not mean to imply that a child with brain dysfunction cannot also be psychotic (Rappaport, 1965, pp. 59-61). It only means that this writer has found the vast majority of children with brain dysfunction to have either an acting-out or passive-resistive behavioral disorder and, in both cases, a flight into relationship. Moreover, citing these two major categories of behavioral disorder does not imply a uniformity of behavior within each of these two categories. Children with brain dysfunction show a variety of individual differences in cognitive style and personality (see Gardner, Morse, and Adamson in Cruickshank, 1966, Chapters 9, 17, and 18, respectively), as well as in temperament (Thomas, Chess, and Birch, 1968). The individuality of this child is a product primarily of the interaction of his constellation of skills and deficiencies and his experiences with these. Recognizing the individuality of the child, the teacher can help him more easily by being prepared to cope with behavior of the acting-out or passive-resistive type.

Both for the child who shows acting-out behavior and for the child who shows passive-resistive behavior, there are three main stages of psychotherapy. These stages overlap and are not

153

absolute. They are cited only to denote areas of emphasis during the child's ego development. The first stage focuses on the child as an individual, on what is tormenting him within himself, regardless of his environment. It addresses itself to the child's hurt pride, to his imperiled identity, and to his maladaptive attempts to cope with these. During that stage of psychotherapy, the child should become sufficiently able to accept his limitations to begin to realize that he also has assets. Then he can start to use those assets to find genuine, as opposed to maladaptive, gratification. Concurrently, as he is able to recognize that he often defeats his own goals by how he handles situations, he moves into the second stage of psychotherapy. In that stage, his interpersonal relationships are stressed. At that time the psychotherapist, the teacher, and the parents emphasize the delimitation of the child's opportunity for failures that began in the first stage of therapy. That is necessary because for the most part the child does not as yet have an adequate enough ego to enable him to make decisions that will lead him into genuine gratifications. As his ego skills develop, he is afforded more and more opportunities for making his own decisions, which in turn contributes to his ego strength. At the same time, all who work with him continue to recognize with him that they are helping persons who will not turn on him, but who daily will provide him with new opportunities for success. The third stage of psychotherapy emphasizes the child's socialization. There he is helped to ready himself for a normal classroom with all the attendant normally expected stresses. He is helped to become a member of his community, as a playmate and as a neighbor, with all that is expected there. It is at this point that the therapist prepares the child to meet crises successfully, such as attending his first party. The therapist is supportive and sees the child through the crisis to help him continue in his ego development. Concurrently, the therapist helps the child to reconcile his self-concepts with his idealized goals for himself. To accomplish this, the child must be sufficiently comfortable with himself to assess realistically his entire constellation of assets and liabilities and to match those with what can be rewarding and gratifying life goals for himself. Unless he bridges the gap between his self-concept and his idealized goals, the child has little chance for lasting adaptation and success.

Early in the first stage of psychotherapy, the child should be asked for his ideas about his problems. He may attribute his school failure to a reading problem, for example, or to an inability to do math. He may have rationalized away all self-depreciation with a conviction such as, "I had poor teachers." Often there is a parent behind the scene who has helped him to establish a rationalization such as: "If I just had decent teachers, then I would have been swell." Or, if he or his parent is a bit more sophisticated, he might assert: "If schools would hire teachers at higher pay, they would do a better job of teaching; then I wouldn't be a reading problem." Starting with the child's understanding of what is wrong with himself, the therapist can help him to recognize that his brain got hurt and that this caused his problems. This is a frightening concept to some adults, particularly parents. Many parents equate brain dysfunction with death, insanity, or hopelessness. In contrast, most of these children, underneath whatever rationalization or defense they have erected, already have some awareness that something is basically wrong with themselves, that something does not let them do what they want to do. Usually they feel tremendous relief when helped to recognize what that comes from and that (within realistic bounds) it can be remedied. Often there follows a gradual reduction in their anxiety and tension, which in turn frequently diminishes the hyperactivity and other classical symptoms.

If a parent counselor is available to help the parents with their anxieties about brain dysfunction, there is a good chance of making an early inroad into the child's ego insufficiencies and deviations. For the parents to be comfortable in discussing brain dysfunction with the child helps him to focus his anxiety so

155

that it no longer is global and pervasive: "Yes, my brain got hurt; it's not that I'm totally no good. I can't read (or compete in sports or whatever) *because* that part of me got hurt."

To explain his hurt brain to the child, two analogies that are within his realm of understanding have been helpful: "If you broke your arm, you couldn't stay out of school for a long time, and so your other arm would have to learn to write. That would not be easy at first, but when properly taught, it would write well. The same things happen when one part of your brain gets hurt, another part is taught how to do what you want it to do." The second analogy reminds the child of how ugly looking and sore his knee was when it got skinned, but that it healed. His brain can get better too. His knowing this makes the world less alien and frightening. Being told this by the psychotherapist also means: "There is another human being in the world who isn't as scared of my problem as I am. There is someone who can face up to this with me, share this with me." This is extremely supportive to the child. If, during this initial stage of psychotherapy, the parents also can be helped to be comfortable with their child's problem and prognosis, he has a sense of support and security never before available to him.

Some readers might question helping the child to know the nature of his problem, feeling that the natural thing would be to disguise or minimize his problem and *not* have him think about it. Opening this up with the youngster is important because it involves, first of all, his strong feelings that something is wrong with him and that he is hopeless. From this child's earliest, preverbal experiences he has strongly sensed: "Your face doesn't look the same toward me as it does toward my brother. You're not happy with me. You are displeased with me. You don't hold me in a loving way." As he gets older and verbalizes his feelings to the therapist he trusts, he expresses fears such as: "I feel like a basket case. Nobody will ever want to marry me. No one will ever want to give me a job. I'll never be a daddy. What will happen to me if my parents die? I'll never be able to make it on my own." At the same time, there is evidence of a keen resentment against this pervasive sense of inadequacy, coupled

156

with an attempt to fight against it to establish some sense of identity. One youngster who was a manipulator par excellence put it this way: "I can't boss me and make me do what I want, so next best thing is to boss my mom around." Discussing with the child how he understands and feels about his problems is also important to help him to clarify why this happened to him. He has a strong need to know: "Why am I different? Who did this to me? Was it Mother? Was it Father? Did God punish me because I was bad?" The hurt and anger form the nucleus of an intense struggle within the child. As a result, when he is helped to see that although something went wrong in the process of development, he is not to blame and the parents are not to blame. It was an accident of nature. This helps the child to mobilize a different kind of feeling both within himself and in relationship to the family. It removes the mystery and fear from "What's wrong with me?" and puts it in the realm of "Yes, there is something wrong with me, through no fault of mine or my family, but something can be done about it."

In the initial stage of psychotherapy, both the acting-out and passive-resistive child are helped to recognize that although they do have a problem, it is not something from which they must flee. They are helped to see that they have the potential to learn and to succeed and to do what the other children can do. Then, depending on the maladaptive efforts the child has made toward adaptation, depending on whether he shows the acting-out or the passive-resistive type of behavior, the therapist addresses himself to how the child has tried to cope with himself and the world around him. The therapist acknowledges that there is nothing wrong with the child's goals. For example, both the passive resister and the acting-outer want people to like them, but they try to achieve this by manipulating people all the time. There is nothing wrong with their *goal*. What is wrong is how they go about trying to achieve it. The psychotherapist's job is to help the child to recognize that he does not become the teacher's pet by disrupting the class every ten seconds, that he does not endear himself to his teacher or to his mother or to the safety patrol by constantly wanting attention that interrupts

157

the other person's activities, and that if he continues such behavior he can expect this person to get annoyed with him.

A great deal of time, usually into and throughout the second stage of therapy, is required to work this through in concrete example after concrete example. While working it through, the therapist continually helps the child to see his positive attributes. For example, the therapist might point out to the child: "You know, when you first came here, you couldn't jump. You couldn't catch a ball. Instead it bopped you on the beezer every time you tried to catch it. You ran away from all kinds of games, because you felt so hurt about the other kids laughing at you, and you felt so hurt because you couldn't do anything they did. That's all changed now. You can do all these things. Learning these things is no tougher a job than not bugging everybody for constant attention. A guy who can run and jump and catch so well can also do that." The therapist constantly helps the child to see that there are positive aspects of himself and that what the therapist currently expects of him, in the reorientation of the child's attempts at adaptation, *is* something he can accomplish.

During the first stage of psychotherapy, the therapist reflects to the child that feelings are natural and human and that the therapist is capable not only of emoting, but also of allowing the child to show emotion. Although the child may not know the meaning of the word *fear*, he has experienced the feeling of fear. That is equally true of anger and other emotions. The child is also aware of the intensity of emotions from a person's voice, facial expressions, gestures, or body movements. When the child is afraid to express his feelings directly, play materials can be useful as a medium through which the child can communicate his experiences. The playthings become an object outside of himself, a third person, on which he can begin to risk the displacement of his feelings.

In the emerging relationship with the therapist, it is important to be aware of what the youngster is feeling so as not to inundate him, but to lead him gradually into a new reality concerning feelings. The therapist should remember that in the

158

very process of leading him into that reality, the child is being led away from what was his reality with his parents. This is frightening, because it means separating from the familiar. It means moving toward a new person and a new experience, and the fear of what this may involve. It is like Plato's allegory of trying to get the people to move out of the cave into the light. The wagons and the soldiers walking along the road were pointed out to them as the real people, instead of the shadows on the cave wall with which they had always lived. This was so overwhelming that they wanted to go back to the cave. They preferred to stay with the familiar, where they were comfortable.

The therapist should also recognize that these youngsters are concrete. They have difficulty organizing percepts, let alone going from there into the higher abstractions of concepts. Emotions, for communication purposes, are concepts. When a child who has had the experience of an emotion is not able to communicate it, it is frequently because he does not have the language, the conceptual ability, with which to do so. Yet, he needs to communicate it because the feeling is uncomfortable, or because he is afraid of it, or because he is afraid of his response to it. It can be very helpful to the child to put into words for him what the therapist perceives he is feeling.

At times, the child will deny what the therapist says. To respond appropriately to a child's denial, the therapist has to consider where the youngster is in relationship both to the treatment process and to the development of his ego skills. Maybe he is not ready to accept the confrontation. If he is not ready, he should be allowed the use of that denial. Until he has achieved the ego growth to be ready to deal with it, there is no point in insisting that he do so. On the other hand, if this occurs in a later stage of therapy when the denial represents, for example, an attempt to control the therapeutic situation, then the child should be helped to see that he is resisting the confrontation and why. The main point is that just as there is a pattern of biological and social growth, so is there a pattern to the treatment process. To know where the child is, concerning

159

his defenses against taking further steps of ego growth, is an important aspect of the therapist's skill.

When the therapist mirrors to a child with brain dysfunction what he is quite certain to be the child's feeling, and the child responds that he is wrong, the therapist usually can believe him. This is especially true of the younger children. Therapists have no special omniscience simply because there happens to be a certain degree appended to their name. By the same token, many of the children are candid enough so that when the therapist has put a feeling into words for them, they are extremely grateful. They exclaim: "Yea, yea, *that's* what I've been trying to tell you." They show great relief. On the other hand, if the therapist makes a wrong interpretation, these children often say so matter-of-factly. It is similar to communication with a child who is difficult to understand because of his mutilated speech. In that case as well, he usually lets one know whether the interpretation was correct or incorrect.

A child with brain dysfunction may also practice denial in therapy for the same reason he does it in the classroom: he is in a situation that is too hot for him to handle, and he has to get out. He might overturn the therapist's desk, or open a window and start to crawl out, or do any of the things he would in the classroom when the teacher presents him with a learning task that is in advance of his level of skill development. In that case, the therapist should recognize with the child that he is unable to handle the interpretation successfully, the same as he is unable to handle, say, number concepts in the classroom successfully at that point in time. It means that the therapist has made a correct interpretation, but has misjudged when to present it to him. Based on a longitudinal understanding of the child, if the therapist thinks he is almost ready to accept the interpretation and is giving only a token fight to stay away from seeing the point, the therapist might say: "Okay, I know this is bugging you right now, and I know that you don't feel quite brave enough to take a look at this today, so we'll let it go. Maybe next time I see you you'll feel brave enough to want to talk about this." In that way the therapist is not backing off, but is letting the child know that he is expected, when ready, to handle this issue, because to do so is vital to his ego growth. At the same time, the therapist is not jamming it down the child's throat at that moment. On the other hand, if the therapist's evaluation of the child's ability to cope with the issue indicates that he will not be able to do so for another six or eight months, the therapist can back off gracefully, without making the expectation imminent.

Both the psychotherapist and the classroom teacher will find that note-taking facilitates such decisions. Nothing keeps one in touch with the child more than does a series of notes. Taking a look at one therapy session does not provide the opportunity to evaluate what is going on longitudinally with the child. Keeping notes serially does. Obviously, keeping them on some shelf is not the key, but reviewing them regularly provides the opportunity to understand what is going on with the child. There is much less chance then of not staying with the child or going off on one's own vagaries, which can have a devastating effect on the success of treatment. One of the best safeguards against that is the use of anecdotal records in the classroom and continuous case notes for the therapist.

With practice, it is not necessary to write such notes during the therapy session. When first starting to make observations, the tendency is to write voluminous notes on a particular situation. After further experience in taking notes and in reviewing them regularly, the essential factors can be readily pinpointed. Then fewer notes are required, and these can be made after the child leaves. Similarly, the teacher can, within a half hour of quiet contemplation after class, summarize what happened during the day. Within that period of time, many teachers can highlight succinctly the key points in their eight children's reactions during the course of the day. To write something down, one must focus attention on what is most significant and sort out all the irrelevancies. This in itself is a learning process that allows the teacher to review what went on today to be better able to anticipate and prepare for tomorrow.

To illustrate the use of the initial stage of therapy to help a child overcome his defective self-concept and hurt pride, it might be helpful to describe Dr. Adamson's procedure with a youngster at The Pathway School. This little boy, in correcting a paper on which he was doing arithmetic, erased his errors to the point of tearing his paper. Then the youngster became very upset. The paper was torn; it was defective. The teacher skillfully handled this by saying, "We can fix that," mending the paper with tape and then saying, "All right, now you can go on."

During a psychotherapy hour, this same boy was enjoying a real feeling of accomplishment by flying an airplane around, when it broke. He asked the therapist to put it back together, and as the therapist started to do this, it became apparent that to repair it would be a major job. At that point the therapy time had come to an end. There was the youngster, with the plane broken, furious and insisting that it be mended immediately. He was projecting his own sense of inadequacy onto the plane. Moreover, his feeling of failure and hurt pride were being denied to himself: "I'm not the one who's broken. The plane is broken." Therefore, the plane had to be mended right away. The therapist said: "I'm sorry, but you know we do have to stop now. We can finish this the next time I see you." The youngster lay on the floor, kicking and crying, expressing all the pathos of his hurt pride, of failure, of frustration, of trying to control the situation by getting the therapist to alter the reality of time in order to meet the child's demand to have the plane fixed immediately. While the youngster was showing this infantile behavior, the therapist said: "You're very mad at me because I'm not going to let you finish this now, even though we will fix it up later. But instead of lying down and acting angry like a little baby, stand up and tell me you're angry

162

at me, that you think I'm a mean old doctor." The youngster got up and took a stance like he was ready to take on the therapist. In that minute, the youngster had moved from feeling totally inadequate, and therefore needing to control the environment and make it treat him like a baby, to being ready to take on the therapist in a challenge. In that moment there was some organization, a readiness to cope with the situation more adaptively, because the therapist had allowed him to be angry for being held to reality, which the child then could accept.

This type of situation was repeated a number of times. However, the child soon became a little more open, allowing the therapist to indicate to this boy that he was upset *because* he felt like that broken plane. Next the therapist helped him to see his feelings about being unable to deal with things when they are imperfect.

The therapist also worked with the teacher, supporting the fact that she did the right thing in the classroom when the page was torn by giving the boy the tape and helping him through that moment. Later, as therapy progressed, the youngster began to understand why he reacted the way he did, and he showed a beginning awareness of his reactions to the feeling of disability within himself. Then the teacher followed through by indicating, when the paper again got torn: "Well, it looks like you're kind of angry. You're upset because the paper is torn, as you sometimes feel things aren't just right with *you*." At that point the youngster knew that the teacher understood him. Thus, there was a meshing of psychotherapy and the classroom learning situation. As John Dewey pointed out, education is learning, not preparation for learning. Education is living, not merely preparation for living.

The acting-outer, such as the child whose case was just cited, requires the delimitation of opportunity for failure for a long time. Usually he has had limits set for him only in the sense of "thou shalt not." What he has needed instead is the setting of limits to insure his having a successful experience. He needs

163

delimitation of the opportunities to act out in ways that are self-defeating and self-devaluating or in ways that will result either in guilt or fear of his own power.

Usually, these children are basically bright, even though they have not realized their good intellectual potential. Therefore, they often use that intellectual capacity in deviant ways, motivated by the drive for psychic survival; that is, the preservation of some sense of identity. As a result, many become master manipulators. One child, for example, when sent to the principal's office, climbed out the window and stayed just out of reach. When the adults began to anticipate that move on his part, he switched to running out into the parking lot and hiding under a car. This controlled not only the principal, but the entire school; because no cars could move until he was found. To do this requires intelligence, as it requires planning and creativity. Moreover, such deviant use of intelligence is well practiced. Because the child is a master at such manipulations, he cannot be ordered to stop. To help him give up being manipulative, the environment and the relationships with him must be structured so that he does not have the opportunity to get into trouble. In particular, the opportunity for his getting into the kind of trouble that makes him terrified of his own power is to be avoided. Much of the child's extremely hostile behavior stems from his being terrified that nobody can stop him. Therefore, he behaves more and more hostilely and antisocially, hoping that someone finally will stop him, thereby reducing his anxiety about being powerless to curb himself.

To recognize with this child, in the classroom, in the home, and in psychotherapy, that he does manipulate and that the opportunity for him to do so must be delimited before he goes out of control—before he becomes drunk with his own power and terrified that he, a child, does have such power—can eventually lead him into more constructive response patterns. He can be helped to channel his energy adaptively by being shown realistic ways of doing so in each situation that is threatening or troublesome to him. He must feel that those who are helping him genuinely do not want to change his goals, that they do

164

want him to be proud of himself, and that they do want him to be a person of whom others are proud, but not in a way that terrifies them and himself.

Now let us consider the passive-resistive child in the first stage of psychotherapy. Concerning the etiology of passive resistance, it is difficult to make generalities. My experience indicates that this child has been a member of a forceful, authoritarian family that has high intellectual striving. Perhaps father and mother are both professional people, and the siblings are extremely bright. Maybe the mean IQ in the family is 125 or more, fostering a high degree of intellectualization, verbalization, and competition. The child with brain dysfunction cannot hold his own, let alone compete, with members of such a family. In one such family, everyone practiced one-upmanship. The youngster with brain dysfunction obviously could not compete this way, so he competed by being a bottleneck. For example, when everybody else was ready to go out to dinner, he was not dressed yet, thereby making everyone wait for him.

Too often the tendency is simply to let the passive resister be. Because he is less of a problem, he can be ignored while the teacher concentrates on the child who will not be ignored. Sometimes this child is ignored because the teacher regards him as hopeless or unapproachable, which really is a reflection of the child's own feelings about himself. The teacher must be aware that his problem is equal to that of the acting-out child, although it is less obvious.

To break the stalemate with such a child, the therapist must help him to see what he is doing: that he is balking or delaying everyone; or being dependent in dressing, for example; or being helpless by maintaining that he cannot do what is requested of him. In time, he begins to realize that he enjoys manipulating people in such ways, and that he does not do such things because of inadequacy. This is an important first differentiation for the teacher and the therapist to make for him: "You do have the skill; you choose not to use it, because you get your jollies by seeing people jump through hoops to help you." When the child sees that he really does have the skills he chooses not

165

to use, then he can be helped to find better ways in which to achieve the goal of feeling important. While working on this with the child, the therapist must be able to reach the key people in the child's life, so that they do not play his game. If anyone does play his game, everyone else's work with the child will be nullified, because the child then has the opportunity to practice his habituated maladaptive behavior. That is so much easier for him than having to risk trying new ways of coping with situations. Only when *all* situations make the same demands on him can he be helped to give up the habituated maladaptation.

Take, for example, the child who always misses the school bus, forcing his mother to drive him to school. His mother should be counseled to tell him ahead of time, not during the crisis: "You know, Johnny, you really make me feel like a fool, and I'm tired of feeling like I'm a dumb mother. Every morning I know you're going to pull this on me, but I drive you to school anyway. I really feel like a fool." Firstly, the child basically does not want to have a dumb mother. Secondly, she has confronted him with what he is doing, and she has indicated that she does not want to continue to participate in his manipulative game. If she is able to follow through, with proper support from parent counseling, she will convey to him: "You're too big for me to treat you like a baby who can never be on time. You have accomplished X and Y and Z, so you certainly can be responsible for catching the bus. Starting tomorrow, that is *your* responsibility." If she then does not get upset and does not allow the manipulation, she is no longer contributing to the perverse gratification he gets from manipulating her. Because of his own inner dynamics, he must then seek another way to get gratification. He can now be helped to find a more constructive, more realistically gratifying way of doing so than by making his mother jump through hoops each morning. Helping this child is not easy. It usually requires a stronger therapist, more support for parents, and a longer time than are required to help the acting-out child effect impulse controls.

Both therapist and teacher must not allow themselves to get into a power struggle with the passive-resistive child. This can happen if reality confrontation is ill-timed. The child has wrestled his parents to the ground every time they tried to overpower him. Only after he has recognized, perhaps begrudgingly, that the teacher and the therapist and the others working with him really want to help him, has the time come for reality confrontation. A reality confrontation cannot come in the beginning of therapy, because it would only create a power struggle. At the proper time, usually in the second or third stage of therapy, the child, parents, therapist, teacher, and possibly other members of the team, can meet to help him to take a hard look at reality. For example, if a child has six months in which to prepare himself to return to regular class full-time, as he says he wants to do, how much work in each subject does he really need to accomplish? Can he accomplish that if he continues to drag his feet as often as he still does today? Such a conference is then followed through by all concerned, and additional conferences are scheduled periodically so that reality is continually present. When properly timed, that kind of reality confrontation can mobilize sufficient motivation to help the child to find better ways of coping than passive resistance, and it can nurture a more realistic sense of achievement and adequacy.

By adolescence, it is more difficult to help both the passive resister and the acting-outer to internalize more adaptive means of fulfilling their goals. Nevertheless, there is reason to believe that internalization can take place as early as the first year of life and can continue indefinitely. We all know persons who at fifty and sixty years of age are able to incorporate into their makeup that which is truly important to them. Perhaps the crux of the problem is that the adolescent has become so rigidly defended that he can fend off internalization, so that he can push key adults away by saying, "I don't want any part of you or what you stand for." If this is the case, it takes a great deal of work to help the adolescent accept the fact that there are those who care about him and who want to help him, regardless of how hard he pushes them away and regardless of how disruptive he tries to be. Frequently, adolescents wear the armor of self-righteousness and disdain for others, which is very provocative and sorely tries the patience of adults. Even though it is difficult, it is absolutely essential to convey to such an adolescent that he is important to the adult and that the adult will not abandon him.

In brief, delimiting the opportunity for failure and, concurrently, channeling the child's impulses and motivation into activity that is realistically gratifying to him, instead of progressively devaluating or terrifying to him, is important to the first stage of therapy. It is the responsibility of those who work with him to use their egos for decision-making, rather than to give him the opportunity to use his inadequate ego for decision-making that can lead only into failure. This does not mean that decisions should be made for him forever. In later stages of therapy, as he is capable of making appropriate decisions, he is given greater opportunity to do so, because that aspect of his ego needs to be strengthened through practice so that he develops facility with it. Not understanding this concept, some educators protest that this approach is unrealistic, because the child must live in the real world. What they ignore is that making decisions for him comprises only one stage in preparing him to live in that real world. Those same educators would not start toilet training a newborn in preparation for living in the real world. Instead, they would advocate keeping pace with what the child needs at that stage of his development. No child can achieve healthy, self-satisfying ego function in one giant step. Not to be cognizant of where the child is developmentally and to push him too hard or prematurely becomes extremely uneconomical in the sense that the child must fight back to maintain some form of identity. Moreover, no one, especially a child such as this, gives up a coping mechanism until he can find a better, more gratifying one.

As the child moves into the second stage of psychotherapy, in which interpersonal relationships are emphasized, he feels

168

more worthwhile. In fact, the new feeling of self-worth may show up in openly challenging the teacher's authority. This must be dealt with by the teacher before the youngster begins to stir up feelings in the other children, so that they respond similarly, or before it deteriorates into an explosive situation. The teacher must recognize with the youngster what he is feeling, but, at the same time, that he cannot be permitted to disrupt the class. If the child does not have the capacity to cope with what he is feeling, it may be necessary to remove him from the group at that time, with the opportunity to rejoin the group when he has a greater degree of inner control. His newly manifested aggression in the classroom should also be picked up in therapy. Then the therapist can help the child to see that he has developed certain generalized patterns of handling hostility; for example, how he is handling situations in the classroom is no different than how he is handling situations at home. As the child becomes aware that he reacts the same way to many apparently different situations, because he perceives in each of them the same threat to his hurt pride or felt inadequacy, for example, he develops a conceptual framework that enables him to begin to evaluate and to monitor his reactions for himself.

In general, the object of this second stage of therapy is to broaden the child's understanding of himself in all situations, thereby widening his field of successful interaction and gradually enabling him to extend his coping skills from the therapy hour into the classroom and then into the home.

The reader might question what is done about the child's instinctual drives when therapy is addressed only to building the ego functions. When these drives, such as sexual impulses, do emerge in a child's acting-out behavior, they can be handled without using the classic approach of delving into all aspects of the drive and the genesis of the attendant conflict. This may mean that a given child may need two different types of psychotherapy: first, the ego-supportive, ego-building kind under discussion; then, after he achieves sufficient ego intactness, a more classical type of treatment that would help him to resolve his inner conflicts, perhaps with a different therapist. Nevertheless, as conflicts centered on instinctual drives are expressed in the first type of psychotherapy, the therapist does not back away from them. He does not show the child that this is a forbidden subject or an area to be afraid of. The therapist recognizes with the child that this is a problem area, often being quite directive and ego-supportive in terms of how to handle the specific impulses and the specific situations. The therapist further indicates to the child that this area requires further work at another time, when the child is able to do so. Most of these children are able to accept this. They often recognize their limitations, especially during the second stage of therapy. By then they can recognize that they have achieved certain aspects of being "boss" over themselves, which they did not have before, and that with additional work they will be able to be boss over themselves in certain other ways at a later time.

As was mentioned earlier, during both the first and second stages of psychotherapy, the child may have to be excluded from the class temporarily. To help this child appropriately requires the administrative support discussed in the early chapters of this book, so that the necessary changes in certain conventional school procedures and policies can be made. For example, an aide in the classroom is not as unheard of today as it was several years ago. Today many administrators acknowledge that an aide is more than another person to add to the payroll. They know that an aide is vital to the effective functioning of the class, especially when a child has a blowup.

Before deciding what to do with the child who cannot handle the expected classroom situation, the teacher must first understand where he is in ego development, what he needs, and what will be effective for him. The youngster who has little ego development at that point needs a *quiet* room, a small space in which to feel secure, a place to be alone with another human being who understands him and will help him to pull himself together. Many youngsters ask for this, legitimately saying to the teacher, "I'm losing control; I need to get out." They do not regard this as punishment or harassment. Another youngster, at a higher level of ego organization, needs to leave the classroom only for the moment, because he cannot stand the stress of a given situation. He could benefit as much from a three-minute walk with the teacher on the grounds or on the sidewalk as from the quiet room. Still another child should not be permitted to leave the class, because he uses that as a means of avoidance or of manipulating the teacher. For that child, it is much better to help him understand, for example, that although his assignment is not what he wants to do at that moment, he should do his assignment first and what he wants to do at a later time. Learning to delay impulse gratification is an important part of ego development. Another child should be taken to the principal's office, when he requires the setting of limits to be reinforced by the principal. (The interrelated roles of teacher, principal, and therapist will be discussed later in this chapter.) Still another child may need what Fritz Redl (1959, 1966) terms the life-space interview, in which the therapist is available to help the child work through his disturbance at the time of crisis. And still another child might be helped best by having his school day shortened.

The following anecdote, taken from Dr. Adamson's treatment of a child at Pathway, illustrates the use of the life-space interview with a child who has brain dysfunction. At lunch time a boy who had some spasticity in one arm was asked to join an already-established group. As he walked into the classroom, one of the boys there became very agitated, shouting: "Get him out of here! He bothers me!" Then a great deal of assaultive gesturing and language was expressed to the newcomer. As a result, the youngster who was overreacting was taken out of the group, and his therapist was asked to see him. The teacher privately asked the therapist: "Could this reaction have been to the new boy's spastic arm because of his own defective image?" The teacher was correct. As the student walked in, it stirred up fantasies and fears in this boy, who himself had a weakness in the same arm. However, the teacher could not quite accept this, telling the therapist: "Intellectually this is fine, but it's hard for

171

me to believe that it actually happens like this." Then the teacher returned to class. Turning to the youngster, the therapist asked what happened.

Student: "He bothered me! He bothered me!"

Therapist: "Do you know why?"

Student: "No. All I know is he bothers me. Every time I see him coming into our room or getting on the bus, he bothers me. I just can't sit next to him on the bus. I don't know why."

Therapist: "When did he first bother you?"

Student: "I don't remember. I just can't remember."

Therapist: "Do you know what I mean? When did you first notice that seeing him upset you?"

Student: "Yes, I remember. The first time I saw him, when he came into this school, I hoped he wouldn't be put in my class."

Therapist: "What do you suppose it was about him that bothered you so much?"

Student: (after a long pause) "I think it's his arm. It's weak. It's crippled. Uh! I don't like to talk about it!"

Therapist: "Do you know why it's so hard to talk about it?"

Student: "Yes. I guess it's because I thought my arm would get like that."

Therapist: "You'd been afraid, then, for a long time, because he reminded you of your injury, and the weakness in your own arm."

Student: "Yes, that's right. But I'm not like him. He's crippled, and I'm not."

Therapist: "That's why you felt the way you did when you first saw him, but how do you feel now?"

Student: "I guess I'm a little weak in my arm. I know I can't always use it as well as I would like to use it. But, you know, he can't really change me. He can't make my arm any worse than it is. It'll always be weak, but it won't be like his. And he won't make me like him."

Therapist: "Do you think you can let yourself look at him now and not be afraid? Can you let him come into your class without being so bothered?"

Student: "I think so."

The therapist ended the five-minute life-space interview by saying, "Well, suppose you let me know tomorrow how it goes when you are with him again in class." In the regular therapy session the following day, the youngster said: "You know, we're

172

friends now. He doesn't bother me any more." As a result of the many therapy hours spent with this youngster in helping him to become aware of his feelings about the nature of his problems and about his feelings of inadequacy, he was able, in a very short period of time, to work through the crisis and the attendant fear. In turn, this also helped the teacher to accept what she perceived in this youngster.

To conduct a life-space interview does not require Utopian conditions, such as a skillful therapist who is available at all times. Many times a teacher who has had one to two years of fairly close supervision can conduct a life-space interview even within the classroom. Sometimes the teacher also can use the group interaction to help with the life-space interview, focusing on a specific incident in the classroom that all the youngsters were either a witness to or a part of. Of course, this has to be carefully done. If the teacher plays the role of the hanging judge, it is doomed to failure. On the other hand, after a year or two of fairly close supervision, the teacher should be able to "read" the situation, to understand why the child reacted as he did, and to see how this incident is related to the feelings and impulses of the other children in the class.

As an example, the class could be getting ready to go to the gym for an activity, when a passive-resistive child just happens to drop his coat. As he picks it up, he accidentally falls on the ankles of the child who is in front of him in line. In trying to get back into line, by chance, he bumps another child who has an injured leg. If the teacher does not intervene, then, the class and the activity to which they are going will be disrupted. If the teacher moves into the situation like a hanging judge, the child will be scapegoated rather than helped. By understanding the use of the life-space interview, the teacher could approach the child with: "Gee, Johnny, I'm sorry that you're afraid to go to the gym today." The teacher could recognize with him that he is still scared of failure in this area of his life and that he is trying, in the only way he knows how, to get out of the situation he does not want to face. The child can be helped to see this without the teacher's worrying about probing some deep, dark,

173

unconscious motive. Firstly, in that situation the teacher is not dealing with instinctual drives. Secondly, the child's fear of failure and his response to it have been worked on for some time. As part of handling that situation, the teacher recognizes with the class that Jimmy and Allen and several others in the class have the same fear, but they handle it differently. When those boys want to crucify Johnny for delaying them, the teacher can point out to them that this is a problem that Johnny is working on, and it is no different than Allen's getting to the gym and wanting to tear around and not put his sneaks on, which is Allen's way of handling his fear of failing. In that type of interaction the teacher accomplishes a great deal, not only maintaining the integrity of the group and directing the group toward the goal of a constructive activity, but also reinforcing what the therapist has been working on for quite some time. In my experience, for the teacher and the therapist to have such complementary roles enables the child to return to regular class in a shorter period of time.

It should also be noted that such an interaction requires only a small amount of time. A teacher who understands both the class and the situation at hand should be able to handle it in a "30-second conference." This requires sufficient understanding to crystallize the essential points into a few succinct sentences. If the teacher cannot do that, but rambles on instead, the child will tune the teacher out.

Another alternative in handling a disruptive child is shortening his school day. This can be used effectively in public schools. When faced with the reality of being inadequately staffed, of not having an aide for every classroom, and perhaps of not having a principal who is able to behave in other than a belligerent, authoritarian fashion toward a child, the child might be best helped by arranging for him to be in school for only part of the day. Both the child and his family should be helped to see this not as a defeat, but as an opportunity to succeed. Hopefully, if at the beginning of the term the child shows every indication of not being able to succeed in class on a full-time basis, the teacher will arrange for him to come to class only part time in the beginning. That can be readily accomplished when each child is brought in individually for diagnostic teaching during the first days of school, as indicated in Chapter VI. Then the teacher can tell the child: "This is as much of an experience at school as we think you can handle right now. As you are able to show us that you're grown up enough to do more things in class, we will be delighted to have you for a longer time each day." Both at Pathway and in public schools, children have earned their way into being in a class full time. It has taken them six to eight months to do so, and at times they had to have the day shortened again because their progress was not continuous, but in time they were able to profit from being in class for the whole day. When necessary, a child who has been having difficulty maintaining himself for an entire day can have his day shortened and then earn back the privilege of full-time class.

Some administrators have objected to this procedure saying: "You're giving those children a bonus. You're playing right into their hands. They don't want to come to school." That has not been my experience with these children. To them, to be in school and to do what the other children do is to have a sense of adequacy. They do not want a chance to play hooky; they want to belong.

Shortening the school day works successfully when under-girded by a relationship structure in which those involved in shortening his day are helping persons who do not reject the child simply because he failed to meet an expectation. This is contrary to his previous experiences, in which many people have been so sick and tired of all the things he could not do and of all the things he botched that they have clearly shown him their antipathy. For his current relationships to serve as a contrast to such experiences, all who work with the child must indicate carefully and assiduously that if he cannot succeed today, he will have another opportunity tomorrow.

Let us turn now to the problem the child with brain dysfunction often has in making the transition into the third state of psychotherapy. Although he has overcome his consider-

175

able and long-standing skill deficiencies, he often continues to react as if he were still deficient. In that case, he has lived so long with his maladaptive patterns that he finds in them a kind of security. Therefore, he is not yet ready to relinquish them completely and risk investing his psychic energy entirely in the use of his newfound skills for adaptive, realistic gratification. If that child is not helped to redeploy his energy from maladaptations to newfound skills, his progress could be aborted. Here again, those who help him allow him to draw upon their own ego bank when he is unable to move himself into the next phase of development. For example, the therapist may say to him: "You know, Johnny, your hurt brain is better. Your brain is fine. You can do most of the things you want to do. Now what we have to work on is the way you see yourself and how you handle yourself." In this approach the youngster comes to appreciate, with the therapist's help, the areas in which he no longer has skill deficiencies. For example, he begins to pride himself on what he can do in running and in baseball and on the trampoline. He takes pride in what he can do academically in reading and in arithmetic. He takes pride in doing independent library work. He is proud of being able to concentrate for two hours on homework. These achievements become increasingly real and gratifying to him, so that in time he relinquishes the old ways of trying to cope with the world around him. As the therapist zeroes in on the youngster's new achievements, continually contrasting the "new" child with the "old" one, the child begins to disassociate himself from the image of being damaged or defective. He begins to risk seeing himself as a successful member of a normal group. This transitional stage is preparatory to his leaving the special group and returning to interaction in a regular class, in his family, in his neighborhood, and in society.

To review briefly, the child was first helped to accept the fact that his brain had been hurt but is reparable. This enabled him to focus his anxiety, instead of continuing to have global anxiety that dissipates attempts to motivate him and fosters avoidance of all learning situations in which his pride has been hurt. Next he "accepted" his handicap and became quite comfortable with the opportunity for success afforded him by the supportive environment in which most decisions were made for him. Then he began to acquire the skills required to return to regular class. To help him expand his armamentarium of skills, both the therapist and the teacher dispensed liberal doses of "rub in," wherein the child's already achieved successes were recited to him and he was reassured that he could achieve what was currently expected of him, just as he had achieved all those other skills. As a result, he began to see himself as a person who *can*, as opposed to a person who cannot, as he had seen himself previously. Nevertheless, he did not yet see himself as wholly adequate and, therefore, did not behave accordingly. Therefore, he needed further help to disassociate himself from the self-concept of defectiveness and to risk seeing himself as capable of being a successful member of a normal group.

In the third stage of therapy, "rub in" is continued. Concurrently, the child is helped to practice making decisions about his own behavior that will best lead him to his own goals. To help the child practice making decisions, the therapist might say to a child: "Johnny, you have learned pretty well to be boss over yourself. You don't blow up any more when your teacher gives you something that you think is hard and you're a little scared of it. You don't have to disrupt the whole class any more. You don't need to go to the quiet room any more. This is great. You're really a junior executive now. I'd like to see you be the top executive of yourself, of your own corporation, 'Johnny, Incorporated.' As the top executive, you have to pass judgment upon everything that comes across your desk. You have to decide whether this is the best thing for the whole corporation or not. You have to make this decision constantly." Many therapy sessions then could be spent practicing how to make appropriate decisions about specific situations involving interaction. This technique may sound contrived, but most children with brain dysfunction never had the opportunity to learn how to make such decisions. Here again, they have lived deprived lives because of their handicap. This technique gives them practice in the volitional decision-making with which they have had little previous experience. As the child acquires some

177

skill in decision-making, anxiety is relieved for him in the same way that repetitive play relieves anxiety for the average child. He then knows he does not have to be afraid of making decisions. When the ability to make wise decisions becomes easy, it is internalized and becomes incorporated into his self-concept. *Then* he is one who *can* make wise decisions.

As part of the third stage of therapy, the child is prepared to return to a regular class where he can succeed and realistically feel proud of himself. To accomplish this, he needs help to accept himself as a part of the new, "normal" group. There usually are two aspects of such help to the child. The first is his reconciliation of self-concept with his idealized image of himself. The second is his bringing others, with whom he interacts socially, to recognize his current adequacy.

The reconciliation of self-concept with idealized image, which must be accomplished to pave the way for modifying how others see him socially, is illustrated in Figure 20. The core of his hurt pride lies in the discrepancy between his current self-concept on the one hand and the idealized goals and expectations of himself that comprise his ego ideal on the other.

As has been discussed in Chapter IV and earlier in this chapter, his self-concept is the product of past and present experiences centered about his skills and deficiencies, both from the standpoint of how he has perceived and felt about these, and from the standpoint of how others have reacted to him. The more serious his deficiencies have been and/or the more vituperative have been the responses of others to his deficiencies, the more he would have developed a devaluated self-concept. The resultant hurt pride would have led him to establish proportionately intense and pervasive means of salving that hurt pride. One way he would have done this is by seizing opportunities to prove himself, whether or not his actions were socially acceptable and in fact accomplished his own goal of being an accepted, desirable person, both in his own eyes and in those of others. This might have led him to walk on roofs or set fires, because none of the other boys were "brave" enough to do so; or disrupt the class, because it requires great "power"; or

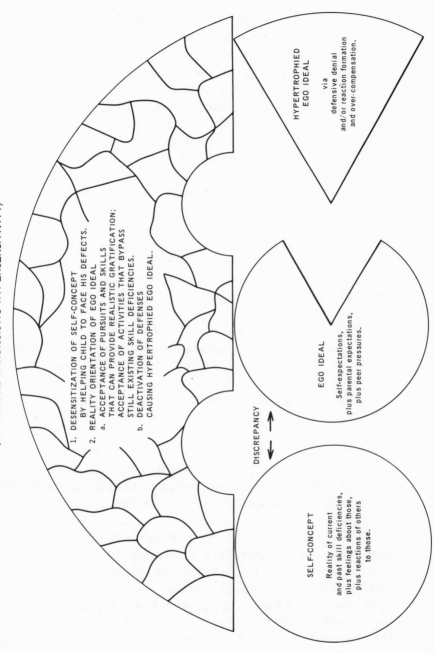

RECONCILIATION BETWEEN SELF-CONCEPT AND IDEALIZED IMAGE

(TO REDUCE NARCISSISTIC HYPERSENSITIVITY)

1. DESENSITIZATION OF SELF-CONCEPT BY HELPING CHILD TO FACE HIS DEFECTS.
2. REALITY ORIENTATION OF EGO IDEAL
   a. ACCEPTANCE OF PURSUITS AND SKILLS THAT CAN PROVIDE REALISTIC GRATIFICATION; ACCEPTANCE OF ACTIVITIES THAT BYPASS STILL EXISTING SKILL DEFICIENCIES.
   b. DEACTIVATION OF DEFENSES CAUSING HYPERTROPHIED EGO IDEAL.

HYPERTROPHIED EGO IDEAL

via
defensive denial
and/or reaction formation
and over-compensation.

EGO IDEAL

Self-expectations,
plus parental expectations,
plus peer pressures.

DISCREPANCY

SELF-CONCEPT

Reality of current
and past skill deficiencies,
plus feelings about those,
plus reactions of others
to those.

Figure 20. Reconciliation between self-concept and idealized image

179

run away from home, because it necessitates great "self-sufficiency" and "resourcefulness." Such attempts to salve his hurt pride have molded his self-expectations and thereby influenced his ego ideal. Equally influential factors have been parental expectations and peer pressures. Often these three factors—self-expectations, parental expectations, and peer pressures—have been antagonistic, serving only to increase the discrepancy between self-concept and ego ideal. Frequently, the result has been an exaggerated ego ideal. By means of defenses such as denial and reaction formation, the child has felt that he must be perfect in whatever he does, or win every time he plays a game, or be a straight-A student, or be a college graduate, or when he becomes an adult to earn in excess of $50,000 a year. Obviously, the more unrealistic the goals are that stem from his exaggerated ego ideal, the more difficult it is to reconcile the self-concept and the ego ideal. If these are not brought to compatibility, the child has little chance for a productive, gratifying life.

To produce the desired compatibility requires work on both the self-concept and the ego ideal. As far as the self-concept is concerned, the child should be aided in accurately assessing what skill deficiencies he used to have, which of those he has overcome and to what degree, and the current status of his collective skills. Concurrently, he needs help to realize what defense he has used to hide his deficiencies from his own awareness and from others. Once the reconciliation between his goals and skills has taken place within himself, he is ready to devote a major portion of his energy to reorienting the attitudes and responses of others toward him, so that they can appreciate his current worth.

As there is a desensitization of his hurt pride, he becomes aware that the defenses he has relied on are no longer needed and, in fact, hinder the achievement of his own goals. Part of that process is to help him to see which activities and roles, both present and future, can provide him real gratification. If he has a residual deficiency that will probably always remain with him, he needs the opportunity to learn about activities and roles that can bypass his deficiency and still be rewarding. Before he is willing to deactivate the exaggerated ego ideal, to recognize it as self-defeating, he must experience in class, in social situations, on the playing field, and in the family that there is a way for him to feel worthwhile. And the therapist must see him through all such situations many times over. Acknowledging this, plus the fact that *everyone* has both assets and liabilities, strengths and weaknesses, he can become comfortable with his current constellation of skills. Then he can be helped to construct goals that are realistically in keeping with those skills. In school, if given the opportunity to spend part of his day in the special class to strengthen his weaknesses and the balance of the day in a regular class, he can show that he can cope more effectively with situations such as recess and the lunchroom. He also can cope better with the children in the neighborhood and with their changing impressions of him. He may have more difficulty with the neighbors' stereotyped viewpoint of him, because adults often are much more rigid in maintaining a stereotype of a child than are children. Since this is an area of great concern and anxiety to the parents and to the child, it should be the school's concern too. This is an important part of the child's reintegration into society.

All who work with the child must acknowledge with him that how he was treated in his neighborhood has been a sore spot: "When you got kicked out of the game and got yelled at, it hurt like the devil. It made you want to cry inside. And sometimes you cried inside so much that you got mad and decided you didn't want anybody tramping around on your feelings any more; they just hurt too badly." Equally important to acknowledging what he has been through is to help him see it in contrast to today's reality. Now he does not have to get kicked out of the group, because he *can* play ball: "Remember when you hit a home run last week? It was the teacher, not just another kid pitching, and he wasn't just lobbing the ball over to be nice to you." Repeatedly emphasized is the point that even though now he can do these things well, the cloud of hurt still hangs over him. Part of the desensitization is to let him talk

181

about it, to let his feelings come out about the resentment and the hurt. Another part is to help him to see that he is not the only person in the world who has had problems, that everybody has problems to some degree. This can be a miraculous revelation to these children. Often they do not believe it in the beginning. They are firmly convinced that everybody else has a life that is blithe and carefree, that they are the only poor slobs with problems in the whole universe. An example is a youngster with brain dysfunction who went on to graduate from college. However, when faced with being on her own and getting a job and handling sexual situations, she required many months of resumed psychotherapy to recognize that other people also have problems and situations with which they must learn to cope. She really had believed that other people handled everything easily and smoothly.

With support, the child can recognize that he does have the ability, the bravery, the intelligence, and the charm to handle these situations, to let people know that he *has* changed. One youngster, for example, who had been the scourge of the neighborhood for years, at age nine had achieved a great deal of skill proficiency and impulse control. He went to each neighbor's house, politely rang the doorbell, and said: "I know I've been a lot of trouble to you, and I'm very sorry. But I'm a different boy now. Will you give me another chance?" This took tremendous courage and ego strength. Not in an uninhibited way, but in a matter-of-fact way, he stated what he needed from the neighbors: a second chance. When helped to bridge the gap between self-concept and ego ideal, many youngsters have responded as dramatically as did this child. Nevertheless, too often the biggest problem is not the child with brain dysfunction, but the adults who never let objective fact interfere with their bias. When such adults in the neighborhood refuse to acknowledge his progress, the child needs consistent support to see that it is the adult who has the problem: "The very fact that she can't see how much you've changed and that she has to keep on cutting you down shows that it is her problem, not yours." It is not unholy or dishonest to tell a child that it is the adult's problem and not his. Moreover, this is an opportunity to help the child learn how to handle such a difficult situation adaptively, which is also important to his reintegration into society.

Inherent in the third stage of psychotherapy is the availability of lifetime planning. As an example of this, when a child is ready to graduate from Pathway into his home community, the new school into which the child will be moving is contacted ahead of time. The principal, the guidance counselor, and the teacher are visited, to help them understand the child's past and his current status and needs. The books that will be used by the class into which the student will move are obtained, and these are included in the remainder of his studies at Pathway. The child, accompanied by his therapist or the Placement Officer or his parents, goes to visit the new school, thereby having the opportunity to go through a classroom experience in the new program. Arrangements are also made for the child to continue in therapy, either at Pathway, if he is a day student, or in some other setting that will answer the child's needs. This is not with the idea of prolonging dependency, but with the idea of gradual weaning, of helping him through another important transitional period back into an environment that harbors many unknowns for him. When the child is ready to terminate therapy, by mutual agreement, it is recognized that there may be difficult times ahead; perhaps in adolescence, perhaps in a crucial situation such as a death in the family. The child is encouraged to feel that he may seek help from the therapist whenever it is needed. The availability and the continuity of this kind of supportive help is an important part of the lifetime-planning concept.

Actually, this is not much different from what is normally expected in adolescence, when there is a recrudescence of the child's former problems and a second-chance opportunity to work them through, as there is a reorganization of certain ego functions during the transition from childhood to adulthood. The adolescent has sore spots about which he turns to his doctor, or parent, or minister, or guidance counselor, or psychotherapist, from whom he needs help over that particular crisis. The child who has had a brain dysfunction is also expected to have certain sore spots recrudesce as he continues to grow following his return to regular class. For him to require occasional help should be no greater a cause for dismay.

To facilitate the success of all stages of the therapeutic process by which the child learns to manage his own behavior adaptively, the teacher, the principal, and the therapist must know their own roles with the child. Although consistency of approach to the child is important, each of these persons plays a different role in the therapeutic process.

The teacher's role is to provide the child with opportunities for successful learning, not to be a junior psychotherapist. When the teacher regards being a psychotherapist as more prestigious than being a teacher, confidences told the teacher by the therapist often are disclosed to the child simply to inflate the teacher's false sense of pride. That type of teacher also often purposely or unwittingly maneuvers the child into a blowup simply to obtain an opportunity to play at being a therapist.

The teacher should use relationship structure solely to make constructive inroads into behavior that interferes with the child's learning. However, this does not mean that the teacher spends the major portion of the day "helping" a child with his "problems." When that occurs it often is a sign that the teacher does not understand at which developmental level to begin the child's educational program, and so finds it easier to provide therapy than to teach. It may also be a sign that the teacher is afraid of the child's behavior and therefore cannot be convincing in the expectations held out to the child. Many teachers have been surprised to find that when they spoke with authority, looking the child straight in the eye, even those youngsters with "incorrigible" behavior listened.

Frequently the teacher who is insecure or who is afraid of the child's behavior vacillates in expectations or tries to justify the classroom rules. Too often such teachers try to ingratiate themselves with a difficult child by citing the principal as the culprit responsible for the rule, as though the teacher had nothing to do with it, or worse, sided with the child against the rule. Such teachers do not realize that children with brain dysfunction usually cannot handle being given alternatives of behavior, but feel more secure knowing that what is expected of them at that point in their development is invariant because it will help them most. At the same time, this does not mean that the teacher relates in a way that is dictatorial, unfeeling, or vituperative toward the child. If a child broke his arm and screamed because he was afraid of the doctor, the adult would be expected to take him to the doctor in a way that was sympathetic and reassuring to the child's upset feelings, yet quietly firm. The adult would not be expected to cart the child off while heaping invectives on him for screaming, punctuated by swats on the fanny, and loudly declaring that he deserves whatever happens to him for not being more careful.

The role of the principal in the therapeutic process is to reinforce, not to be a substitute for, the teacher's authority. The principal should represent rules and procedures designed to promote the child's growth. This cannot be represented to the child by heavy handedness, by shaming or devaluating him, by severe rigidity, or by demanding instant maturity. The child's improvement in behavior is contingent upon ego development, and all development requires time. As the principal quietly but firmly reinforces the teacher's authority and expectations, the child is confronted with the reality that he cannot manipulate the entire school, and, as a result, often calms down quickly. In some instances the principal need do nothing more than say: "Sit down in that chair. I have something important to finish at my desk. I'll be with you then." That provides the child with a cooling-off period in which he possibly can remuster his controls. On the other hand, the principal's launching himself at the child with a high concentration of anxiety and great consternation over the immensity of the child's unspeakable offense will not provide the needed cooling-off period.

At times the principal is called upon to deal with mutual hostility between teacher and child, often with each demanding immediate banishment of the other. It is not the occasion for an

I'll-defend-you-to-the-death loyalty on the part of the principal. It is a time when the principal should recognize with both the teacher and the child that each of them is upset and needs a cooling-off period, after which there will be a conference to clarify the situation and decide next steps. When that conference is held, the principal can help both the teacher and the child by first indicating that everyone gets angry sometimes, and that is no federal offense. Then the specific point of contention can be discussed and guidelines spelled out concerning how such a situation will be handled in the future. As an example, an eleven-year-old boy became increasingly resistive to doing work properly assigned him by the teacher. On one such occasion, the boy made crude and offensive noises at the teacher, who in turn punched him and summarily marched him to the principal.

In the conference that followed the cooling-off period, both teacher and youngster, with the teacher taking the lead, acknowledged that each had lost control and had not handled the situation constructively. Then it was spelled out that if another occasion arose in which the boy refused to do his assignment, he would know that he would be expected to continue at that assignment, at the expense of participating in activities he enjoyed, including after-school play, until he satisfactorily completed the assignment. The rule had to be invoked only a few times before the boy and teacher developed a healthy respect for each other that helped the boy to accomplish his work better. That crisis could not have been resolved so happily if the principal had felt forced into siding with either the teacher or the child. The crisis also provided the boy the opportunity to see that he did not have to run from a difficult and angry situation, but could stay in it and resolve it to his own satisfaction, which was important to his particular stage of ego growth.

At other times, the principal is asked to expel a child who is disrupting the class by means of offensive behavior for which all his classmates constantly pick on him. This is an opportunity for the principal to help the teacher and the class to realize that one child's problem is no worse than any other child's problem. This can be accomplished through a conference with the entire class present, in which the reason for each child's being in that class is pointed out matter-of-factly. The class is helped to recognize that each of them is in the class to overcome his own problem. Then the discussion can be guided into how each member of the class can help the child whose behavior is offensive to overcome his particular problem, thereby helping not only him but the entire class. Because children with brain dysfunction feel so inadequate, they often resort to a seesaw reaction—knocking the other fellow down, so that by comparison they can feel that they are on top. Such a situation provides the opportunity for helping them to see the maladaptation of the seesaw reaction and to find a more gratifying way to handle the situation.

The role of the therapist in the therapeutic process is to help the child cope more adaptively with his hurt pride, recognize his maladaptive behavior, and replace that with truly gratifying means of managing his own behavior. Like the principal, the therapist cannot be expected to produce instant maturity. If called upon by the teacher for a life-space interview with a child who is in a crisis, the therapist cannot be expected to make the child immediately conform to the teacher's wishes. For the therapist even to make such an attempt would be alien to his role and would sabotage the trusting relationship imperative to accomplishing the goals of psychotherapy. Recognizing that ego development requires much time and the working through of many crises, the therapist enters the crisis with the child only for the purpose of helping him to resolve it in a way that can be used to promote ego development. The therapist should help the teacher recognize this. Moreover, the therapist should help the teacher understand that to bring the therapist into a crisis as "The Big Stick" also implies to the child that the teacher is afraid of and incapable of handling the situation. Often, the more "Big Sticks" called upon in a crisis, the more the child is made to feel omnipotent to the point of panicking at his own power.

Inherent in the therapist's role is the self-awareness of knowing whether he can be effective with various types of behavioral problems. Depending on his level of training and self-understanding, the personality of the therapist can be an important factor in the success of treatment. That factor is particularly relevant to the treatment of children with brain dysfunction, who require from the therapist a great deal of interaction and communication. This cannot be accomplished without putting a great deal of one's personality into it. Usually, the quiet, placid therapist has not been successful with the passive-resister, nor the passive, indecisive therapist with the acting-outer.

The psychotherapist can also make a significant contribution to the habilitation of children who have brain dysfunction by working with the teacher of these children as a group. Such a group meeting is not for the purpose of providing psychotherapy for the teachers. It is for the purpose of allowing the teachers an opportunity to air their feelings and to examine all aspects of problem situations that arise within the classroom and within the school. Everybody under stress feels the need to share the stressful situation with someone who can help them to reduce that stress. Teachers need a regular opportunity, at least on a once-a-week basis, to air classroom problems. The focus of the meeting is on how to handle problems that interfere with learning. The therapist does not delve into the intrapsychic conflicts of the individual teachers, but helps them to recognize the defenses that interfere with their effectiveness as teachers, without going into the causes of such defenses.

To be effective in discussing how to handle behavioral problems within the classroom, the therapist must know how to deal with such problems when they occur within the group. By virtue of training and experience, the therapist often is knowledgeable only about handling behavioral problems on an individual basis. The latter does not meet the teacher's needs, who must deal with such problems within the group setting. By observing in the classroom and by seeing the behavioral problems from the vantage point of the teacher's responsibilities, the therapist can translate what he knows about helping the child on an individual basis into meaningful suggestions to the teacher for helping the child as a member of the group. The therapist should make tentative suggestions to the teacher about handling behavior, recommend that the teacher observe the results, and be prepared to discuss those results at the next meeting. In so doing, the therapist divorces himself from the role of omniscience and encourages the teacher to contribute observations to and participate in the resolution of the problems.

Group therapy for children who have brain dysfunction has proven to be of significant value at Pathway. In many cases, it has been a more effective medium than individual therapy in helping the child to resolve his difficulties in relating with his peers. That is understandable in view of group interaction being inherent in this type of treatment. Moreover, group therapy is much more economical than individual therapy, thereby lending itself better to a public school program. It certainly seems that group therapy can be well suited to the needs of these children in the second and third stages of psychotherapy, in which problems associated with interpersonal relations and socialization are worked through. Nevertheless, experience thus far does not indicate that it can be substituted for individual therapy in most cases. Instead, the child seems to profit best from having both individual and group therapy.

No discussion of behavioral management would be complete without mentioning medication. As the noted Dr. Leon Eisenberg has said, drugs are a path neither to a brave new world nor to the gateway of hell. Present-day drugs are not a magical solution to anything. However, work going on in biochemistry does hold promise for the future. In the meantime, a review of those drugs most commonly used with children who have brain dysfunction could be helpful. The intent is not to enable the educator to prescribe medications, but to familiarize the educator with the possible effects of drugs on the child's ability to learn and to manage his behavior more effectively. Such information can enable the educator to communicate

189

better with a child's physician, if drugs are being used, concerning observations about behavior that may be in response to the medication.

The present review is not an exhaustive one, and it is based on clinical observations made primarily on those children at Pathway for whom medication has been prescribed.

When a child has shown a markedly unstable electro-encephalogram, whether or not this indicates any seizure activity, coupled with driven and explosive emotion, anticonvulsants have been tried. Some such youngsters have responded dramatically to anticonvulsants. Take for example the child who had a history of complete incorrigibility. He was hyper-everything to the point that he had been taken from his home and put into one of the state hospitals for containment. Despite the fact that there was a history of EEG abnormality, he had not been given anticonvulsants. Within a very short time after receiving no treatment but anticonvulsants, he showed a dramatic gain in ability to contain himself and to be much less hyper. He could control his impulses well enough to return home and to be in a regular classroom. Some neurologists call such lack of control a "subclinical" seizure; others call it a seizure "equivalent," in the sense that it is not the usual psychomotor, petit-mal, or grand-mal seizure. Regardless of label, it is something educators should be cognizant of when they see repeatedly driven and explosive behavior.

It was discovered quite some time ago that although the amphetamines pep adults up, they often have the reverse effect on children. Whether or not the electroencephalogram was stabilized when the child showed hyperactivity, agressive behavior, and lack of inhibition, amphetamines were often prescribed. Frequently, the child initially showed dramatic improvement, only to revert to his original behavioral difficulties, apparently because he built up a tolerance for the amphetamines. At times higher dosages of the drug sustained the behavioral improvement for a time, but side effects were more likely to become prominent. The prolonged use of high doses of amphetamines in some cases produced a kind of paranoia. More recently, however, Ritalin has been used as an alternative to the amphetamines. In the case of Ritalin, the tolerance factor has not been so pronounced. In addition to slowing down the hyperactive child to some extent, Ritalin also seems to have an organizing effect on his performance in general. At the same time, Ritalin seems to activate the lethargic, poorly organized, flabby child. This apparent paradox, where a hyperactive child is somewhat calmed by Ritalin and a lethargic child is speeded up by it, is probably explained by some third factor not yet identified.

The tranquilizers have not proven too effective in reducing hyperactivity or other symptoms customarily associated with brain dysfunction. To the contrary, when a drug such as Valium has been used in an effort to reduce anxiety or depressive feelings of inadequacy, in some cases it seemed to make the child worse, resulting in a moderately agitated depression. On the other hand, Mellaril has been useful for some children who had severe neurotic and thought-process disturbances associated with their brain dysfunction.

In general, the majority of children who have brain dysfunction do not seem to be helped appreciably by medication. With the exception of the relatively rare child who has a seizure equivalent, medication is not a substitute for a comprehensive habilitative program. Moreover, although biochemical research holds future promise for this child, especially in the area of the central nervous system's metabolic processes, that promise is not yet fulfilled. For the present, there is no substitute for an effective educational program conjoined with ego-building relationships and behavioral management.

The basic theme of this chapter has been that because the child with brain dysfunction is a totality, his behavior must be regarded and dealt with as one manifestation of his overall development. His functional systems of learning give rise to his primary ego skills, from which his higher ego skills emerge as they are forged on the anvil of life experience. Because his behavior is contingent upon the status of his ego, and because his ego is fashioned by a developmental process, this child cannot be ordered to manifest instant maturity. For him to be able to manage his own behavior adaptively and with resultant genuine gratification requires much time, in which he patiently must be seen through many crises, and in which he must be given many opportunities for successful experiences in all aspects of his life.

REFERENCES

Cruickshank, W. M. *The Teacher of Brain-Injured Children.* Syracuse: Syracuse University Press, 1966.

Rappaport, S. R. (ed.) *Childhood Aphasia and Brain Damage: Volume II, Differential Diagnosis.* Norristown: The Pathway School, 1965.

Thomas, A., Chess, S., and Birch, H. G. *Temperament and Behavior Disorders in Children.* New York: New York University Press, 1968.

Redl, Fritz. "Strategy and Technique of Life Space Interview," *American Journal of Orthopsychiatry*, XXIX (1959), 1-18.

_____. *When We Deal with Children.* New York: The Free Press, 1966.

X. Parent Counseling

As both public schools and parents recognize that the child who has brain dysfunction is a totality and that his progress in overcoming his learning and behavioral disorders is as much affected by his life away from school as by his educational program, parent counseling will become an integral part of the school's function. This has already become a reality in some school districts, where social workers are full-time members of the staff. In other school districts, psychologists and guidance counselors are beginning to assume some responsibility for counseling the parents of these children.

Regardless of the disciplinary background of the person who assumes the role of parent counselor, that person must understand normal child development, the functional systems of learning, the educational program, his problems at home, and all that comprises the parents' struggles with the problems of the child with brain dysfunction. Moreover, the parent counselor cannot work solely with parents, because that militates against providing them with the help they need. Parents have two basic questions that constantly gnaw at them: "Why did this happen to my child?" and "What can I do about it?" The parent counselor cannot answer those questions effectively without having a thorough knowledge of the child and of all aspects of his total habilitative program. Therefore, the parent counselor needs time for observation in the child's classroom and time to communicate with the teacher and all others who are working with the child, as well as time to work with the parents.

Ideally, parent counseling should begin before the child enters the class (see Chapter III). In an evaluative conference, the parent counselor and whoever else was involved in the preadmission examination of the child should share their findings with the parents. The aim of the evaluative conference is to help the parents to understand the nature of the child's problems, how these manifest themselves, both in test situations and in everyday situations, and why certain recommendations seem to be appropriate to help him overcome those problems. To be effective the evaluative conference must focus on the needs of the parents. Parents need explanations of their child's difficulties that are couched in plain language, not in professional jargon and mystique. They need to know IQ's *and* that IQ's are not absolute *and* what those IQ's mean in terms of their child. They need many examples of how the child responded in various test situations, so that they can integrate that information with how the child responds to the many similar situations at home. As they do integrate and thereby understand this information, they in turn will cite examples of performance at home to match the performance described in the test situation. Apropos of this, at The Pathway School the motto for evaluative conferences is *esse quam videre*. Stepping out of his usual role of Director of Child Development and into the role of Latin scholar, Dr. Getman has translated this as "Show 'em, don't snow 'em."

Parents also need the opportunity to air their anxieties and to raise questions. That may require the evaluative conference to extend over several meetings. When the press of time does not permit those several meetings, several follow-up telephone discussions with the parent counselor can serve as a substitute.

In attempting to explain why their child has problems, the counselor should share neurological, medical, and all other information factually but in a fashion that makes sense to the parents. It is no kindness to handle parents as though they were preschool children who had to be spared the more difficult or upsetting facts of life. Parents should be helped to understand that the entire field of inner space is in the process of being explored, that the interrelatedness of the brain and the functional systems of learning presents a frontier yet to be conquered, and that their child can have even a severe learning

194

and behavioral disorder without its cause having been definitively established. Parents must know that if the professionals
have not as yet identified all the causes of brain dysfunction,
they cannot blame themselves for their child's problems. Parents
should also be helped to realize that etiology is important only
as a means of defining the appropriate habilitative program.
Identifying the etiology is not meant to stigmatize or to indict
them as being biologically or in any other way inferior.

In some cases, parents have legitimate concern that their
child's difficulties have a hereditary basis. That, of course,
should be explored by the appropriate medical persons. In other
cases, parents should know that there are many possible factors
that could disrupt genetic coding and could appear to be
hereditary. As an example, research currently being done by
Doctors Carl and Hally Sax at the Cranbrook Institute of
Science indicates the possibility of relatively small amounts of
alcohol and coffee acting synergistically to have a deleterious
effect on genetic coding equivalent to a radiation dosage that
exceeds the limit for safety. Thus, it is conceivable that several
generations could enjoy drinking whiskey and coffee, which
would have an injurious effect on their offspring, which in turn
could be misconstrued as hereditary. Probably another decade
will pass before ways of preventing the causes of brain
dysfunction are known.

Stepping back into his role in child development, Dr. Getman
has stressed that parents need help in their three R's: their *role*
with their child, their *responsibility* in helping their child, and
their *response* to the information given to them by the professionals. As with the other three R's, one does not learn them
through a single exposure, but through continued practice,
evaluation, and refinement, and this takes time. Therefore,
parent counseling cannot be viewed as a one-shot opportunity
to impress parents and to inundate them with the professional's
superior knowledge. Counseling is a learning process that
requires repeated interactions and communications. That is one
reason why counseling parents of children with brain dysfunction should be conceived as being educative in nature. The other

reason is that these parents have lived for many years with the harrassment of the child's behavioral and learning disorders and with the frustration and humiliation of not being able to do anything to help their own child. What they need is someone to help them understand how to "read" their child and to guide them in how to aid their child successfully. Certainly most of these parents do not initially need to explore their deepseated conflicts concerning their child.

In most cases, when parents do have emotional disturbances that interfere with their ability to help their child, if first given educative counseling, they themselves realize their need for psychotherapy. Such parents have said to the parent counselor: "I understand why my child does those things now. What you have said makes sense. And I see how his teacher handles him in those situations, but I can't do it. Something won't let me. I have to find out why." At that point in time the parent is much better motivated to benefit from psychotherapy than if it had been thrust on him or her at the outset of parent counseling. If the latter had been done, it probably would have resulted only in heightened guilt and defensiveness. It is as important to start the parents' educative process with what *they* need at that moment as to start the child's educative process with what *he* needs at that moment.

As the parents are helped to understand why their child responds as he does (see Chapter IV), they are better able to carry out relationship structure (see Chapters IV and IX) in the home, so that their child's experiences there will be commensurate with those at school. As they learn to read their child, they feel less frustrated and inadequate, therefore less in need of being punitive, rejecting, and dictatorial toward the child. Then, with help, they can take the initiative to interrupt the longstanding power struggle they have had with him. One way they can do so is not to expect more of the child than he is capable of at that particular time.

When the parents really read their child, they know that a "simple" expectation, such as to tie his own shoelaces, is simple for them but not for him. Like the teacher, before expecting the child to perform any task, they accurately analyze it to discover what it asks of the child and whether he is developmentally ready to succeed at it. They recognize that tying shoelaces, for example, requires many discrete steps, which the child will have to learn one at a time. Therefore, they present that task to him expecting him to learn only one step at a time. Like the teacher, they also realize that it will probably require weeks or months for him to learn the entire series of steps involved and to integrate those so that he can perform the act of tying his shoes easily. By expecting this to take time, the parents can be content with his progress and can express pleasure with each small accomplishment of their child. The parents thereby convey to their child: "I will help you for as long as you need it. I will help you now because you can't do it for yourself. Tomorrow you'll do a little better."

Another way in which the parents can interrupt the power struggle is to know which situation the child cannot yet handle and not expose him to such before he is ready to succeed in them. For example, it is no favor to the child to give him a large, festive birthday party while he is incapable of handling a large group of children. As he develops, there will be a right time to give him such a party. Knowing that, the parents are better able to gear what they expect of themselves as "good" parents to what the child needs at that point in time. Similarly, if the parents have been trained to read the child, they can anticipate when he is headed for a failure or a blowup. Then they can take steps to avoid it. They can call their child aside and quietly let him know, for example, that his feelings are getting out of hand and that they want to help him to get back into control before he has an embarrassing experience. Then they can indicate to him, quietly but firmly, which route they will take to accomplish that.

In the process of establishing a new role with their child, the parents need to feel comfortable in acknowledging with their child that this is a new role for them, that they will not play the old kinds of "games" with him any more, because now they know they cannot help him by doing so. Some parents may fear that to acknowledge that the former role they played with him was wrong and that they understand how hurt and angry he felt in response to them would be to undermine his love and respect for them. Those parents should be helped to see that an adult can place no greater burden on a child than that of always being right. As the child goes through the process of learning, of making mistakes and noting the consequences, he knows that *he* cannot always be right. If the parents are always right, that must make him seem very inept and inadequate by comparison. On the other hand, when his parents can comfortably admit being wrong, then he does not have to feel like a nothing when he makes a mistake. To remove such a burden from their child can only cause him to respond to them with heightened love and respect. Nevertheless, the parents cannot expect him to show that immediately. Before he can do that, he will have to air his accumulated hurt and angry feelings, establish some sense of self-worth, and test his parents to see whether he can safely entrust his feelings to them again. That also will take a long time.

Because of their accumulated stress, the parents are not likely to accomplish their transition of roles simply and smoothly. They should be helped to be comfortable with the likelihood of becoming irritable and at times losing their temper with their child's behavior. They should not feel it necessary to try to hide such feelings from the child. Indeed all they could do would be to try, because they could not succeed in hiding their true feelings. If they attempted to do so, the child would know this. These youngsters usually are extremely sensitive to nonverbal expressions of feeling. When the youngster saw that his parents contradicted with their words what they actually felt toward him, he again would have confirmation that they were not to be trusted.

Being candid with the child will help to build a better relationship even when the parents show anger. Because, in many cases, the parents are trying to help their child learn how to handle his anger effectively, they can set him a good example by sharing their feelings with him before they lose their own

198

control. They can say to him: "All right, I've had it with that behavior. I've been trying to help you handle this so you can feel proud of yourself, and all you do is turn me off. Okay, that's it for now. I can't try to help you with it any more today. I hope that when we try it again tomorrow you won't try to turn me off." It is a relief to the child to find all at the same time that he cannot manipulate his parents' feelings like a Yo-Yo and that they do not have to pretend to be all-perfect and that they have not rejected and abandoned him.

Obviously, to handle such a situation effectively is not a simple task. It involves judging the extent of one's own patience, the volatility of one's rising anger, the child's reason for that behavior, when it would be best to terminate the situation, how to communicate the crux of the situation clearly and concisely to the child, and which activity to direct his attention to next. No one learns to handle something that complex in one counseling conference, by attending a single seminar, or by reading a book. As in any other learning process, one must perform the task, evaluate the performance, and practice refining it. Parents are no exception. To learn how to put relationship structure into effect at home, they need the opportunity for continued guidance in their performance of it.

When parents recognize that their only innate qualifications for parenthood are sexual fertility and potency, they should not feel ashamed to need guidance in how to be effective parents. Moreover, when the goal is to aid a child with brain dysfunction in overcoming his complex ego insufficiencies and deviations, it is the parents' responsibility to avail themselves of such help. Therefore, not only should the school require parent counseling as a condition for accepting the child into the class, but the parents should require it of themselves as part of their responsibility to their child.

As counseling enables the parents to become more knowledgeable about their child's learning and behavioral disorders and as they learn to understand him in the gamut of everyday situations in which he has difficulty, they can more willingly and effectively work at tailoring their roles and relationships

199

with him to have greatest impetus on his habilitation. Hopefully, by that time, whatever wishes for a magical solution the parents may have had initially have given way to the realization that to habilitate their child will place extra demands of time, energy, and patience on each member of the family for a long time. Before discussing the parents' role with the other children in the family, however, let us consider the role that is ideally required of them to have optimal impact on the progress of the child with brain dysfunction.

The following "ideal" parental role is an amalgamation of attributes that have been aimed at, and to varying degrees achieved, by parents through the help of educative counseling and later, if needed, psychotherapy. Not all the parents with whom I have had experience had to work on all the attributes. Some traits were inherent in their personalities and emerged quite readily as the parents found relief from some of their inordinately heavy burdens of stress and anxiety. Other traits required a great deal of work to achieve. Some were never achieved. In certain cases, the child had to prove his adequacy, both scholastically and socially, before his parents could accept him at all, or feel any semblance of warmth and approval toward him. Even then they expected him to revert to his old ways. The main point is that both parents and parent counselors should be aware of the ideal role that would best help the child.

First of all, the parents should want their child to be a person in his own right rather than an extension of themselves. It is easy to pay lip service to this, but to live it requires quite a bit of maturity. When parents have their own intrapsychic reasons for feeling insecure or inadequate, they are motivated to place unduly high aspirations on their children to succeed where they did not. Their unconscious hope is to bask in the reflected glory of their children or to prove their own worth through the accomplishments of their children. In such instances, it is apparent that the parents want to get from the child, not to give to him. The child with brain dysfunction, who requires his parents and all others who work with him to be an ego bank (see Chapters IV and IX), therefore is extremely frustrating and

200

noxious to the parent who himself has a shaky sense of self-worth. For any sustained period of time, that parent finds it impossible to give to the child rather than to want to get from him. If that parent has an intrapsychic conflict that focuses on intellectual achievement or on athletic prowess, the child with brain dysfunction is likely to be openly rejected. Because most of his gains are small and because most of them, at least for quite some time, will not be in the area of cognitive or athletic gymnastics, his gains cannot please that parent.

Secondly, and this is often a correlate of the first point, parents should not feel uncomfortable with their child's learning and behavioral disorders. They should not feel so threatened by those disorders that they expect instant remedy. They should be able to accept their child's dependency on them while at the same time they encourage and aid his development. They should be capable of flexibility in the expectations they hold out to their child and in their approach to him, according to his changing needs. Parents are better able to play a helping role in their child's development when they realize that his growth will not always be at a rapid or even a consistent pace. Then they are less likely to be upset by his expected ups and downs. They can also demonstrate to him a greater-than-average patience and frustration tolerance.

Finally, recognizing their child's need for structure and consistency (see Chapter IV), they can conduct their lives and household in an organized, but not rigidly compulsive, manner. This allows the structure to keep pace with the changing needs of the child during the course of his development, as opposed to its being enforced rigidly and with regard only for the parents' need for compulsiveness.

As parents are helped toward such a role with their child, they are better able to accommodate the necessary changes in their personal and family lives during the course of their child's habilitation. Nevertheless, the parent counselor should be careful that the parents do not misconstrue the stated need for them to modify their roles as a moral mandate to give up everything for the child with brain dysfunction. To do that would not be realistic or desirable for them or for their child. These parents are no different than any other parents in needing opportunities for their own personal fulfillments. The structure that is put into effect in the home should be beneficial both to the child, in helping him to develop his ego skills, and also to the parents, in providing them their needed opportunities for personal fulfillment. The structure at home will be more effective as parents realize that it will help them as much as it will help the child. Take, for example, seven-year-old Tommy, a child who would not go to bed when asked, and when finally he did, he would not stay there.

Tommy had never slept through an entire night. From two years of age on, he not only refused to go to bed, but at some time during the night he also got into bed with his parents. Seven years of accumulated fatigue, from broken sleep and frustration, from hurried, tense, and usually unsatisfying sexual relations, had brought Tommy's parents to the brink of desperation. Counseling them involved not only the goal of getting Tommy on a normal sleep schedule, but also the correlative goal of rest and sexual fulfillment for the parents. To achieve those goals, the first step was to analyze Tommy's daily schedule. He still took a nap before supper. His mother encouraged it, because his nap allowed her undisturbed time for the preparation of dinner. In the hope of avoiding disturbing Tommy's siblings, who had homework to do, Tommy's father played with him for a half hour after dinner and then sent him to bed. Able to undress himself, Tommy spent an hour or more running out of his room in various stages of undress. The evening usually ended with father losing his temper, soundly spanking Tommy, and throwing him into bed with threats of dire consequences if he did not go to sleep. Tommy then usually cried himself to sleep. If he awakened before his parents retired for the night, he came to them wanting milk, water, relief from nasal congestion, or many other personal comforts. If they had already gone to bed when he awakened, Tommy came into their bed. This was permitted because by then they were too exhausted to fight him any longer.

Through counseling, the parents reoriented their perspective of Tommy's bedtime situation and his daily routine. His nap before supper was abandoned. Instead, his siblings played a game with him in which he could find success and enjoyment. His mother also rearranged her schedule so that the major portion of preparing dinner was accomplished while Tommy was at school. When dinner was ready, Tommy and his siblings had specific chores in setting the table. Tommy was assigned a task that he could accomplish easily while the others were doing their tasks. The shared activities had the added advantage of providing dinner conversation in which Tommy could participate.

After dinner, he had a longer and quieter period with his father in which he could demonstrate some of his newly emerging skills. This provided his father with an opportunity to express genuine pleasure with Tommy's gains and to relate to him as a boy of seven, rather than roughhousing with him as he had done since Tommy had been a baby. When bedtime arrived, both Tommy and his father had had a satisfying experience. As a result, Tommy was more willing to go to bed and his father was not choked by the rising anger dictating that he should banish Tommy to Lower Slobovia for the next hundred years. Tommy was encouraged to undress and ready himself for bed as quickly as other boys his age did.

When ready for bed, he called his mother, who then spent time alone with Tommy. After he was tucked in, she sat next to his bed and usually read to him. Occasionally they would quietly sing a favorite song. At the established time for sleep, his light was turned off and he was expected to remain in bed until morning. At first he continued to come into his parents' room. Because this was anticipated, by prearrangement they took turns getting up with him, returning to Tommy's room, tucking him in, and reassuring him that he could sleep in his own bed now, since he had accomplished so many other things he was proud of. After enumerating all his accomplishments, he was kissed goodnight and the parent left Tommy's room. After six weeks of transition, both Tommy and his parents were able to find the gratification they needed.

Similarly, parents need help in training someone who can stay with their child so that they can enjoy social and recreational activities. Perhaps such activities cannot be as frequent as desired, but at least the parents do not feel that they are trapped in the house with their child. Frequently a male college athlete has proven successful as a babysitter. The child admires him and often will do almost anything to please him. With some preparatory training from the parent counselor as well as from the parents, the college student can be of significant help to the child's ego development.

Just as the parents cannot aid in the child's habilitation by avoiding or denying their child's disorders (see Chapter IX), they cannot help their other children by avoiding the issue of the child with brain dysfunction. The family has to make certain adjustments to this child just as it must to the child who has diabetes or cystic fibrosis or any other type of difficulty. The sooner the other children are helped to understand this child's problems and what they can do to help him overcome those problems, the sooner each member of the family will find his desired gratification. To accomplish that, especially with young children, is not easy, but there is no substitute for it. Regardless of age, each child in the family needs individual attention, and this has to be scheduled to avoid the parents' suddenly realizing that they have lost contact with a child for the past month. When the other children understand the problem and are helping toward its solution *and* have their individual needs met, helping their sibling can contribute substantially to their own ego development. To find gratification in being of service to someone who needs help certainly fosters the growth of the higher ego skills.

To answer all the needs of these parents, the parent counselor must know the family's routine and all its daily problems. The counselor and the parents then must work out a tentative attack on each problem situation, revising that plan in accordance with how effective the suggestions prove to be, until the problem situation is resolved. Both the counselor and the parents must remember that they cannot launch a plan to resolve all the areas of problem at once. They must begin with the most pressing problem and bring that under control before they attempt to alleviate others. This means that the parents will have to ignore some aspects of their child's difficulties for a while. It is a reality that cannot be disregarded. If the parents attempt to move in on the child on all fronts simultaneously, taking away his maladaptations before he is ready to replace them with behavior that is genuinely gratifying, his psychic survival will be imperiled and he will be unable to respond in the desired manner.

In attempting to find the time to do the kind of parent counseling required, group parent meetings should not be overlooked. These have many advantages in addition to conservation of time. Parents take comfort and courage from learning that they are not the only ones struggling with such a problem. They also can support each other emotionally in living through a crisis or a particularly difficult time. This is especially true when the group is helped to be thoroughly familiar with each of the children being discussed. Then each member of the group invests emotionally in the solution of each child's problems. This is much more beneficial to all than to wait impatiently until the person talking gets through, so that they can get time to discuss what is really important; namely, their own child. The parent counselor leading the group will find that to have each member thoroughly familiar with each child does not waste the group's time. In addition to the personal support each parent can give to the other, the problem situations have enough in common so that each parent can learn from the resolution of another parent's problem and apply it to his or her own home situation and the child's level of development.

This chapter has attempted to highlight the main needs of parents, together with the responsibilities of both parent counselors and parents toward the habilitation of the child with brain dysfunction. Guidelines to resolve the plethora of problems attendant to everyday living is beyond the scope of this chapter. However, hopefully, the parent counselor and the parents will find the points highlighted herein useful in evolving

205

a plan whereby each of the daily problems can be resolved. Helpful suggestions can also be found in Cruickshank (1967), in Baruch (1949), and in Ginott (1965). In applying any suggestions, parents and counselors must be sure to adapt them to the needs of the child and to the home situation in its entirety. When that is done, and when the "hopeless" situations are worked through to solutions, there is no greater gratification for the parents.

REFERENCES

Cruickshank, W. M. *The Brain-Injured Child in Home, School, and Community.* Syracuse: Syracuse University Press, 1967.
Baruch, D. *New Ways in Discipline.* New York: McGraw-Hill, 1949.
Ginott, H. *Between Parent and Child.* New York: Macmillan, 1965.

XI. Conclusions

Today, we are experiencing perhaps the most exciting frontier era of all times. The frontiers no longer involve covered wagons and gold mines, but adventures of the mind and explorations of its treasures, which are so awesome as to stagger even those whose imagination was honed on Flash Gordon and Rod Serling. When Man first gazed into the atom and used what he found there to lift exploratory fingers into outer space, his mind was stretched into a new dimension. Shortly thereafter, his mind reached new proportions as he found the means of probing inner space as well. There he found the key to the mystery that had gone unanswered throughout time: How life is created.

It took him 5,000 years to traverse the distance between the thought that gave rise to the wheel and the thought that smashed the atom to take from its innards the power to nullify the law of gravity. Yet within a single decade, both Sputnik and the double helix arose to establish frontiers on the measureless reaches of outer and inner space. The current speed with which knowledge and technology are being accelerated makes this not an age of despair but an age of hope.

As knowledge and technology push back the frontier of inner space, surely brain dysfunction will be remedied with facility and dispatch, and in time its causes will be prevented. To help in those accomplishments there is a clarion call to the educator to join ranks with professionals from other disciplines. The call is not for educators to do biochemical or psychophysical research, but to do what they can do best—observe the child's processes of learning and discern the how and why of tasks that best aid it. As education makes that singularly significant contribution, the resultant data, shared with other disciplines, will foster and further refine the knowledge of inner space. In turn, the findings of the other disciplines, when shared with education, will facilitate and heighten education's contribution.

This frontier era of ours requires that all who participate in it be professionals, not solely by virtue of the degree appended to their names, but largely by virtue of their attitude. That attitude is rooted in the realization that what one has already learned and practiced is not absolute and certainly is not to be cherished as holy simply because one has already learned and practiced it. The validity and effectiveness of everything that has been learned and practiced must be examined in the light of all that is known today. This is demanded by the speed with which knowledge and technology have been accrued during the past decade. It is demanded by the fact that laws of nature, long regarded as absolute, now have been either repealed or amended. Today proteins *can* be synthesized. Today even the patriarch of all such laws, the law of gravity, is amended by the contingency that what goes up must come down *unless* it reaches an escape velocity of 6.9 miles per second.

The professional attitude is also rooted in the recognition that knowledge cannot be hoarded. It cannot be the province of a select few. It cannot be employed for the purpose of self-aggrandizement. Knowledge is the province of everyone. Nonetheless, that does not provide license to misuse it, nor does it bestow on those who wish to have it without the required training the freedom to practice pediatrics or neurology or optometry or anything else. The sharing of all existing knowledge only insures the freedom of opportunity to apply it to the enrichment and effectiveness of one's own professional pursuits.

The professional attitude requires still more. It necessitates a respect for the efforts and contributions of all others who are working toward the solution of a problem. It calls for the realization that one is not omnipotent, that nobody has a monopoly on the best solution or the right route to it, and that one can not singlehandedly solve the inordinately intricate problems of inner space. It demands that one be unwilling to dissipate time and energy in the clannishness and competitiveness that manifests itself as "my degree is better than your degree" or "my discipline's approach to the problem is all right and yours is all wrong." It rises above the spurious use of research as an instrument to discredit the work of others or to establish one's own cause, such as by "proving" that all behavior is unequivocally a conditioned response to the printed word *because* since Smokey-the-Bear signs were posted in the subways, the city of New York has not had a single forest fire. And the professional attitude requires the extraordinary ego strength that enables one to feel secure when working in a field that has many uncertainties and unknowns, while constantly questioning and evaluating one's own work. Those circumstances would make a person of lesser ego strength seek security by embracing and defending dogmas or by collecting grievances about and dispensing anxiety to all with whom one works.

Educators cannot become professionals solely by attaining status through graduate degrees or by obtaining collective bargaining through labor unions. They can become professionals primarily through better training and through developing the professional attitude. Thus equipped, they are prepared to join ranks with their colleagues from other disciplines and to make a noteworthy contribution to the frontier of inner space. Whether or not recognized as such, that frontier is where educators have always lived and labored.

Those educators who have undertaken the responsibility of helping children to overcome the learning and behavioral disorders of brain dysfunction cannot have arrived at that responsibility by chance, caprice, or default. These children have problems of such scope and complexity that they must have educators who are among the most talented, the most dedicated, and the best trained. To habilitate these children cannot be accomplished by mini-persons who use mini-talents to carry out mini-concepts. The selection both of those who are to habilitate these children and of the program by which they are to be habilitated is not the responsibility of the school alone. It is the responsibility of the entire community. When it is recognized that there are probably close to 8,000,000 such children in the United States, that responsibility is a grave one. How it is

209

executed can have a telling impact on the nation's economy, strength, and well-being.

Public education did not of itself decide that it no longer would be available only to the well child. Society decided that public education should be available to *all* children. In support of that decision, now society must decide that it is in its own best interests to expect and to provide the means for public education to produce programs that will in fact habilitate children with brain dysfunction. For if society does not habilitate these children, then it will doom most of them to lifelong ineptitude; and it will contribute to the waste of a society's most precious resource, mentality. Its decreed wastefulness will be compounded by the forced expenditure of billions of dollars to maintain them later in life, in mental and correctional institutions from which they will not emerge as self-respecting and tax paying citizens. Society must not miss this opportunity to insure its own future success by investing in this large segment of its children.

Society and public education conjointly must realize that the expenditure of large sums of money alone will not in itself habilitate children with brain dysfunction. Federal, state, and local funding does not comprise the Garden of Eden. Unless ample effort and thought and planning and training also go into its cultivation, the habilitative program's most abundant crop will be weeds.

Fortunately a wave of popular interest in these children has been generated by their parents. That wave can help to carry public education forward to new heights. To accomplish that public schools must formulate habilitative programs that: (1) view this child as a total organism who needs a total, comprehensive program in order to have the most effective opportunity for learning; (2) insure the continuous consideration of all aspects of his development and performance in his educational program; (3) acknowledge learning opportunities to be present both before and after school hours, so that more than classroom programming is considered, and so that the teacher is not charged with the sole responsibility for the child's habilitation; (4) see this child not only as a pupil, but also as a member of a family and of society, with the result that the home and the community assume their responsibilities in providing adequate and appropriate environments for his development. Because the required programs are comprehensive and necessitate interdisciplinary teamwork, public schools cannot effect them without the cooperative efforts and talents of their communities.

To be sound, a habilitative program must be based on a comprehensive conceptual model, such as the one presented in this book, that provides guidelines for carrying out all aspects of the program in both the school and the home. Guidelines are needed to build relationship structure and educational structure, which serve as a matrix in which the child can overcome his skill deficiencies and maladaptations and can develop all aspects of his ego. These guidelines also enable the teacher to evaluate more accurately all aspects of the child that are involved in answering the questions that a given task poses to him. At the same time, the guidelines help the teacher to ascertain specifically what each task asks of the child and how it relates to the child's current needs and levels of development. Both teacher and parents also need guidelines that concern both an overview of the child's developmental strengths and deviations and a microscopic enlargement of one aspect of his development as a total child, his functional systems of learning. For all children learning takes place through these functional systems, and so they are important, but for the child who has brain dysfunction, these functional systems are of critical importance. Armed with such understanding, the teacher and the parents can effect the necessary melding of the child's performance with appropriate opportunities for successful learning and for other aspects of his ego growth.

It is inconceivable that an effective habilitative program can be established unless it is rooted in a comprehensive conceptual model, which would guide the understanding of the child as a totality, the setting up of the classroom, the establishment of a prescriptive educational program, and the evaluation of the

211

effectiveness both of the whole program and of the model itself. Otherwise, misconceptions and inadvertencies that over the years have come to be regarded as correct procedure cannot be identified and replaced by concepts and instrumentations that serve this child more effectively.

In the conceptual model presented, the child with brain dysfunction is seen as a totality. Therefore, it advocates that his behavior be regarded and dealt with as one manifestation of his overall development. His functional systems of learning give rise to his primary ego skills, from which his higher ego skills emerge as they are forged on the anvil of life experience. Because his behavior is contingent upon the status of his ego, and because his ego is fashioned by a developmental process, this child cannot be ordered to manifest instant maturity. For him to be able to manage his own behavior adaptively and with resultant genuine gratification requires much time, in which he patiently must be seen through many crises both at school and at home, and in which he must be given many opportunities for successful experiences in all aspects of his life. Those opportunities that have to do with his education are not conceived as being rooted in any one physical environment or set of learning materials, but in the teacher's ability to assess all aspects of all educational materials and of various environmental arrangements to determine whether each does in fact contribute to the child's opportunity for successful learning, and if so, at what stage of his development. As the teacher learns to judge the child's developmental levels and needs, primarily from observations of how the child performs the task required of him, and as the teacher learns to make expectations about what the child should perform, only after the task to be presented to him has been accurately analyzed in terms of what questions it asks the child and in terms of at which developmental levels the questions are asked, the child can be provided with learning opportunities that are truly prescriptive to his needs. Then teachers can fulfill their responsibility to help this segmented and fragmented child learn how to make his functional systems operate in accord with their natural design, so that he can become a unified and effective

212

being. If teachers of these children are able to accomplish that, the complex processes that are involved in learning will be better understood than ever before, and as a result, the education of all children will reach a new level of effectiveness.

If today's habilitative programs are able to provide the child who has brain dysfunction with truly successful opportunities both for learning and for ego development in general, history will record this era of special education not as the worst of times, but as the best of times.

The goal of effective habilitative programs for these children is not so formidable when placed in its proper perspective. If the earth's entire history is regarded as analogous to a calendar year, January through August would be devoid of life. The next two months would be devoted to primeval creatures ranging from viruses and single-cell bacteria to jellyfish. Mammals would not appear until the middle of December. Modern man would not make his entrance until 11:45 on New Year's Eve. Written history would begin only one minute before midnight. Awareness of the child with learning and behavioral disorders due to brain dysfunction would occur as the clock chimed to usher in the New Year. Thus, in this exciting frontier era of ours, we can take heart that for these children and their families and for education, as well as for the entire professional community, this is an age of hope; for "Every dragon gives birth to a St. George who slays it."—Kahlil Gibran.

Glossary

Cephalocaudal—The head-to-feet direction in which the nervous system develops.

Cortical Inhibition—The ability to restrain or control a movement that previously had been a reflex or automatic response. This takes place as the central nervous system develops and is an important milestone in the child's development because it paves the way for volitional practice.

Endogenous—The child who functions at a retarded level of achievement, intelligence, and adaptation, who shows no indication of rising above that level of function, is regarded as endogenously retarded. This retardation is considered genetically based.

Epigenesis—A series of interrelated developmental phases in which each phase is rooted in the one that preceded it and paves the way for the next, more refined or more complexly differentiated phase.

Etiology—The cause or origin, in contrast to the symptoms of, any abnormality or dysfunction.

Exogenous—The child who functions at a retarded level of achievement, intelligence, or adaptation, who indicates a potential for a higher level of function, is regarded as exogenously retarded. This retardation is considered to arise from factors not inherent in the organism and therefore is potentially reversible.

Gustation—The sense of taste.

Habilitation—Because most children with brain dysfunction never had the adequate skills to enable them to adapt to their environment successfully, they cannot be "*re*habilitated," or restored to normal function. Instead they require a habilitative program that builds their skills and results in their being able to function effectively.

Kernicterus—A condition accompanied by widespread degeneration of various parts of the brain and spinal cord. It is associated with jaundice in the infant and has often occurred when the incompatibility between the RH blood factor of the mother and the child has not been treated at birth.

Ophthalmologist—A physician who has received additional training that concentrated on the organic pathology and surgery of the eye. In contrast, the optometrist, not a physician, usually receives training in the function of vision.

Organismic—Consideration of the organism, or individual, as a functional whole. It connotes a holistic approach to the child and a concern for his total functioning.

215

Otologist—A physician who has received additional training that concentrated on the diseases, organic pathology, and surgery of the ear. In contrast, the audiologist, not a physician, is trained to deal with the function of hearing. Usually the otologist and audiologist collaborate on problems of hearing and the ear.

Phenylpyruvic Oligophrenia—A congenital metabolic disorder, also known as phenylketonuria (PKU). It appears in infancy and, unless treated early, results in extreme intellectual retardation.

Physiatrist—A physician who specializes in physical medicine, or the diagnosis and treatment of disease or disorder by physical means, such as radiation, heat, cold, water, electricity, and exercise. The physiatrist is trained in the muscle systems and their functions. The physical therapist, not a physician, is trained to carry out such physical therapies under the direction of a physiatrist.

Pronation—When the foot is rotated so that its inner edge is flattened and bears more weight than its outer edge, it is said to be pronated. The hand is pronated when the forearm is rotated toward the body, resulting in the palm being turned backward or downward.

Psychobiological Totality—The integration of the child's mind and body and the interrelatedness of the organic and functional adequacies and inadequacies from which his performance results.

Reality Confrontation—Helping the child to become sufficiently comfortable, both with himself and with those who are working with him, to carefully examine the consequences of his acts, so that he can guide his behavior according to the goals he really wishes to accomplish. It is a technique used to free the child from enslavement brought on by his habituated maladaptive attempts to reach his goals.

Rubella—The cause of this disease (German measles) is a virus which was particularly strong in the epidemic of 1964-65. Although the symptoms are similar to those of ordinary measles, when a pregnant woman gets rubella, her infant is likely to be born with some combination of cardiac, visual, and hearing defects, as well as brain dysfunction or retardation.

Synapse—The space between the end of one neuron (nerve fiber) and the beginning of the next. This is the region of electrochemical contact among neurons, where neural signals are relayed.

Index

217